MW01603154

OPTAVIA
AIR FRYER
Cookbook 2021

The complete Optavia Air Fryier Cookbook; 500+ Lean &
Green, Delicious and Effortless Recipes to Kill your Hunger
and Boost your Energy for a Long-Term Transformation

Amber Moore

TABLE OF CONTENTS

OPTAVIA LEAN & GREEN BREAKFAST RECIPES

OPTAVIA LEAN & GREEN LUNCH RECIPES

OPTAVIA LEAN & GREEN POULTRY AIR-FRY RECIPES

OPTAVIA LEAN & GREEN TURKEY AIR-FRY RECIPES

OPTAVIA LEAN & GREEN LOW BUDGET RECIPES

OPTAVIA LEAN & GREEN PORK AIR-FRY RECIPES

OPTAVIA LEAN & GREEN SEAFOOD AIR-FRY RECIPES

OPTAVIA GREENS & VEGETABLES AIR-FRY RECIPES

OPTAVIA LEAN & GREEN DESSERT AIR-FRY RECIPES

OPTAVIA LEAN & GREEN BREAKFAST RECIPES

1. Delicious Breakfast Soufflé

Preparation time: 10 minutes | Cooking duration: 8 minutes | Serves: 4

Ingredients:
* 4 eggs, whisked
* 4 tbps heavy cream
* A pinch of red chili pepper, crushed
* 2 tbps parsley, diced
* 2 tbps chives, diced
* Salt and black pepper to the taste

Cooking Instructions:

In a bowl, mix the eggs with salt, pepper, cream, red pepper, parsley and chives, mix well and divide into 4 soufflé plates.

Place the dishes in the air fryer and cook the soufflés at 350 ° F for 8 minutes.

Serve hot.

Nutritional Value (Amount per Serving):
* Calories 102
* Fat 8 g
* Carbohydrates 0.7 g
* Sugar 0 g
* Protein 5 g
* Cholesterol 23 mg

2. Egg Muffins

Preparation time: 10 minutes | Cooking duration: 15 minutes | Serves: 4

Ingredients:
* 1 egg
* 2 tbps olive oil
* 3 tbps milk
* ounces white flour
* 1 tablespoon baking powder
* 2 ounces parmesan, grated
* A splash of Worcestershire sauce

Cooking Instructions:

In a bowl, mix the egg with the flour, oil, baking powder, milk, Worcestershire and Parmesan, beat well and divide into 4 silicone muffin cups.

Place the cups in the cooking basket of the air fryer, cover and cook at 392 ° F for 15 minutes.

Serve hot for breakfast.

Nutritional Value (Amount per Serving):
* Calories 108
* Fat 7.1 g
* Carbohydrates 0.5 g
* Sugar 0.3 g
* Protein 9 g
* Cholesterol 23 mg

3. Croissant with Ham, Mushroom and Egg

Preparation: 5 minutes | Cooking duration: 8 minutes | Serves: 1

Ingredients:
* 1 store-bought Croissant
* 3 slices honey shaved ham
* 4 honey cherry tomato, halved
* 4 small button mushroom, quartered
* 1 Egg
* 1.8 oz. shredded cheddar cheese
* Handful salad greens
* 1/2 Rosemary Sprig, roughly diced (optional)

Cooking Instructions:
* Lightly grease a baking dish with margarine.
* Arrange the ingredients in two layers, placing the cheese in the middle and top layer. Create a space in the center of the ham mixture, break the egg.
* Sprinkle the mixture with black pepper, salt and rosemary and place on the basket of the Air fryer together with the croissant.
* In the oven at a preheated temperature at 325 ° F for 8 minutes. (Remove the croissant from the air fryer basket after 4 minutes).
* Serve croissants and cheese baked eggs on the plate along with some salads.

Nutritional Value (Amount per Serving):
* Calories 120
* Carbohydrates 0.7 g
* Sugar 0.3 g
* Protein 5 g
* Cholesterol 20 mg

4. Delicious Potato Hash

Preparation time: 10 minutes | Cooking duration: 25 minutes | Serves: 4

Ingredients:
* 1 and 1/2 potatoes, cubed
* 1 yellow onion, diced
* 2 tsp.s olive oil
* 1 green bell pepper, diced
* Salt and black pepper to the taste
* 1/2 tsp. thyme, dried
* 2 eggs

Cooking Instructions:

Heat up your air fryer at 350 °F, add oil, heat it up, add onion, bell pepper, salt and pepper, stir and cook for 5 minutes.

Add potatoes, thyme and eggs, stir, cover and cook at 360 °F for 20 minutes.

Divide among plates and serve for breakfast.

Nutritional Value (Amount per Serving):
* Calories 120
* Fat 10 g
* Carbohydrates 0.7 g
* Sugar 0.2 g
* Protein 5 g
* Cholesterol 22 mg

5.   Polenta Bites

Preparation time: 10 minutes | Cooking duration: 20 minutes | Serves: 4

Ingredients:

For the polenta:

- 1 tablespoon margarine
- 1 cup cornmeal
- 3 cups water
- Salt and black pepper to the taste

For the polenta bites:

- 2 tbps powdered sugar
- Cooking spray

Cooking Instructions:

In a pan, mix the water with the cornmeal, margarine, salt and pepper, mix, bring to a boil over medium heat, cook for 10 minutes, remove from heat, blend once more and refrigerate until it's cold.

Collect 1 tablespoon of polenta, form a ball and place it on a work surface.

Repeat with the rest of the polenta, place all the balls in the cooking basket of your air fryer, spray them with cooking spray, cover and cook at 380 ° C for 8 minutes.

Arrange the polenta bites on plates, sprinkle with sugar and serve for breakfast.

Nutritional Value (Amount per Serving):

- Calories 117
- Fat 10.2 g
- Protein 8 g
- Cholesterol 23 mg

6.   Delicious Breakfast Potatoes

Preparation time: 10 minutes | Cooking duration: 35 minutes | Serves: 4

Ingredients:

- 2 tbps olive oil
- 3 potatoes, cubed
- 1 yellow onion, diced
- 1 red bell pepper, diced
- Salt and black pepper to the taste
- 1 tsp. garlic powder
- 1 tsp. sweet paprika
- 1 tsp. onion powder

Cooking Instructions:

Grease the basket of the air fryer with olive oil, add the potatoes, season and season with salt and pepper.

Add the onion, pepper, garlic powder, paprika and onion powder, mix well, cover and cook at 370 ° F for 30 minutes.

Divide the potato mixture on plates and serve for breakfast.

Nutritional Value (Amount per Serving):

- Calories 107
- Fat 9 g
- Carbohydrates 0.5 g
- Sugar 0.3 g
- Protein 9 g
- Cholesterol 22 mg

7.   Tasty Cinnamon Toast

Preparation time: 10 minutes | Cooking duration: 5 minutes | Serves: 6

Ingredients:

- 1 stick margarine, soft
- 12 bread slices
- 1/2 cup sugar
- 1 and 1/2 tsp. vanilla extract
- 1 and 1/2 tsp. cinnamon powder

Cooking Instructions:

In a bowl, mix soft margarine with sugar, vanilla and cinnamon and whisk well.

Spread this on bread slices, place them in your air fryer and cook at 400°F for 5 minutes,

Divide among plates and serve for breakfast.

Nutritional Value (Amount per Serving):

- Calories 120
- Fat 10.1 g
- Carbohydrates 0.4 g
- Sugar 0.3 g
- Protein 7 g
- Cholesterol 22 mg

8.   Sweet Breakfast Casserole

Preparation time: 10 minutes | Cooking duration: 30 minutes | Serves: 4

Ingredients:

- 3 tbps brown sugar
- 4 tbps margarine
- 2 tbps white sugar
- 1/2 tsp. cinnamon powder
- 1/2 cup flour

For the casserole:

- 2 eggs
- 2 tbps white sugar
- 2 and 1/2 cups white flour
- 1 tsp. baking soda
- 1 tsp. baking powder
- 2 eggs
- 1/2 cup milk
- 2 cups margarinemilk
- 4 tbps margarine
- Zest from 1 lemon, grated
- 1 and 2/3 cup blueberries

Cooking Instructions:

In a bowl, mix the eggs with 2 tablespoons of white sugar, 2 and 1/2 cups of white flour, baking powder, baking soda, 2 eggs, milk, margarine, 4 tablespoons of margarine, lemon and blueberries, mix and pour into a pan that fits your air fryer.

In other bowls, mix 3 tablespoons of brown sugar with 2 tablespoons of white sugar, 4 tablespoons of margarine, 1/2 cup of flour and cinnamon, mix until crumbled and spread over the blueberry mixture.

Place in a preheated air fryer and bake at 300 ° F for 30 minutes.

Divide between plates and serve for breakfast.

Nutritional Value (Amount per Serving):

- Calories 106
- Fat 9.8 g
- Carbohydrates 0.5 g
- Sugar 0.2 g
- Protein 9 g
- Cholesterol 26 mg

9. Air Fried Sandwich

Preparation time: 10 minutes | Cooking duration: 6 minutes | Serves: 2

Ingredients:

- 2 English muffins, halved
- 2 eggs
- 2 bacon strips
- Salt and black pepper to the taste

Cooking Instructions:

Break the eggs in your air fryer, add the bacon on top, cover and cook at 120 ° C for 6 minutes.

Heat the English muffin halves in the microwave for a few seconds, divide the eggs into 2 halves, add the bacon on top, season with salt and pepper, cover with the other 2 English muffins and serve for breakfast.

Nutritional Value (Amount per Serving):

- Calories 108
- Fat 7.9 g
- Carbohydrates 0.7 g
- Sugar 0 g
- Protein 6 g
- Cholesterol 15 mg

10. Air Fried French Toast

Preparation: 4 minutes | Cooking duration: 6 minutes | Serves: 4

Ingredients:

- 2 slices of sourdough bread
- 3 eggs
- 1 tablespoon of margarine
- 1 tsp. of liquid vanilla
- 3 tsp.s of honey
- 2 tbps of Greek yogurt Berries

Cooking Instructions:

Preheat the air fryer to 356 ° F.

Pour the vanilla into the eggs and whisk to mix. Spread the margarine on all sides of the bread and dip the eggs into absorb.

Place the bread in the basket of the air fryer and bake for 3 minutes. Turn the bread over and bake for another 3 minutes.

Transfer to a place, garnish with yogurt and berries with a sprinkle of honey.

Nutritional Value (Amount per Serving):

- Calories 104
- Fat 8.8 g
- Carbohydrates 0.2 g
- Sugar 0.2 g
- Protein 7 g
- Cholesterol 20 mg

11. Rustic Breakfast

Preparation time: 10 minutes | Cooking duration: 13 minutes | Serves: 4

Ingredients:

- 7 ounces baby spinach
- 8 chestnuts mushrooms, halved
- 8 tomatoes, halved
- 1 garlic clove, minced
- 4 chipolatas
- 4 bacon slices, diced
- Salt and black pepper to the taste
- 4 eggs
- Cooking spray

Cooking Instructions:

Grease a pan with oil and add the tomatoes, garlic and mushrooms.

Add the bacon and fries, also add the spinach and the broken eggs at the end.

Season with salt and pepper, place the pan in the cooking basket of your air fryer and cook for 13 minutes at 350 ° F.

• Divide between plates and serve for breakfast.

Nutritional Value (Amount per Serving):

- Calories 109
- Fat 8.2 g
- Carbohydrates 0.6 g
- Sugar 0 g
- Protein 9 g
- Cholesterol 25 mg

12. Turkey Burrito

Preparation time: 10 minutes Cooking duration: 10 minutes Serves: 2

Ingredients:

- 4 slices turkey breast already cooked
- 1/2 red bell pepper, sliced
- 2 eggs
- 1 small avocado, peeled, pitted and sliced
- 2 tbps salsa
- Salt and black pepper to the taste
- 1/8 cup mozzarella cheese, grated
- Tortillas for serving

Cooking Instructions:

In a bowl, beat the eggs with salt and pepper to taste, pour them into a pan and place them in the basket of the air fryer.

Cook at 400 ° F for 5 minutes, remove the pan from the fryer and transfer the eggs to a plate.

Arrange the tortillas on a work surface, divide the eggs on them, also divide the turkey meat, pepper, cheese, salsa and avocado.

Roll up the burritos and place them in the air fryer after coating it with aluminum foil.

Heat the burritos to 300 ° F for 3 minutes, divide them into plates and serve.

Nutritional Value (Amount per Serving):

- Calories 122
- Fat 8.4 g
- Carbohydrates 0.3 g

- Sugar 0.2 g
- Protein 5.4 g
- Cholesterol 16 mg

13. Breakfast Egg Bowls

Preparation time: 10 minutes | Cooking duration: 20 minutes | Serves: 4

Ingredients:

- 4 dinner rolls, tops cut off and insides scooped out
- 4 tbps heavy cream
- 4 eggs
- 4 tbps mixed chives and parsley
- Salt and black pepper to the taste
- 4 tbps parmesan, grated

Cooking Instructions:

Arrange the dinner rolls on a baking tray and break one egg into each.

Divide the cream, mixed herbs into each roll and season with salt and pepper.

Sprinkle parmesan over the rolls, place them in the air fryer and cook at 350 ° F for 20 minutes.

Divide bowls of bread on plates and serve for breakfast.

Nutritional Value (Amount per Serving):

- Calories 104
- Fat 8.2 g
- Carbohydrates 1 g
- Sugar 0 g
- Protein 9 g
- Cholesterol 23 mg

14. Tasty Baked Eggs

Preparation time: 10 minutes | Cooking Time: 20 minutes | Serves: 4

Ingredients:

- 4 eggs
- 1 pound baby spinach, torn
- 7 ounces ham, diced
- 4 tbps milk
- 1 tablespoon olive oil
Cooking spray
- Salt and black pepper to the taste

Cooking Instructions:

Heat a pan with the oil over medium heat, add the spinach, cook for a couple of minutes and remove from the heat, stirring.

Grease 4 molds with cooking spray and divide the spinach and ham.

Break an egg into each mold, also divide the milk, season with salt and pepper, place the molds in an air fryer preheated to 350 ° F and bake for 20 minutes.

• Serve baked eggs for breakfast.

Nutritional Value (Amount per Serving):

- Calories 110
- Fat 8.3 g
- Carbohydrates 1 g
- Sugar 0 g
- Cholesterol 19 mg

15. French Toast Delight

Preparation: 15 minutes | Cooking duration: 10 minutes | Serves: 2

Ingredients:

- 4 bread slices
- 2 tbps margarine
- 1/2 tsp. cinnamon
- 2 Eggs
- Pinch salt
- Pinch ground cloves
- Pinch Nutmeg
- Icing sugar and maple syrup, to serve

Cooking Instructions:

Preheat the air fryer to 350 ° F. Whisk together eggs, cloves, cinnamon, nutmeg, cloves and salt in a bowl. Margarine on the sides of each slice of bread and cut into strips.

Dip the strips of bread with the margarine one after the other in the egg mixture and place them in the pan. (Cook in twice as needed).

Cook for 2 minutes and then remove the strips. Lightly coat the bread strips with cooking spray on both sides. Return the pan to the deep fryer and cook for another 4 minutes, making sure they cook evenly.

Remove the bread from the air fryer once it is golden brown. Sprinkle with powdered sugar and drizzle with maple syrup.

Nutritional Value (Amount per Serving):

- Calories 120
- Fat 9.1 g
- Carbohydrates 0.4 g
- Sugar 0.3 g
- Protein 7 g

16. Rarebit Air-Fried Egg

Preparation: 5 minutes | Cooking duration: 5 minutes | Serves: 2-4

Ingredients:

- 4 Slices Sourdough
- 4 Eggs
- 1/3 cup ale
- 1 & 1/2 cups cheddar, grated
- 1 tsp. mustard powder
- 1/2 tsp. paprika
- Black Pepper to taste
- 2 tsp. Worcestershire Sauce

Cooking Instructions:

Fry the eggs, sunny side up and set aside. Preheat the air fryer to 350 ° F.

In a bowl, combine the cheddar, beer, paprika, mustard powder and Worcestershire sauce.

Spread only one side of each slice of sourdough with the cheddar mixture.

Place the slices of bread in the tray of the air fryer. Cook for about 3 minutes until lightly browned.

Garnish the rare pieces with fried eggs and spices with pepper to taste.

Nutritional Value (Amount per Serving):

- Calories 120

- Fat 9.4 g
- Carbohydrates 0.6 g
- Sugar 0.3 g
- Protein 6 g
- Cholesterol 22 mg

17.   Garlic and Cheese Bread Rolls

Preparation: 10 minutes | Cooking duration: 5 minutes | Serves: 2

Ingredients:
- 8 tbps of grated cheese
- 6 tsp.s of melted margarine
- Garlic bread spice mix
- 2 bread rolls

Cooking Instructions:

Slice the sandwiches from the top crosswise but do not cut them at the bottom.

Place all the cheese in the slots and brush the tops of the sandwiches with the melted margarine. Sprinkle the garlic mix on the rolls.

Heat the air fryer to 350 ° F. Place the rolls in the basket and cook until the cheese has melted for about 5 minutes.

Nutritional Value (Amount per Serving):
- Calories 120
- Fat 9 g
- Carbohydrates 0.5 g
- Sugar 0.2 g
- Protein 6 g
- Cholesterol 20 mg

18.   Wheat &Seed Bread

Preparation: 70 minutes | Cooking duration: 18 minutes | Serves: 4

Ingredients:
- 31/2 ounces of flour
- 1 tsp. of yeast
- 1 tsp. of salt
- 3 &1/2 ounces of wheat flour ¼ cup of pumpkin seeds

Cooking Instructions:

Mix the wheat flour, baking powder, salt, seeds and 00 flour in a large bowl. Stir ¾ cup of warm water and keep stirring until the dough becomes soft.

Knead for another 5 minutes until the dough becomes elastic and smooth. Shape into a ball and cover with a plastic bag. Leave to rise for 30 minutes.

Heat the air fryer to 392 ° F.

Transfer the dough to a pizza pan and place it in the air fryer. Cook for 18 minutes until golden brown. Remove and place on a wire rack to cool.

Nutritional Value (Amount per Serving):
- Calories 118
- Fat 9.2 g
- Carbohydrates 0.2 g
- Sugar 0.2 g
- Protein 9 g
- Cholesterol 23 mg

19.   Thai Style Omelette

Preparation: 5minutes | Cooking duration: 10 minutes | Serves: 2

Ingredients:
- 3 & 1/2 oz minced Pancetta
- 2 Eggs
- 1 cup onion, diced
- 1 tablespoon fish salt

Cooking Instructions:

Beat the eggs until it is light and fluffy. Preheat the Air fryer to 280°F.

In a bowl, add together all the ingredients. Pour the mixture into the air fryer tray.

Remove after 10 minutes or once omelet is golden brown. Cut and serve.

Nutritional Value (Amount per Serving):
- Calories 122
- Fat 8.7 g
- Carbohydrates 0.6 g
- Sugar 0.2 g
- Protein 6 g
- Cholesterol 15 mg

20.   Apple-Cinnamon Empanadas

Preparation: 15 minutes | Cooking duration: 30 minutes | Serves: 2-4

Ingredients:
- 2-3 baking apples, peeled & diced
- 2 tsp.s of cinnamon
- 1/4 cup white sugar
- 1 tablespoon brown sugar
- 1 tablespoon of water
- 1/2 tablespoon cornstarch
- ¼ tsp. of vanilla extract
- 2 tbps of margarine or margarine
- 4 pre-made empanada dough shells (Goya)

Cooking Instructions:

In a bowl, combine the white sugar, brown sugar, cornstarch and cinnamon; set aside. Put the diced apples in a saucepan and put them on the stove.

Add the dry ingredients combined to the apples, then add the water, vanilla extract and margarine; stirring well to mix.

Cover the pot and cook over high heat. Once it starts to boil, lower the heat and simmer, until the apples are soft. Remove from heat and let cool.

Place the empanada shells on a clean surface. Pour the apple mixture into each of the shells, being careful to avoid spilling on the edges. Fold the shells to completely cover the apple mixture, seal the edges with water, pressing down to secure them with a fork.

Cover the air fryer basket with aluminum foil but leave the edges uncovered so that air can circulate through the basket. Place the empanadas shells in the foil-lined air fryer basket, set the temperature to 350 ° F and timer for 15 minutes.

Halfway through cooking, remove the basket and turn the empanadas with a spatula. Remove from the oven when

golden and serve directly from the basket onto plates.
Nutritional Value (Amount per Serving):

- Calories 122
- Fat 8.7 g
- Carbohydrates 0.7 g
- Sugar 0.2 g
- Protein 6 g
- Cholesterol 23 mg

21.   Baked Eggs
Preparation: 2 minutes | Cooking duration: 15-20 | minutes Serves: 4

Ingredients:

- 7 Oz. leg ham
- 4 eggs
- 4 tsp.s full cream milk Margarine
- 1 lb baby spinach
- 1 tablespoon olive oil Salt and Pepper to taste

Cooking Instructions:

Preheat the air fryer to 350 ° F. Place four molds with the margarine.
Divide the spinach and ham equally in the four molds. Break 1 egg into each and add a teaspoon. of milk. Season with salt and pepper.
Place in the air fryer for about 15-20 minutes. For a runny yolk, cook for 15 minutes, when fully cooked; 20 minutes.
Nutritional Value (Amount per Serving):

- Calories 125
- Fat 8.1 g
- Carbohydrates 0.3 g
- Sugar 0.2 g
- Protein 7 g
- Cholesterol 15 mg

22.   Light Blueberry Muffins
Preparation: 15 minutes | Cooking duration: 15 minutes | Serves: 11-12

Ingredients:

- 1 cup of fresh, ripe blueberries, rinsed
- 1&1/2 cups all-purpose flour
- 1/2 cup of white sugar
- 2 tsp.s of baking powder
- 1/3 cup of vegetable oil
- 1 medium-sized egg
- 1/2 tsp. of salt ¼ cup unsweetened yogurt
- 1 tablespoon brown sugar
- 2 tsp.s vanilla extract

Cooking Instructions:

Lightly sprinkle the blueberries with flour, shake and set aside. Combine the yeast, sugar, flour, and salt in a large bowl, mixing well to combine evenly.
In a smaller bowl, whisk the egg, oil, yogurt and vanilla extract together until a uniform combination is achieved. Pour it into the larger bowl containing the dry ingredients and mix well with a whisk or fork.
Add the blueberries, using a wooden spoon or spatula to gently fold them. Arrange the muffin tins on the baking sheet and place them on the basket of the air fryer (make

two batches). Pour the batter into the muffin tins, filling about ¾ away.
Now sprinkle with brown sugar. Set at 350 ° F for 10 minutes. To remove. (Muffins are ready when a toothpick inserted in the center comes out dry. Otherwise, return the basket and return the air fryer to 320 ° F and a cooking duration of 2 minutes).
Let the muffins cool for a while.

23.   Simple Egg Soufflé
Preparation Time: 5 minutes Cooking Time: 8 minutes Serving: 2

Ingredients:

- 2 eggs
- 1/4 tsp chili pepper 2 tbsp heavy cream 1/4 tsp pepper
- 1 tbsp parsley, chopped Salt

Cooking Instructions:

In a bowl, whisk eggs with remaining gradients.
Spray two ramekins with cooking spray.
Pour egg mixture into the prepared ramekins and place into the air fryer basket.
Cook soufflé at 390 F for 8 minutes.
Serve and enjoy.
Nutritional Value (Amount per Serving):

- Calories 112
- Fat 10 g
- Carbohydrates 1.1 g
- Sugar 0.4 g
- Protein 6 g
- Cholesterol 184 mg

24.   Milky Semolina Cutlets
Preparation: 45 minutes | Cooking duration: 15 | minutes Serves: 2

Ingredients:

- 3 tbps of vegetable oil
- 1 cup of semolina
- 12 ounces of mixed vegetables (any of your choice), diced
- 2 & 1/2 pounds of milk
- 1/2tsp. salt
- 1/2 tsp. black pepper, ground

Cooking Instructions:

Pour the milk into a saucepan and heat. Add the mixed vegetables and cook until soft for about 3 minutes.
Add the pepper and salt and then the semolina. Cook until the mixture has thickened; this will take about 10 minutes.
Grease a flat plate with oil; spread the semolina mixture over it. Refrigerate for about 4 hours until it is very firm.
Heat the air fryer to 350 ° F.
Remove from the refrigerator and cut into flat round shapes. Brush the cutlets with oil and place them in the air fryer.
Cook for 10 minutes. Serve hot with a sauce of your choice.
Nutritional Value (Amount per Serving):

- Calories 119

- Fat 8.1 g
- Carbohydrates 0.2 g
- Sugar 0.2 g
- Protein 7 g
- Cholesterol 20 mg

25. Oatmeal Muffins

Preparation: 5minutes Cooking Duration: 15 minutes | Serves: 2-4

Ingredients:
- 2 Eggs
- 31/2 ounce oats
- 3 ounce margarine, melted
- 1/2 cup flour
- 1/4 tsp. vanilla essence
- 1/2 cup icing sugar Pinch baking powder
- 1 tablespoon raisins
- Cooking spray

Cooking Instructions:

Combine the sugar and margarine until soft. Whisk together the eggs and vanilla essence. Add it to the sugar / margarine mixture until soft peaks form.

Combine flour, raisins, baking powder and oats in a separate bowl. Add it to the blended ingredients.

Lightly grease the muffin tins with cooking spray and fill them with batter. Preheat the air fryer to 350 ° F.

Place the muffin tins in the tray of the air fryer.

Cook for 12 minutes.

Nutritional Value (Amount per Serving):
- Calories 105
- Fat 9.4 g
- Carbohydrates 0.5 g
- Sugar 0.3 g
- Protein 5 g
- Cholesterol 22 mg

26. Mushroom Oatmeal

Preparation time: 10 minutes Cooking duration: 20 minutes Serves: 4

Ingredients:
- 1 small yellow onion, chopped
- 1 cup steel cut oats
- 2 garlic cloves, minced
- 2 tbps margarine
- ½ cup water
- 14 ounces canned chicken stock
- 3 thyme springs, chopped
- 2 tbps extra virgin olive oil
- ½ cup gouda cheese, grated
- 8 ounces mushroom, sliced
- Salt and black pepper to the taste

Cooking Instructions:

Heat a pan suitable for an air fryer with the margarine over medium heat, add the onions and garlic, stir and cook for 4 minutes.

Add the oats, water, salt, pepper, broth and thyme, mix, place in the air fryer and cook at 360 ° F for 16 minutes.

Meanwhile, heat a pan with olive oil over medium heat, add mushrooms, cook for 3 minutes, combine with oatmeal and cheese, mix, divide into bowls and serve for breakfast.

Nutritional Value (Amount per Serving):
- Calories 113
- Fat 8.2 g
- Carbohydrates 0.3 g
- Sugar 0.2 g
- Protein 8 g

27. Corn Kernel Fritters

Preparation: 5 minutes | Cooking duration: 5 minutes | Serves: 1

Ingredients:
- 1 Egg
- 1 cup corn kernels 3/4 cup milk
- 1 cup flour
- 1&1/2 tsp.s baking powder
- 1/2 tsp.s salt
- 1/4 tsp.s pepper
- 2 tbps margarine, melted

Cooking Instructions:

Preheat the air fryer to 375 ° F. In a bowl combine the flour, yeast, salt and pepper.

In another bowl, whisk together egg, milk and margarine and combine with dry ingredients, mixing well. Stir in the corn and leave for 5 minutes to allow the batter to sit well.

Now, form the batter into small rounded pancakes. Place the pancakes on a baking sheet and let them freeze for 5 minutes to keep the shape.

Finally, place the pancakes in the tray of the air fryer, set the timer for 4-5 minutes. Serve and enjoy with yogurt sauce or gravy.

Nutritional Value (Amount per Serving):
- Calories 122
- Fat 8.2 g
- Carbohydrates 0.2 g
- Sugar 0.2 g
- Protein 5.2 g
- Cholesterol 17 mg

28. Biscuits Casserole

Preparation time: 10 minutes Cooking duration: 15 minutes Serves: 8

Ingredients:
- 12 ounces biscuits, quartered
- 3 tbps flour
- 1/2 pound sausage, diced
- A pinch of salt and black pepper
- 2 and 1/2 cups milk
- Cooking spray

Cooking Instructions:

Grease your air fryer with cooking spray and heat it over 350 °F.

Add biscuits on the bottom and mix with sausage.

Add flour, milk, salt and pepper, toss a bit and cook for 15 minutes.

Divide among plates and serve for breakfast.

Nutritional Value (Amount per Serving):

- Calories 122
- Fat 8 g
- Carbohydrates 0.4 g
- Sugar 0.2 g
- Protein 5.1 g
- Cholesterol 18 mg

29.   Breakfast Sandwich

Preparation: 5minutes | Cooking duration: 7minutes | Serves: 1

Ingredients:
- 2 Bacon Slices
- 1 Egg
- 1 English muffin Salt& Pepper to taste

Cooking Instructions:

Beat the egg into a soufflé cup and add salt and pepper to taste.

Heat the air fryer to 390°F and place the soufflé cup, English muffin and bacon into the tray.

Cook all the ingredients for 6-10 minutes. Assemble sandwich and enjoy.

Nutritional Value (Amount per Serving):
- Calories 109
- Fat 9 g
- Carbohydrates 0.7 g
- Sugar 0.2 g
- Protein 6 g
- Cholesterol 22 mg

30.   Walnuts and Pear Oatmeal

Preparation time: 5 minutes Cooking duration: 12 minutes Serves: 4

Ingredients:
- 1 cup water
- 1 tablespoon margarine, soft
- ¼ cups brown sugar
- ½ tsp. cinnamon powder
- 1 cup rolled oats
- ½ cup walnuts, chopped
- 2 cups pear, peeled and chopped
- ½ cup raisins

Cooking Instructions:

In a heat proof dish that fits your air fryer, mix milk with sugar, margarine, oats, cinnamon, raisins, pears and walnuts, stir, introduce in your fryer and cook at 360°F for 12 minutes.

Divide into bowls and serve.

Nutritional Value (Amount per Serving):
- Calories 122
- Fat 8.2 g
- Carbohydrates 0.3 g
- Sugar 0.2 g
- Protein 5.1 g
- Cholesterol 18 mg

31.   French Toast Delight

Preparation time: minutes Cooking time: minutes Serves: 2

Ingredients
- 4 bread slices 2 tbps margarine 1/2 tsp. cinnamon 2 Eggs
- Pinch salt
- Pinch ground cloves Pinch Nutmeg Icing sugar and maple syrup, to serve

Cooking Instructions

Preheat AirFryer to 350 ° F. Whisk together eggs, cloves, cinnamon, nutmeg, cloves and salt in a bowl. Margarine on the sides of each slice of bread and cut into strips.

Dip the strips of bread with the margarine one after the other in the egg mixture and place them in the pan. (Cook in twice as needed).

Cook for 2 minutes and then remove the strips. Lightly coat the bread strips with cooking spray on both sides. Return the pan to the airfryer and cook for another 4 minutes, making sure they cook evenly.

Remove the bread from the AirFryer once it is golden brown. Sprinkle with powdered sugar and drizzle with maple syrup.

Nutritional Value (Amount per Serving):
- Calories 122
- Fat 8.1 g
- Carbohydrates 0.3 g
- Sugar 0.2 g
- Protein 5.3 g
- Cholesterol 16 mg

32.   Milky Semolina Cutlets

Preparation time: 45 minutes Cooking time: 15 minutes Serves: 2

Ingredients

3 tbps of vegetable oil 1 cup of semolina 12 ounces of mixed vegetables (any of your choice), chopped 2½ pounds of milk ½ tsp. salt ½ tsp. black pepper, ground

Cooking Instructions

Pour the milk into a saucepan and heat. Add the mixed vegetables and cook until soft for about 3 minutes.

Add the pepper and salt and then the semolina. Cook until the mixture has thickened; this will take about 10 minutes.

Grease a flat plate with oil; spread over the semolina mixture. Refrigerate for about 4 hours until it is very firm.

Heat the Airfryer to 350 ° F.

Remove from the refrigerator and cut into flat round shapes. Brush the cutlets with oil and put them in the airfryer.

Cook for 10 minutes. Serve hot with a sauce of your choice.

Nutritional Value (Amount per Serving):
- Calories 120
- Fat 8.4 g
- Carbohydrates 0.3 g
- Sugar 0.2 g
- Protein 5.4 g
- Cholesterol 17 mg

33. Light Blueberry Muffins

Preparation time: 15 minutes Cooking time: 15 minutes Serves: 11-12

Ingredients

1 cup of fresh, ripe blueberries, rinsed 1½ cups all-purpose flour ½ cup of white sugar 2 tsp.s of baking powder 1/3 cup of vegetable oil 1 medium-sized egg ½ tsp. of salt ¼ cup unsweetened yogurt 1 tablespoon brown sugar 2 tsp.s vanilla extract.

Cooking Instructions

Lightly sprinkle the blueberries with flour, shake and set aside. Combine the yeast, sugar, flour, and salt in a large bowl, mixing well to combine evenly.

In a smaller bowl, whisk the egg, oil, yogurt and vanilla extract together until a uniform combination is achieved. Pour it into the larger bowl containing the dry ingredients and mix well with a whisk or fork.

Add the blueberries, using a wooden spoon or spatula to gently fold them. Arrange the muffin tins on the baking sheet and place them on the air fryer basket (make two batches). Pour the batter into the muffin tins, filling them about ¾ apart.

Now sprinkle with brown sugar. Set at 350 ° F for 10 minutes. To remove. (The muffins are ready when a toothpick inserted in the center comes out dry. Otherwise, return the basket and reset the air fryer to 320 ° F and 2 minutes cooking.)

Let the muffins cool for a while and then enjoy!

Nutritional Value (Amount per Serving):
- Calories 120
- Fat 7 g
- Carbohydrates 0.3 g
- Sugar 0.2 g
- Protein 8 g

34. Corn Kernel Fritters

Preparation time: 5 minutes Cooking time: 5 minutes Serves: 1

Ingredients
- 1 Egg
- 1 cup corn kernels 3/4 cup milk
- 1 cup flour
- 1½ tsp.s baking powder
- 1/2 tsp.s salt 1/4 tsp.s
- pepper 2 tbps margarine, melted

Cooking Instructions

Preheat AirFryer to 375 ° F. In a bowl combine flour, baking powder, salt and pepper.

In another bowl, whisk together the egg, milk and margarine and add to the dry ingredients, mixing well. Stir in the corn and leave for 5 minutes to allow the batter to sit well.

Now, form the batter into small rounded pancakes. Place the pancakes on a baking sheet and let them freeze for 5 minutes to keep the shape.

Finally, place the pancakes in the AirFryer pan, set the timer for 4-5 minutes. Serve and enjoy with yogurt sauce or gravy.

Nutritional Value (Amount per Serving):
- Calories 125
- Fat 8.4 g
- Carbohydrates 0.3 g
- Sugar 0.2 g
- Protein 5.1 g
- Cholesterol 18 mg

35. Apple Oat Sunrise Fritters

Preparation time: 10 minutes Cooking time: 5 minutes Serves: 2

Ingredients
- 2 Apples, peeled, cored & sliced into rings 1/2 cup + 2 tbps sugar 1½ tsp.s ground cinnamon, divided 1/2 cup rice flour 2 tbps cornstarch 1 tsp. baking powder 1/2 cup club soda
- 1 cup oats
- Egg
- 3/4 tsp. kosher salt

Cooking Instructions

Combine 1 tsp. of cinnamon and 1/2 cup of sugar in a shallow bowl, whisking well. Next, preheat the air fryer to 350 ° F.

In a food processor, blend the oats into a coarse powder. Put in a large bowl and add the rice flour, baking powder, cornstarch, salt, cinnamon and the rest of the sugar, whisking well.

Add the egg and club soda, stirring more soda, a little at a time, until the mixture is like pancake batter.

Dip the apple rings into the batter, then place them in the AirFryer tray, one set at a time. Bake until golden and crisp for about 4 minutes.

Serve the pancakes sprinkled with the reserved cinnamon sugar.

Nutritional Value (Amount per Serving):
- Calories 115
- Fat 8.2 g
- Carbohydrates 0.3 g
- Sugar 0.2 g
- Protein 6 g
- Cholesterol 14 mg

36. Egg Cups

Preparation Time: 10 minutes Cooking Time: 18 minutes Serves: 12

Ingredients:
- 12 eggs
- 4 oz cream cheese
- 12 bacon strips, uncooked 1/4 cup buffalo sauce
- 2/3 cup cheddar cheese, shredded Pepper
- Salt

Cooking Instructions:

In a bowl, beat the eggs, pepper and salt together.

Line each silicone muffin mold with a strip of bacon.

Pour the egg mixture into each muffin pan and place it in the basket of the air fryer. (In batches)

Cook at 350 F for 8 minutes.

In another bowl, mix the cheddar and cream cheese and microwave for 30 seconds. Add the buffalo sauce and mix well.

Remove the muffin tins from the air fryer and add 2 teaspoons of cheese mixture to the center of each egg cup.

Return the muffin tins to the air fryer and cook for another 10 minutes.

Serve and enjoy.

Nutritional Value (Amount per Serving):

- Calories 215
- Fat 17 g
- Carbohydrates 1 g
- Sugar 0.4 g
- Protein 10 g
- Cholesterol 172 mg

37.   Cherries Risotto

Preparation time: 10 minutes Cooking duration: 12 minutes Serves: 4

Ingredients:

- 1 and ½ cups Arborio rice
- 1 and ½ tsp.s cinnamon powder
- 1/3 cup brown sugar
- A pinch of salt
- 2 tbps margarine
- 2 apples, cored and sliced
- 1 cup apple juice
- 3 cups milk
- ½ cup cherries, dried

Cooking Instructions:

Heat a pan that wraps the fryer with the margarine over medium heat, add the rice, stir and cook for 4-5 minutes.

Add sugar, apples, apple juice, milk, cinnamon and cherries, mix, place in air fryer and cook at 350 ° F for 8 minutes.

Divide into bowls and serve for breakfast.

Nutritional Value (Amount per Serving):

- Calories 122
- Fat 8.7 g
- Carbohydrates 0.5 g
- Sugar 0.2 g
- Protein 5.6 g
- Cholesterol 20 mg

38.   Apple Oat Sunrise Fritters

Preparation: 10 minutes | Cooking duration: 5 minutes | Serves: 2

Ingredients:

- 2 Apples, peeled, cored & sliced into rings
- 1/2 cup + 2 tbps sugar
- 1&1/2 tsp.s ground cinnamon, divided
- 1/2 cup rice flour
- 2 tbps cornstarch
- 1 tsp. baking powder
- 1/2 cup club soda
- 1 cup oats
- 1 Egg
- 3/4 tsp. kosher salt

Cooking Instructions:

Combine 1 tsp. of cinnamon and 1/2 cup of sugar in a shallow bowl, whisking well. Next, preheat the air fryer to 350

° F.

In a food processor, blend the oats into a coarse powder. Transfer to a large bowl and add the rice flour, baking powder, cornstarch, salt, cinnamon and the rest of the sugar, whisking well.

Add the egg and club soda, stirring more soda, a little at a time, until the mixture is like pancake batter.

Dip the apple rings into the batter and place them in the plate of the air fryer, one set at a time. Bake until golden and crisp for about 4 minutes.

Serve the pancakes sprinkled with the reserved cinnamon sugar.

Nutritional Value (Amount per Serving):

- Calories 113
- Fat 8.2 g
- Carbohydrates 0.3 g
- Sugar 0.2 g
- Protein 5.2 g
- Cholesterol 17 mg

39.   Rice, Almonds and Raisins Pudding

Preparation time: 5 minutes Cooking duration: 8 minutes Serves: 4

Ingredients:

- 1 cup brown rice
- ½ cup coconut chips
- 1 cup milk
- 2 cups water
- ½ cup maple syrup
- ¼ cup raisins
- ¼ cup almonds
- A pinch of cinnamon powder

Cooking Instructions:

Place the rice in a pan suitable for an air fryer, add water, heat on the stove over medium-high heat, cook until the rice is soft and drain.

Add the milk, coconut drops, almonds, raisins, cinnamon and maple syrup, mix well, place in the air fryer and cook at 360 ° for 8 minutes.

Divide the rice pudding into bowls and serve.

Nutritional Value (Amount per Serving):

- Calories 120
- Fat 7.5 g
- Carbohydrates 0.3 g
- Sugar 0.2 g
- Protein 6 g
- Cholesterol 15 mg

40.   Dates and Millet Pudding

Preparation time: 10 minutes Cooking time: 15 minutes Serves: 4

Ingredients:

- 14 ounces milk
- 7 ounces water
- 2/3 cup millet
- 4 dates, pitted
- Honey for serving

Cooking Instructions:

Put the millet in a pan that fits your air fryer, add dates, milk and water, stir, introduce in your air fryer and cook at 360 °F for 15 minutes.

Divide among plates, drizzle honey on top and serve for breakfast.

Nutritional Value (Amount per Serving):

- Calories 113
- Fat 8.4 g
- Carbohydrates 0.3 g
- Sugar 0.2 g
- Protein 5.9 g
- Cholesterol 16 mg

41.   Tomato and Bacon Breakfast

Preparation time: 10 minutes Cooking duration: 30 minutes Serves: 6

Ingredients:

- 1 pound white bread, cubed
- 1 pound smoked bacon, cooked and diced
- ¼ cup olive oil
- 1 yellow onion, diced
- 28 ounces canned tomatoes, diced
- 1/2 tsp. red pepper, crushed
- 1/2 pound cheddar, shredded
- 2 tbps chives, diced
- 1/2 pound Monterey jack, shredded
- 2 tbps stock
- Salt and black pepper to the taste
- 8 eggs, whisked

Cooking Instructions:

Add oil to the air fryer and heat it to 350 ° F.

Add the bread, bacon, onion, tomatoes, chilli and broth and mix.

Add the eggs, cheddar and Monterey Jack and cook for 20 minutes.

Divide on plates, sprinkle with chives and serve.

Nutritional Value (Amount per Serving):

- Calories 115
- Fat 9 g
- Carbohydrates 0.3 g
- Sugar 0.2 g
- Protein 6 g
- Cholesterol 20 mg

42.   Creamy Hash Browns

Preparation time: 10 minutes Cooking duration: 20 minutes Serves: 6

Ingredients:

- 2 pounds hash browns
- 1 cup whole milk
- 8 bacon slices, diced
- 9 ounces cream cheese
- 1 yellow onion, diced
- 1 cup cheddar cheese, shredded
- 6 green onions, diced
- Salt and black pepper to the taste
- 6 eggs

- Cooking spray

Cooking Instructions:

Heat your air fryer to 350 ° F and grease it with cooking spray.

In a bowl, mix the eggs with the milk, cream cheese, cheddar cheese, bacon, onion, salt and pepper and beat well.

Add the fried potatoes to the air fryer, add the eggs mixed on top and cook for 20 minutes.

Divide between plates and serve.

Nutritional Value (Amount per Serving):

- Calories 117
- Fat 9 g
- Carbohydrates 0.5 g
- Sugar 0.2 g
- Protein 6 g
- Cholesterol 18 mg

43.   Breakfast Casserole

Preparation Time: 10 minutes Cooking Time: 28 minutes Serves: 4

Ingredients:

- 2 eggs
- 4 egg whites
- 4 tsp pine nuts, minced 2/3 cup chicken broth
  1 lb Italian sausage
- 1/4 cup roasted red pepper, sliced 1/4 cup
  pesto sauce
- 2/3 cup parmesan cheese, grated 1/8 tsp pepper
- 1/4 tsp sea salt

Cooking Instructions:

Preheat the air fryer to 370 F.

Spray the air pan with cooking spray and set aside.

Heat another skillet over medium heat. Add the sausage to a skillet and cook until golden brown.

After cooking, drain the excess oil and spread it in the prepared pan.

Whisk the remaining ingredients except the pine nuts in a bowl and pour over the sausage.

Place the pan in the air fryer and cook for 25-28 minutes.

Garnish with pine nuts and serve.

Nutritional Value (Amount per Serving):

- Calories 650
- Fat 41 g
- Carbohydrates 2 g
- Sugar 2.1 g
- Protein 42 g
- Cholesterol 210 mg

44.   Vegetable Quiche

Preparation Time: 10 minutes Cooking Time: 24 minutes Serves: 6

Ingredients:

- 8 eggs
- cup coconut milk
- 1 cup tomatoes, chopped 1 cup zucchini, chopped
  1 tbsp butter
- 1 onion, chopped
- 1 cup Parmesan cheese, grated 1/2 tsp pepper

- tsp salt

Cooking Instructions:

Preheat the air fryer to 370 F.

Melt the butter in a skillet over medium heat, then add the onion and sauté until the onion is slightly golden.

Add the tomatoes and courgettes to the pan and brown for 4-5 minutes.

Transfer the cooked vegetables to the pan of the air fryer.

Beat the eggs with cheese, milk, pepper and salt in a bowl.

Pour the egg mixture over the vegetables in a pan.

Place the dish in the air fryer and cook for 24 minutes or until the eggs have solidified.

Slice and serve.

Nutritional Value (Amount per Serving):
- Calories 245
- Fat 15 g
- Carbohydrates 8.5 g
- Sugar 4.5 g
- Protein 23 g
- Cholesterol 251 mg

45. Spinach Muffins

Preparation Time: 10 minutes Cooking Time: 20 minutes Serves: 8

Ingredients:
- 4 eggs
- 1/2 tsp baking powder 1 zucchini, grated
- 1/4 cup parmesan cheese, grated 1/2 cup feta cheese, crumbled
- 4 onion spring, chopped 1/3 cup coconut flour 1/4 cup butter, melted
- 4 tbsp parsley, chopped 1/2 tsp nutmeg
- 1/4 cup water
- 1/2 cup spinach, cooked 1/4 tsp pepper
- 1/4 tsp salt

Cooking Instructions:

Preheat the air fryer to 370 F.

In a bowl, whisk together the eggs, water, butter and salt.

Add the baking soda and coconut flour and mix well.

Add the onions, nutmeg, parsley, spinach and courgettes. Mix well.

Add the parmesan and feta and mix well. Season with pepper and salt.

Pour the batter into the silicone muffin molds and place in the basket of the air fryer.

Bake the muffins for 20 minutes.

Serve and enjoy.

Nutritional Value (Amount per Serving):
- Calories 215
- Fat 16 g
- Carbohydrates 4.1 g
- Sugar 1.1 g
- Protein 15 g

46. Broccoli Muffins

Preparation Time: 10 minutes Cooking Time: 24 minutes Serves: 6

Ingredients:

19

- 2 large eggs
- 1 cup broccoli florets, chopped 1 cup unsweetened almond milk 2 cups almond flour
- tsp baking powder
- tbsp nutritional yeast 1/2 tsp sea salt

Cooking Instructions:

Preheat the air fryer to 325 F.

Add all ingredients into the large bowl and mix until well combined.

Pour mixture into the silicone muffin molds and place into the air fryer basket.

Cook muffins for 20-24 minutes.

Serve and enjoy.

Nutritional Value (Amount per Serving):
- Calories 240
- Fat 23 g
- Carbohydrates 12 g
- Sugar 1.7 g
- Protein 14 g
- Cholesterol 61 mg

47. Zucchini Gratin

Preparation Time: 10 minutes Cooking Time: 24 minutes Serves: 4

Ingredients:
- large egg, lightly beaten
- 1 1/4 cup unsweetened almond milk 3 medium zucchinis, sliced
- 1 tbsp Dijon mustard 1/2 cup nutritional yeast 1 tsp sea salt

Cooking Instructions:

Preheat the air fryer to 370 F.

Arrange the courgette slices in the pan of the air fryer.

In a saucepan, heat the almond milk over low heat and mix in the Dijon mustard, nutritional yeast and sea salt. Add the beaten egg and mix well.

Pour the sauce over the courgette slices.

Place the dish in the air fryer and cook for 20-24 minutes.

Serve and enjoy.

Nutritional Value (Amount per Serving):
- Calories 110
- Fat 3.4 g
- Carbohydrates 13 g
- Sugar 2 g
- Protein 11 g
- Cholesterol 50 mg

48. Vegetable Egg Soufflé

Preparation Time: 10 minutes Cooking Time: 20 minutes Serves: 4

Ingredients:
- 4 large eggs
- 1 tsp onion powder 1 tsp garlic powder
- 1 tsp red pepper, crushed
- 1/2 cup broccoli florets, chopped 1/2 cup mushrooms, chopped

Cooking Instructions:

Spray four molds with cooking spray and set aside.

In a bowl, beat the eggs with the onion powder, garlic powder and chilli.

Add mushrooms and broccoli and mix well.

Pour the egg mixture into the prepared molds and place the molds in the basket of the air fryer.

Cook at 350 F for 15 minutes. Make sure the souffle is cooked if the souffle is not cooked, then cook for another 5 minutes.

Serve and enjoy.

Nutritional Value (Amount per Serving):
- Calories 95
- Fat 5.5 g
- Carbohydrates 4.1 g
- Sugar 2.6 g
- Protein 8 g
- Cholesterol 180 mg

49. Breakfast Egg Muffins

Preparation Time: 10 minutes Cooking Time: 20 minutes Serves: 12

Ingredients:
- 6 eggs
- lb ground pork sausage 3 tbsp onion, minced
- 1/2 red pepper, diced 1 cup egg whites
- 1/2 cup mozzarella cheese 1 cup cheddar cheese

Cooking Instructions:

Preheat the air fryer to 325 F.

Brown the sausage over medium-high heat until the meat turns pink.

Divide the red pepper, cheese, cooked sausages and onion into each silicone muffin mold.

In a large bowl, whisk together the egg whites, egg, pepper and salt.

Pour the egg mixture into each muffin pan and place it in the basket of the batch air fryer.

Cook the muffins in the air fryer for 20 minutes.

Serve and enjoy.

Nutritional Value (Amount per Serving):
- Calories 193
- Fat 12 g
- Carbohydrates 2 g
- Sugar 0.7 g
- Protein 12 g
- Cholesterol 125 mg

50. Cinnamon and Cream Cheese Oats

Preparation time: 10 minutes Cooking duration: 25 minutes Serves: 4

Ingredients:
- 1 cup steel oats
- 3 cups milk
- 1 tablespoon margarine
- ¾ cup raisins
- 1 tsp. cinnamon powder
- ¼ cup brown sugar
- 2 tbps white sugar

- 2 ounces cream cheese, soft

Cooking Instructions:

Heat a pan suitable for air fryer with margarine over medium heat, add oats, mix and toast for 3 minutes.

Add the milk and raisins, mix, place in the air fryer and cook at 350 ° F for 20 minutes.

Meanwhile, in a bowl, mix the cinnamon with the brown sugar and stir.

In a second bowl, mix the white sugar with the cream cheese and whisk.

Divide the oats into bowls and garnish each with cinnamon and cream cheese.

Nutritional Value (Amount per Serving):
- Calories 95
- Fat 5.5 g
- Carbohydrates 4.1 g
- Sugar 2.6 g
- Protein 8 g
- Cholesterol 180 mg

51. Cheese Pie

Preparation Time: 10 minutes Cooking Time: 16 minutes Serves: 4

Ingredients:
- 8 eggs
- 1/2 cups heavy whipping cream 1 lb cheddar cheese, grated Pepper
- Salt

Cooking Instructions:

Preheat the air fryer to 325 F.

In a bowl, whisk together the cheese, eggs, whipping cream, pepper and salt.

Spray the air fryer pan with cooking spray.

Pour the egg mixture into the prepared dish and place it in the basket of the air fryer.

Cook for 16 minutes or until the egg is ready.

Serve and enjoy.

Nutritional Value (Amount per Serving):
- Calories 725
- Fat 61 g
- Carbohydrates 3.2 g
- Sugar 1.3 g
- Protein 42 g
- Cholesterol 502 mg

52. Parmesan Breakfast Casserole

Preparation Time: 10 minutes Cooking Time: 20 minutes Serves: 3

Ingredients:
- 5 eggs
- 2 tbsp heavy cream
- 3 tbsp chunky tomato sauce
- 2 tbsp parmesan cheese, grated

Cooking Instructions:

Preheat the air fryer to 325 F.

In the mixing bowl combine the cream and eggs.

Add the cheese and tomato sauce and mix well.

Spray the air fryer pan with cooking spray.
Pour the mixture into the pan and place it in the basket of the air fryer.
Cook for 20 minutes.
Serve and enjoy.
Nutritional Value (Amount per Serving):
- Calories 175
- Fat 12 g
- Carbohydrates 2 g
- Sugar 1.2 g
- Protein 12.3 g
- Cholesterol 280 mg

53.   Spinach Egg Breakfast
Preparation Time: 10 minutes Cooking Time: 20 minutes Serves: 4
Ingredients:
- 3 eggs
- 1/4 cup coconut milk
- 1/4 cup parmesan cheese, grated 4 oz spinach, chopped
- 3 oz cottage cheese

Cooking Instructions:
Preheat the air fryer to 350 F.
Add the eggs, milk, half parmesan and ricotta to a bowl and beat well. Add the spinach and mix well.
Pour the mixture into the pan of the air fryer.
Sprinkle the remaining half of Parmesan cheese.
Place the dish in the air fryer and cook for 20 minutes.
Serve and enjoy.
Nutritional Value (Amount per Serving):
- Calories 134
- Fat 8.1 g
- Carbohydrates 2.7 g
- Sugar 1.1 g
- Protein 16 g
- Cholesterol 130 mg

54.   Breakfast Egg Tomato
Preparation Time: 10 minutes Cooking Time: 24 minutes Serves: 2
Ingredients:
- 2 eggs
- 2 large fresh tomatoes 1 tsp fresh parsley Pepper
- Salt

Cooking Instructions:
Preheat the air fryer to 325 F.
Cut off the top of a tomato and spoon out the tomato innards.
Break the egg in each tomato and place in air fryer basket and cook for 24 minutes.
Season with parsley, pepper, and salt.
Serve and enjoy.
Nutritional Value (Amount per Serving):
- Calories 91
- Fat 5.3 g
- Carbohydrates 7.2 g
- Sugar 5.1 g

- Protein 8 g
- Cholesterol 162 mg

55.   Mushroom Leek Frittata
Preparation Time: 10 minutes Cooking Time: 32 minutes Serves: 4
Ingredients:
- 6 eggs
- 6 oz mushrooms, sliced 1 cup leeks, sliced
- Salt

Cooking Instructions:
Preheat the air fryer to 325 F.
Spray the pan of the air fryer with cooking spray and set aside.
Heat another skillet over medium heat. Spray pan with cooking spray.
Add the mushrooms, leeks and salt to a frying pan for 6 minutes.
Break the eggs into a bowl and beat well.
Transfer the sautéed mushroom and leek mixture to the prepared pan.
Pour the egg over the mushroom mixture.
Place the dish in the air fryer and cook for 32 minutes.
Serve and enjoy.
Nutritional Value (Amount per Serving):
- Calories 112
- Fat 7.4 g
- Carbohydrates 4.1 g
- Sugar 2.1 g
- Protein 13 g
- Cholesterol 241 mg

56.   Blackberry French Toast
Preparation time: 10 minutes Cooking duration: 20 minutes Serves: 6
Ingredients:
- 1 cup blackberry jam, warm
- 12 ounces bread loaf, cubed
- 8 ounces cream cheese, cubed
- 4 eggs
- 1 tsp. cinnamon powder
- 2 cups half and half
- 1/2 cup brown sugar
- 1 tsp. vanilla extract
- Cooking spray

Cooking Instructions:
Grease your air fryer with cooking spray and heat it to 300 ° F.
Add the blueberry jam to the bottom, overlap half the bread cubes, then add the cream cheese and garnish with the rest of the bread.
In a bowl mix the eggs with half and half, cinnamon, sugar and vanilla, beat well and add to the bread mixture.
Cook for 20 minutes, divide between plates and serve for breakfast.
Nutritional Value (Amount per Serving):
- Calories 110
- Fat 8.6 g

- Carbohydrates 0.3 g
- Sugar 0.2 g
- Protein 6.4 g
- Cholesterol 15 mg

57. Smoked Sausage Breakfast Mix

Preparation time: 10 minutes Cooking duration: 30 minutes Serves: 4

Ingredients:

- 1 and 1/2 pounds smoked sausage, diced and browned
- A pinch of salt and black pepper
- 1 and 1/2 cups grits
- 4 and 1/2 cups water
- 16 ounces cheddar cheese, shredded
- 1 cup milk
- ¼ tsp. garlic powder
- 1 and 1/2 tsp.s thyme, diced
- Cooking spray
- 4 eggs, whisked

Cooking Instructions:

Put the water in a saucepan, bring to a boil over medium heat, add the semolina, mix, cover, cook for 5 minutes and remove from heat.

Add the cheese, stir until it melts and mix with milk, thyme, salt, pepper, garlic powder and eggs and whisk very well.

Heat the air fryer to 300 ° F, grease with cooking spray and add the browned sausage.

Add the grains, mix, distribute and cook for 25 minutes.

Divide between plates and serve for breakfast.

Nutritional Value (Amount per Serving):

- Calories 110
- Fat 8.1 g
- Carbohydrates 0.3 g
- Protein 5.2 g

OPTAVIA LEAN & GREEN LUNCH RECIPES

58. Lunch Shrimp Croquettes

Preparation time: 10 minutes Cooking duration: 8 minutes Servings: 4

Ingredients:

- 2/3 pound shrimp, cooked, peeled, deveined and chopped
- 1 and ½ cups bread crumbs
- 1 egg, whisked
- 2 tbps lemon juice
- 3 green onions, chopped
- ½ tsp. basil, dried
- Salt and black pepper to the taste
- 2 tbps olive oil

Cooking Instructions:

In a bowl, mix half of the breadcrumbs with the egg and lemon juice and mix well.

Add the green onions, basil, salt, pepper and prawns and mix well.

In a separate bowl, mix the rest of the breadcrumbs with the oil and mix well.

Shape the shrimp mix into round balls, roll them in breadcrumbs, put them in a preheated air fryer and cook for 8 minutes at 400 ° F.

Serve them with a dip for lunch.

Nutritional Value (Amount per Serving):

- Calories 112
- Fat 8.1 g
- Carbohydrates 0.3 g
- Protein 5.2 g

59. Scrambled Egg Muffins with Cheese

Preparation time: 20 minutes Servings: 6

Ingredients

- 6 ounces smoked turkey sausage, chopped 6 eggs, lightly beaten
- 2 tbps shallots, finely chopped
- 2 garlic cloves, minced
- Sea salt and ground black pepper, to taste 1 tsp. cayenne pepper
- 6 ounces Monterey Jack cheese, shredded

Cooking Instructions

Simply combine the sausage, eggs, shallot, garlic, salt, black pepper and cayenne pepper in a baking dish. Stir to mix well.

Pour the mixture into 6 standard size muffin tins with paper liners.

Cook in a preheated air fryer at 340 ° F for 8 minutes. Top with the cheese and cook for another 8 minutes. To enjoy!

Nutritional Value (Amount per Serving):

- Calories 110
- Fat 7.4 g
- Carbohydrates 0.3 g
- Protein 5.5 g

60. Spring Chocolate Doughnuts

Preparation time: 20 minutes Servings: 6

Ingredients

- 1 can (16-ounce can margarinemilk biscuits Chocolate Glaze:
- 1 cup powdered sugar
- 4 tbps unsweetened baking cocoa 2 tablespoon margarine, melted
- 2 tbps milk

Cooking Instructions

Bake the cookies in the preheated 350 ° F air fryer for 8 minutes, turning them halfway through the cooking time.

While the cookies are cooking, make the icing.

Beat the ingredients with the whisk until smooth, adding enough milk for the desired consistency; set aside.

Dip the donuts in the chocolate glaze and transfer them to a wire rack to cool.

Nutritional Value (Amount per Serving):

- Calories 115

- Fat 7.1 g
- Carbohydrates 0.3 g
- Protein 5.2 g

61. Sweet Mini Monkey Rolls

Preparation time: 25 minutes Servings: 6

Ingredients
- 3/4 cup brown sugar 1 stick margarine, melted
- 1/4 cup powdered sugar
- 1 tsp. ground cinnamon 1/4 tsp. ground cardamom
- 1 (16-ounce can refrigerated margarinemilk biscuit dough

Cooking Instructions

Spray 6 standard size muffin molds with non-stick spray. Mix the brown sugar and margarine; divide the mixture between the muffin tins.

Mix the icing sugar with the cinnamon and cardamom. Separate the dough into 16 biscuits; cut each into 6 pieces. Roll the pieces over the cinnamon sugar mixture to coat. Divide between muffin cups.

Bake at 340 ° F for about 20 minutes or until golden brown. Flip and serve.

Nutritional Value (Amount per Serving):
- Calories 117
- Fat 8.1 g
- Carbohydrates 0.5 g
- Protein 5.5 g

62. Cranberry Cornbread Muffins

Preparation time: 35 minutes Servings: 4

Ingredients
- 3/4 cup all-purpose flour 3/4 cup cornmeal
- 1 tsp. baking powder
- 1/2 tsp. baking soda 1/2 tsp. salt
- 3 tbps honey
- 1 egg, well whisked 1/4 cup olive oil 3/4 cup milk
- 1/2 cup fresh cranberries, roughly chopped

Cooking Instructions

In a baking dish, carefully combine the flour, corn flour, baking powder, baking soda and salt. In a separate bowl, mix the honey, egg, olive oil, and milk.

Next, mix the liquid mixture into the dry Ingredients; stir to mix well. Incorporate the fresh blueberries and mix to mix well.

Pour the batter into a lightly greased muffin pan; cover with aluminum foil and drill small holes all over the foil. Now bake for 15 minutes.

Remove the foil and cook for another 10 minutes. Transfer to a wire rack to cool slightly before cutting and serving.

Nutritional Value (Amount per Serving):
- Calories 111
- Fat 8.5 g
- Carbohydrates 0.4 g
- Protein 5.1 g

63. Hanukkah Latkes (Jewish Potato Pancakes)

Preparation time: 20 minutes Servings: 4

Ingredients
- 6 potatoes
- 4 onions
- 2 eggs, beaten
- Sea salt and ground black pepper, to taste 1/2 tsp. smoked paprika
- 1/2 cup all-purpose flour

Cooking Instructions

Blend the potatoes and onions in the food processor until smooth. Drain the mixture well and mix in the other ingredients. Stir to mix well.

Put the pancake batter on the baking tray with a teaspoon. Flatten them slightly so that the center can cook.

Cook at 370 ° for 5 minutes; flip and cook for another 5 minutes. Repeat with the additional batter.

Serve with sour cream if desired.

Nutritional Value (Amount per Serving):
- Calories 121
- Fat 8.8 g
- Carbohydrates 0.4 g
- Protein 5.9 g

64. Oatmeal Pizza Cups

Preparation time: 30 minutes Servings: 4

Ingredients
- 1 cup rolled oats
- tsp. baking powder
- 1/4 tsp. ground black pepper Salt, to taste
- tbps margarine, melted 1 cup milk
- slices smoked ham, chopped
- ounces mozzarella cheese, shredded 4 tbps ketchup

Cooking Instructions

Start by preheating the air fryer to 350 ° F. Now lightly grease a muffin mold with a non-stick spray.

Combine the oat flakes, baking powder, pepper and salt in the food processor until coarse.

Add the remaining ingredients and mix to combine well. Pour the mixture into the prepared muffin pan.

Cook in a preheated air fryer for 20 minutes until an inserted toothpick is clean.

Nutritional Value (Amount per Serving):
- Calories 120
- Fat 7.9 g
- Carbohydrates 0.4 g
- Protein 6.1 g

65. Scrambled Eggs with Spinach and Tomato

Preparation time: 15 minutes Servings: 2

Ingredients
- 2 tbps olive oil, melted 4 eggs, whisked
- ounces fresh spinach, chopped

- medium-sized tomato, chopped 1 tsp. fresh lemon juice
- 1/2 tsp. coarse salt
- 1/2 tsp. ground black pepper
- 1/2 cup of fresh basil, roughly chopped

Cooking Instructions

Add olive oil to an air fryer pan. Make sure you tilt the pan to distribute the oil evenly.

Simply combine the remaining ingredients, except the basil leaves; whisk well until everything is well incorporated.

Cook in a preheated air fryer for 8-12 minutes at 280 ° F. Garnish with fresh basil leaves. Serve hot with a dollop of sour cream if desired.

Nutritional Value (Amount per Serving):
- Calories 110
- Fat 7.2 g
- Carbohydrates 0.4 g
- Protein 6.6 g

66. Colby Potato Patties

Preparation time: 15 minutes Servings: 8

Ingredients

- 2 pounds white potatoes, peeled and grated 1/2 cup scallions, finely chopped
- 1/2 tsp. freshly ground black pepper, or more to taste
- 1 tablespoon fine sea salt 1/2 tsp. hot paprika
- 2 cups Colby cheese, shredded
- 1/4 cup canola oil
- 1 cup crushed crackers

Cooking Instructions

First, boil the potatoes until tender. Drain, peel and mash the potatoes.

Mix the mashed potatoes well with the shallot, pepper, salt, paprika and cheese. Then, shape the balls using your hands. Now, flatten the balls to make meatballs.

In a shallow bowl, mix the canola oil with the crushed crackers. Roll the meatballs over the crumb mixture.

Next, cook the meatballs at 360 ° F for about 10 minutes, working in batches. Serve with Tabasco mayonnaise if desired.

Nutritional Value (Amount per Serving):
- Calories 120
- Fat 6.2 g
- Carbohydrates 0.2 g
- Protein 7.6 g

67. Lunch Special Pancake

Preparation time: 10 minutes Cooking duration: 10 minutes Servings: 2

Ingredients:

- 1 tablespoon margarine
- 3 eggs, whisked
- ½ cup flour
- ½ cup milk
- 1 cup salsa
- 1 cup small shrimp, peeled and deveined

Cooking Instructions:

Preheat your air fryer at 400 °F, add fryer's pan, add 1 tablespoon margarine and melt it.

In a bowl, mix eggs with flour and milk, whisk well and pour into air fryer's pan, spread, cook at 350 °For 12 minutes and transfer to a plate.

In a bowl, mix shrimp with salsa, stir and serve your pancake with this on the side.

Nutritional Value (Amount per Serving):
- Calories 120
- Fat 8.4 g
- Carbohydrates 0.3 g
- Protein 5.1 g

68. Zesty Broccoli Bites with Hot Sauce

Preparation time: 20 minutes Servings: 6

Ingredients

For the Broccoli Bites:
- 1 medium-sized head broccoli, broken into florets 1/2 tsp. lemon zest, freshly grated
- 1/3 tsp. fine sea salt 1/2 tsp. hot paprika 1 tsp. shallot powder
- 1 tsp. porcini powder 1/2 tsp. powdered garlic 1/3 tsp. celery seeds
- 1 ½ tbps olive oil
- For the Hot Sauce:
- 1/2 cup ketchup
- 1tbps brown sugar
- 1 tablespoon balsamic vinegar ½ tsp. ground allspice

Cooking Instructions

Throw all the ingredients for the broccoli nuggets into a bowl, covering the broccoli florets on all sides.

Cook them in the preheated 360 ° air fryer for 13-15 minutes. Meanwhile, mix all the ingredients for the hot sauce.

Pause the air fryer, mix the broccoli with the prepared sauce and cook for another 3 minutes.

Nutritional Value (Amount per Serving):
- Calories 122
- Fat 7.2 g
- Carbohydrates 0.2 g
- Protein 8.6 g

69. Sweet Corn and Kernel Fritters

Preparation time: 20 minutes Servings: 4

Ingredients

- 1 medium-sized carrot, grated 1 yellow onion, finely chopped
- ounces canned sweet corn kernels, drained
- 1 tsp. sea salt flakes
- 1 heaping tablespoon fresh cilantro, chopped 1 medium-sized egg, whisked
- 2 tbps plain milk
- cup of Parmesan cheese, grated 1/4 cup of self-rising flour
- 1/3 tsp. baking powder 1/3 tsp. brown sugar

Cooking Instructions

Press the grated carrot into the colander to remove excess liquid. Then, distribute the grated carrot between several sheets of kitchen paper and pat dry.

Then, mix the carrots with the remaining ingredients in the order listed above.

Roll 1 tablespoon of the mixture into a ball; flatten it gently using the back of a spoon or your hand. Now, repeat with the remaining ingredients.

Spitz the balls with a non-stick cooking oil. Cook in a single layer at 350 ° for 8-11 minutes or until they are firm to the touch in the center. Serve hot and enjoy your meal!

Nutritional Value (Amount per Serving):

- Calories 132
- Fat 7.1 g
- Carbohydrates 0.2 g
- Protein 8.2 g

70. Gorgonzola Stuffed Mushrooms with Horseradish Mayo

Preparation time: 15 minutes Servings: 5

Ingredients

- 1/2 cup of breadcrumbs 2 cloves garlic, pressed
- 2 tbps fresh coriander, chopped
- 1/3 tsp. kosher salt
- 1/2 tsp. crushed red pepper flakes 1 ½ tbps olive oil
- 20 medium-sized mushrooms, cut off the stems 1/2 cup Gorgonzola cheese, grated
- 1/4 cup low-fat mayonnaise
- 1tsp. prepared horseradish, well-drained 1 tablespoon fresh parsley, finely chopped

Cooking Instructions

Mix the breadcrumbs with the garlic, coriander, salt, chilli and olive oil; stir to mix well.

Stuff the mushroom caps with the breadcrumb filling. Complete with the grated Gorgonzola.

Place the mushrooms in the pan of the air fryer and insert them into the machine. Grill at 380 ° F for 8-12 minutes or until the filling has heated up.

Meanwhile, prepare the horseradish mayonnaise by mixing the mayonnaise, horseradish and parsley. Serve with the hot fried mushrooms. To enjoy!

Nutritional Value (Amount per Serving):

- Calories 108
- Fat 6.1 g
- Carbohydrates 0.2 g
- Protein 7 g

71. Potato Appetizer with Garlic-Mayo Sauce

Preparation time: 19 minutes Servings: 4

Ingredients

- 2 tbps vegetable oil of choice
- Kosher salt and freshly ground black pepper, to taste 3 Russet potatoes, cut into wedges
- For the Dipping Sauce:
- 2 tsp.s dried rosemary, crushed 3 garlic cloves, minced
- 1/3 tsp. dried marjoram, crushed 1/4 cup sour cream
- 1/3 cup mayonnaise

Cooking Instructions

Lightly grease your potatoes with a thin layer of vegetable oil. Season with salt and ground black pepper.

Place the seasoned wedges in the cooking basket of the air fryer. Bake at 395 ° F for 15 minutes, shaking once or twice.

Meanwhile prepare the dipping sauce by mixing all the sauce ingredients. Serve the potatoes with the dipping sauce and enjoy your meal!

Nutritional Value (Amount per Serving):

- Calories 105
- Fat 7.1 g
- Carbohydrates 0.2 g
- Protein 8 g

72. The Best Sweet Potato Fries Ever

Preparation time: 20 minutes Servings: 4

Ingredients

- 1 1/2 tbps olive oil
- 1/2 tsp. smoked cayenne pepper
- sweet potatoes, peeled and cut into 1/4-inch long slices 1/2 tsp. shallot powder
- 1/3 tsp. freshly ground black pepper, or more to taste 3/4 tsp. garlic salt

Cooking Instructions

Firstly, preheat your air fryer to 360 °F.

Then, add the sweet potatoes to a mixing dish; toss them with the other Ingredients.

Cook the sweet potatoes approximately 14 minutes. Serve with a dipping sauce of choice.

Nutritional Value (Amount per Serving):

- Calories 112
- Fat 6.5 g
- Carbohydrates 0.2 g
- Protein 8 g

73. Spicy Cheesy Risotto Balls

Preparation time: 26 minutes Servings: 4

Ingredients

- ounces cooked rice
- 1 /2 cup roasted vegetable stock 1 egg, beaten
- 1 cup white mushrooms, finely chopped 1/2 cup seasoned breadcrumbs
- garlic cloves, peeled and minced
- 1/2 yellow onion, finely chopped
- 1/3 tsp. ground black pepper, or more to taste 1 ½ bell peppers, seeded minced
- 1/2 chipotle pepper, seeded and minced 1/2 tablespoon Colby cheese, grated
- 1 ½ tbps canola oil
- Sea salt, to savor

Cooking Instructions

Heat a saucepan over medium heat; now heat the oil and sauté the garlic, onions, bell pepper and chipotle pepper until tender. Add the mushrooms and fry until fragrant and the liquid has almost evaporated.

Add the cooked rice and broth; boil for 18 minutes. Now add the cheese and spices; mix to combine.

Allow the mixture to cool completely. Shape the risotto

mixture into balls. Dip the risotto balls in the beaten egg; then, roll them on the breadcrumbs.

Fry the risotto meatballs for 6 minutes at 400 ° F. Serve with marinara sauce and enjoy your meal!

Nutritional Value (Amount per Serving):
- Calories 122
- Fat 6.8 g
- Carbohydrates 0.2 g
- Protein 9 g

74. Turkish Koftas

Preparation time: 10 minutes Cooking duration: 15 minutes Servings: 2

Ingredients:
- 1 leek, chopped
- 2 tbps feta cheese, crumbled
- ½ pound lean beef, minced
- 1 tablespoon cumin, ground
- 1 tablespoon mint, chopped
- 1 tablespoon parsley, chopped
- 1 tsp. garlic, minced
- Salt and black pepper to the taste

Cooking Instructions:

In a bowl, mix beef with leek, cheese, cumin, mint, parsley, garlic, salt and pepper, stir well, shape your koftas and place them on sticks.

Add koftas to your preheated air fryer at 360 °F and cook them for 15 minutes.

Serve them with a side salad for lunch.

Nutritional Value (Amount per Serving):
- Calories 110
- Fat 6.1 g
- Carbohydrates 0.2 g
- Protein 8.4 g

75. Chicken Kabobs

Preparation time: 10 minutes Cooking duration: 20 minutes Servings: 2

Ingredients:
- 3 orange bell peppers, cut into squares
- ¼ cup honey
- 1/3 cup soy sauce
- Salt and black pepper to the taste
- Cooking spray
- 6 mushrooms, halved
- 2 chicken breasts, skinless, boneless and roughly cubed

Cooking Instructions:

In a bowl, mix chicken with salt, pepper, honey, say sauce and some cooking spray and toss well.

Thread chicken, bell peppers and mushrooms on skewers, place them in your air fryer and cook at 338 °F for 20 minutes.

Divide among plates and serve for lunch.

Nutritional Value (Amount per Serving):
- Calories 122
- Fat 6.9 g

- Carbohydrates 0.2 g
- Protein 8.5 g

76. Crispy Wontons with Asian Dipping Sauce

Preparation time: 20 minutes Servings: 4

Ingredients
- 1tsp. sesame oil 3/4 pound ground beef Sea salt, to taste
- 1/4 tsp. Sichuan pepper 20 wonton wrappers Dipping Sauce:
- 1tbps low-sodium soy sauce 1 tablespoon honey
- 1 tsp. Gochujang
- 1 tsp. rice wine vinegar 1/2 tsp. sesame oil

Cooking Instructions

Heat 1 tsp. of sesame oil in a wok over medium-high heat.

Cook the ground beef until it turns pink. Season with salt and Sichuan pepper.

Place a piece of the wonton wrapper on the palm of your hand; add the beef mixture to the center of the paper. Then, fold it up to form a triangle; pinch the edges to seal tightly.

Place the wontons in the basket of the lightly greased air fryer. Cook in the preheated air fryer at 360 ° F for 10 minutes. Work in batches.

Meanwhile, mix all the ingredients for the sauce. Serve hot.

Nutritional Value (Amount per Serving):
- Calories 131
- Fat 8.9 g
- Carbohydrates 0.4 g
- Protein 6.9 g

77. Beef Lunch Meatballs

Preparation time: 10 minutes Cooking duration: 15 minutes Servings: 4

Ingredients:
- ½ pound beef, ground
- ½ pound Italian sausage, chopped
- ½ tsp. garlic powder
- ½ tsp. onion powder
- Salt and black pepper to the taste
- ½ cup cheddar cheese, grated
- Mashed potatoes for serving

Cooking Instructions:

In a bowl, mix the beef with the sausage, garlic powder, onion powder, salt, pepper and cheese, mix well and form 16 meatballs with this mixture.

Place the meatballs in your air fryer and cook them at 370 ° F for 15 minutes.

Serve the meatballs with some mashed potatoes on the side.

Nutritional Value (Amount per Serving):
- Calories 132
- Fat 6.7 g
- Carbohydrates 0.2 g
- Protein 5.5 g

78.   Delicious Chicken Wings

Preparation time: 10 minutes Cooking duration: 45 minutes Servings: 4

Ingredients:

- 3 pounds chicken wings
- ½ cup margarine
- 1 tablespoon old bay seasoning
- ¾ cup potato starch
- 1 tsp. lemon juice
- Lemon wedges for serving

Cooking Instructions:

In a bowl, mix the starch with the seasoning of the old bay leaf and the chicken wings and mix well.

Place the chicken wings in the basket of the air fryer and cook them at 360 ° F for 35 minutes while shaking the fryer from time to time.

Raise the temperature to 400 ° F, cook the chicken wings for another 10 minutes and divide them into plates.

Heat a skillet over medium heat, add the margarine and let it melt.

Add the lemon juice, mix well, remove from the heat and sprinkle with the chicken wings.

Serve them for lunch with lemon wedges apart.

Nutritional Value (Amount per Serving):

- Calories 118
- Fat 7.1 g
- Carbohydrates 0.5 g
- Protein 8.5 g

79.   Easy Hot Dogs

Preparation time: 10 minutes Cooking duration: 7 minutes Servings: 2

Ingredients:

- 2 hot dog buns
- 2 hot dogs
- 1 tablespoon Dijon mustard
- 2 tbps cheddar cheese, grated

Cooking Instructions:

Put hot dogs in preheated air fryer and cook them at 390 °F for 5 minutes.

Divide hot dogs into hot dog buns, spread mustard and cheese, return everything to your air fryer and cook for 2 minutes more at 390 °F.

Serve for lunch.

Nutritional Value (Amount per Serving):

- Calories 128
- Fat 7.7 g
- Carbohydrates 0.5 g
- Protein 7.5 g

80.   Air Fried Crumbed Fish

Preparation time: 10 minutes Cooking time: 12 minutes Servings: 2

Ingredients

4 fish fillets 3.5 oz. breadcrumbs 4 tbps vegetable oil 1 egg, whisked 1 lemon, to serve

Cooking Instructions

Preheat air fryer to 350 °F. Combine breadcrumbs and stir well until crumbly and loose.

Dip the fish fillets into the egg, shake off residual then dip into breadcrumb mix, ensuring that it is thoroughly and evenly coated.

Lay in the air fryer gently and cook for 12 minutes. Serve with lemon.

Nutritional Value (Amount per Serving):

- Calories 122
- Fat 7.5 g
- Carbohydrates 0.3 g
- Protein 7.2 g

81.   Fried Fish With Onions

Preparation time: 40 minutes Cooking time: 40 minutes Servings: 2

Ingredients

- ½ pound fish fillets, wash & cubed ½ onion, minced 1 clove garlic, minced 1 tablespoon oil 1 tablespoon chili paste 1½ tablespoon soy sauce 1 tablespoon sugar ¼ cup water
- 1/2 tablespoon salt 2 tablespoon vinegar

Cooking Instructions

Marinate the fish cubes with salt for 30 minutes. Preheat the deep fryer to 390 F. Sprinkle the fish with oil and place it in the air fryer. Cook for 15 minutes.

Meanwhile, in a saucepan, combine the oil, chilli paste, onion and garlic. Turn on the flame to medium temperature and fry for 5 minutes until the onions turn translucent.

Remove the fish from the air fryer and place it in the pan. Now add the water, soy sauce, sugar, salt and vinegar. Lower the heat, cover and simmer for 10 minutes.

Finally, set the flame to maximum. Remove when the sauce thickens.

Nutritional Value (Amount per Serving):

- Calories 130
- Fat 7.1 g
- Carbohydrates 0.3 g
- Protein 8.2 g

82.   Cod Fish Nuggets

Preparation time: 15 minutes Cooking time: 10 minutes Servings: 4

Ingredients

1 pound cod, cut lengthwise into strips of 1-inch by 2.5

For The Breading: 1 cup all-purpose flour 2 tbps olive oil ¾ cup panko breadcrumbs 2 eggs, beaten 1 pinch salt

Cooking Instructions

Preheat the Airfryer to 390 ° F. Blend the panko, breadcrumbs, olive oil and salt in a food processor.

Set the panko mixture, flour and eggs aside in three separate bowls.

Put the pieces of cod in the flour, eggs and breadcrumbs, pressing firmly to make the breadcrumbs adhere to the fish. Shake off the excess breadcrumbs.

Add the cod croquettes to the cooking basket and cook for 8 to 10 minutes until golden brown.

Nutritional Value (Amount per Serving):
- Calories 120
- Fat 7.9 g
- Carbohydrates 0.3 g
- Protein 8.4 g

83.   Roasted Garlic Bacon And Potatoes

Preparation time: 5 minutes Cooking time: 25 minutes
Servings: 4

Ingredients
- 4 medium sized potatoes, peeled and cut into 2
- 4 strips of streaky bacon 2 sprigs of rosemary
  6 cloves of garlic, smashed, unpeeled 3 tsp.s
  of vegetable oil

Cooking Instructions

Preheat Airfryer to 390°F.

Put the smashed garlic, bacon, potatoes, rosemary and
then the oil in a bowl. Stir thoroughly.

Place into airfryer basket and roast until golden for about
25 minutes.

Nutritional Value (Amount per Serving):
- Calories 114
- Fat 8.1 g
- Carbohydrates 0.3 g
- Protein 6.2 g

84.   Chinese Pancetta Lunch Mix

Preparation time: 10 minutes Cooking duration: 12 minutes Servings: 4

Ingredients:
- 2 eggs
- 2 pounds Pancetta, cut into medium cubes
- 1 cup cornstarch
- 1 tsp. sesame oil
- Salt and black pepper to the taste
- A pinch of Chinese five spice
- 3 tbps canola oil
- Sweet ketchup for serving

Cooking Instructions:

In a bowl, mix five spices with salt, pepper and cornstarch
and mix.

In another bowl, mix the eggs with the sesame oil and beat
well.

Dip the bacon cubes into the cornstarch mixture, then dip
the eggs and place them in the air fryer you greased with
canola oil.

Bake at 340 ° F for 12 minutes, shaking the fryer once.

Serve the bacon for lunch with the sweet ketchup on the
side.

Nutritional Value (Amount per Serving):
- Calories 125
- Fat 7.9 g
- Carbohydrates 0.2 g
- Protein 8.3 g

85.   Meat, Corn And Potato Barbecue

Preparation time: 3 minutes Cooking time: 27 minutes
Servings: 4

Ingredients

2 Pancetta belly bacon slices 2 sausages 1 corn on the cob
1 mealy potato 2 spare ribs 2 shasliks Salt and pepper to
taste Barbecue sauce

Cooking Instructions

Heat the Airfryer to 392 ° F. Place the potato in it and cook
for 15 minutes.

Add the corn and meat skewers, bacon, sausages and spare
ribs and grill for 12 minutes.

Remove and sprinkle with salt and pepper. Serve with barbecue sauce and vegetable salad.

Nutritional Value (Amount per Serving):
- Calories 117
- Fat 8.5 g
- Carbohydrates 0.3 g
- Protein 6.6 g

86.   Teriyaki Glazed Halibut Steak

Preparation time: 30 minutes Cooking time: 10-15 minutes
Servings: 3

Ingredients
- 1 pound halibut steak For The Marinade: 2/3 cup low
  sodium soy sauce ½ cup mirin
- 2 tbps lime juice ¼ cup sugar
- ¼ cup orange juice ¼ tsp. ginger ground ¼ tsp. crushed
  red pepper flakes 1 each garlic clove (smashed)

Cooking Instructions

Place all ingredients for the teriyaki glaze / marinade in a
saucepan. Bring to a boil and reduce by half, then allow to
cool.

When it cools, pour half of the icing / marinade into a zip-
up bag along with the halibut, then refrigerate for 30 minutes.

Preheat Airfryer to 390 ° F. Place marinated halibut in Airfryer and cook 10-12 minutes. Brush some of the remaining glaze on the halibut steak.

Spread on white rice with basil / mint chutney.

Nutritional Value (Amount per Serving):
- Calories 116
- Fat 7.1 g
- Carbohydrates 0.3 g
- Protein 7.2 g

87.   Pancetta Chops With Pineapple-
   Jalapeno Salsa

Preparation time: 20 minutes Cooking time: 20 minutes
Servings: 3

Ingredients
- 3 pieces of Pancetta Chops (roughly 10 ounces each) 2
  tablespoon of finely chopped parsley 1 tablespoon of
  ground Coriander ¾ cup of olive oil
- 1 tablespoon of finely chopped rosemary 4 ounces of
  tomatoes, diced 2 cloves of garlic, chopped 4 ounces of
  pineapple, diced 8 Jalapenos

3 tsp.s of Dijon Mustard 1½ tsp.s of sugar 4 ounces of lemon juice 3 tbps of finely chopped Cilantro 2½ tsp.s of salt

Cooking Instructions

Place the rosemary, sugar, mustard, coriander, ¼ cup of olive oil, 1 tablespoon of coriander, 1 ½ teaspoons of salt and 1 tablespoon of parsley in a mixing bowl and mix thoroughly. Add the bacon cutlets and mix.

Pour the marinade into a resealable plastic bag and refrigerate for about 3 hours.

Heat your deep fryer to 390 ° F.

Place the jalapenos in a bowl and season with 1 tsp. of oil to cover them evenly. Transfer the jalapenos to the airfryer and cook for about 7 minutes. Remove from deep fryer and set aside to cool.

Once cooled, peel, remove the seeds and chop the jalapenos into small pieces and transfer them to a bowl. Add the pineapple, tomatoes, garlic and lemon juice, the rest of the oil, parsley, coriander and salt. Stir and set the sauce aside.

Remove the bacon chops from the refrigerator and allow to rest for 30 minutes at room temperature before cooking.

Place the ribs in the airfryer and roast at 390 ° F for about 12 minutes. The bacon cutlets are well cooked when the internal temperature is 140 ° F.

Nutritional Value (Amount per Serving):
- Calories 104
- Fat 8.7 g
- Carbohydrates 0.3 g
- Protein 6.7 g

88.   Coconut Coated Fish Cakes With Mango Sauce

Preparation time: 20 minutes Cooking time: 14 minutes Servings: 4

Ingredients
- 18 ounces of white fish fillet 1 green onion, finely chopped 1 mango, peeled, cubed 4 tbps of ground coconut 1½ ounces of parsley, finely chopped 1½ tsp.s of ground fresh red chili 1 lime, juice and zest 1 egg
- 1 tsp. of salt

Cooking Instructions

Add ½ ounce of parsley, ½ tsp. of ground red pepper, half of the lime juice and the zest of the mango cubes and mix well.

Using a food processor, blend the fish and add the salt, egg and the rest of the lime zest, lime juice and chilli. Incorporate the green onions, 2 tablespoons of coconut and the rest of the parsley.

Put the rest of the coconut in a deep plate. Shape the fish mixture into 12 round cakes. Put the cakes in coconut to coat them.

Place half of the cakes in the fryer basket and bake for 7 minutes at 356 ° F. Remove when the cakes are golden brown and place the second batch of cakes in the oven.

Serve the cakes with the mango sauce.

Nutritional Value (Amount per Serving):
- Calories 128
- Fat 7.6 g

- Carbohydrates 0.2 g
- Protein 8.2 g

89.   Creamed Asparagus and Egg Salad

Preparation time: 25 minutes + chilling time Servings: 4

Ingredients
- 2 eggs
- 1 pound asparagus, chopped 2 cup baby spinach
- 1/2 cup mayonnaise 1 tsp. mustard
- 1 tsp. fresh lemon juice
- Sea salt and ground black pepper, to taste

Cooking Instructions

Place the grill in the basket of the air fryer; lower the eggs onto the grill. Bake at 270 ° F for 15 minutes.

Transfer them to an ice-cold water bath to stop cooking. Peel the eggs under cold running water; Coarsely chop the hard-boiled eggs and set them aside.

Raise the temperature to 400 ° F. Place the asparagus in the basket of the lightly greased air fryer.

Cook for 5 minutes or until tender. Put in a nice salad bowl. Add the baby spinach.

In a baking dish, carefully combine the remaining ingredients. Season with this dressing on the asparagus in the salad bowl and garnish with the chopped eggs.

Nutritional Value (Amount per Serving):
- Calories 115
- Fat 8.9 g
- Carbohydrates 0.5 g
- Protein 7.9 g

90.   Prosciutto Sandwich

Preparation time: 10 minutes Cooking duration: 5 minutes Servings: 1

Ingredients:
- 2 bread slices
- 2 mozzarella slices
- 2 tomato slices
- 2 prosciutto slices
- 2 basil leaves
- 1 tsp. olive oil
- A pinch of salt and black pepper

Cooking Instructions:

Arrange the mozzarella and ham on a slice of bread.

Season with salt and pepper, place in your air fryer and cook at 400 ° F for 5 minutes.

Pour a drizzle of oil over the ham, add the tomato and basil, cover with the other slice of bread, cut the sandwich in half and serve.

Nutritional Value (Amount per Serving):
- Calories 109
- Fat 7.7 g
- Carbohydrates 0.3 g
- Protein 8.7 g

91. Easy Zucchini Chips

Preparation time: 20 minutes Servings: 4

Ingredients

- 3/4 pound zucchini, peeled and sliced 1 egg, lightly beaten
- 1/2 cup seasoned breadcrumbs
- 1/2 cup parmesan cheese, preferably freshly grated

Cooking Instructions

Dry the courgettes with a kitchen towel.

In a baking dish, carefully combine the egg, breadcrumbs and cheese. Then, cover the courgette slices with the breadcrumbs mixture.

Cook in the preheated air fryer at 400 ° F for 9 minutes, shaking the basket halfway through the cooking time.

Work in batches until the fries are golden.

Nutritional Value (Amount per Serving):

- Calories 119
- Fat 7.9 g
- Carbohydrates 0.5 g
- Protein 7.7 g

92. Japanese Chicken Mix

Preparation time: 10 minutes Cooking duration: 8 minutes-Servings: 2

Ingredients :

- 2 chicken thighs, skinless and boneless
- 2 ginger slices, chopped
- 3 garlic cloves, minced
- ¼ cup soy sauce
- ¼ cup mirin
- 1/8 cup sake
- ½ tsp. sesame oil
- 1/8 cup water
- 2 tbps sugar
- 1 tablespoon cornstarch mixed with 2 tbps water Sesame seeds for serving

Cooking Instructions:

In a bowl, mix chicken thighs with ginger, garlic, soy sauce, mirin, sake, oil, water, sugar and cornstarch, toss well, transfer to preheated air fryer and cook at 360 °F for 8 minutes.

Divide among plates, sprinkle sesame seeds on top and serve with a side salad for lunch.

Nutritional Value (Amount per Serving):

- Calories 148
- Fat 7.1 g
- Carbohydrates 0.5 g
- Protein 8.5 g

93. Salmon And Potato Patties

Preparation time: 10 minutes Cooking time: 29 minutes Servings: 8

Ingredients

- 7 ounces of salmon 1 cup of breadcrumbs 3 russet potatoes (about 4.7 ounce each) peeled, chopped 1 egg, whisked 4 ounces of frozen vegetables, parboiled and drained 1 tablespoon of finely chopped parsley ½ tsp.

of black pepper 1 tsp. of dill Salt to taste
- Oil spray

Cooking Instructions

Place the chopped potatoes in boiling water and cook for 10-12 minutes. Drain the water completely. Mash the potatoes with a wooden mixer and put them in the refrigerator to cool.

Heat the air fryer to 356 ° F for 5 minutes. Add the salmon and grill for 5 minutes. Remove and flake the salmon with a fork.

Remove the mashed potatoes from the refrigerator and add the salmon, vegetables, black pepper, salt, dill and parsley and mix. Add the beaten egg and mix.

Form 8 meatballs and coat the meatballs with the breadcrumbs. Spray the meatballs with oil using spray oil.

Place them in the air fryer and cook for about 12 minutes or until golden brown. You can serve with mayonnaise and lemon with a salad.

Nutritional Value (Amount per Serving):

- Calories 120
- Fat 7.4 g
- Carbohydrates 0.4 g
- Protein 8.2 g

94. Roasted Green Bean Salad with Goat Cheese

Preparation time: 10 minutes + chilling time Servings: 4

Ingredients

- 1 pound trimmed green beans, cut into bite-sized pieces Salt and freshly cracked mixed pepper, to taste
- 1 shallot, thinly sliced
- 1 tablespoon lime juice
- 1 tablespoon champagne vinegar 1/4 cup extra-virgin olive oil
- 1/2 tsp. mustard seeds 1/2 tsp. celery seeds
- 1 tablespoon fresh basil leaves, chopped
- 1 tablespoon fresh parsley leaves 1 cup goat cheese, crumbled

Cooking Instructions

Pour the green beans with salt and pepper into a lightly greased air fryer basket.

Cook in preheated air fryer at 400 ° F for 5 minutes or until tender.

Add the shallots and mix gently to combine.

In a bowl, whisk the lime juice, vinegar, olive oil and spices. Dress the salad and garnish with the goat cheese. Serve at room temperature or cool. To enjoy!

Nutritional Value (Amount per Serving):

- Calories 118
- Fat 8.5 g
- Carbohydrates 0.4 g
- Protein 7.1 g

95. Red Currant Cupcakes

Preparation time: 20 minutes Servings: 3

Ingredients

- 1 cup all-purpose flour 1/2 cup sugar
- 1 tsp. baking powder
- A pinch of kosher salt
- A pinch of grated nutmeg 1/4 cup coconut, oil melted 1 egg
- 1/4 cup full-fat coconut milk 1/4 tsp. ground cardamom 1/4 tsp. ground cinnamon 1 tsp. vanilla extract
- 6 ounces red currants

Cooking Instructions

Mix the flour with the sugar, baking powder, salt and nutmeg. In a separate bowl, whisk the coconut oil, egg, milk, cardamom, cinnamon, and vanilla.

Add the egg mixture to the dry ingredients; stir to mix well.

Now, fold the red currant; mix gently to combine. Scrape the batter into 6 lightly greased standard size muffin tins.

Bake the cupcakes at 360 ° F for 12 minutes or until the tops are golden. Sprinkle some extra powdered sugar on top of each muffin, if desired. To enjoy!

Nutritional Value (Amount per Serving):

- Calories 103
- Fat 7.5 g
- Carbohydrates 0.4 g
- Protein 6.1 g

96. Easy Cheesy Broccoli

Preparation time: 25 minutes Servings: 4

Ingredients

- 1/3 cup grated yellow cheese
- large-sized head broccoli, stemmed and cut small florets 2 1/2 tbps canola oil
- tsp.s dried rosemary 2 tsp.s dried basil
- Salt and ground black pepper, to taste

Cooking Instructions

Bring a medium skillet filled with lightly salted water to a boil. Then, boil the broccoli florets for about 3 minutes.

Then, drain the broccoli florets well; season with canola oil, rosemary, basil, salt and black pepper.

Set your air fryer to 390 ° F; place the seasoned broccoli in the cooking basket; set the timer for 17 minutes. Toss the broccoli halfway through the cooking process.

Serve hot topped with grated cheese and enjoy your meal!

Nutritional Value (Amount per Serving):

- Calories 108
- Fat 7.1 g
- Carbohydrates 0.4 g
- Protein 6.6 g

97. Peppery Roasted Potatoes with Smoked Bacon

Preparation time: 15 minutes Servings: 2

Ingredients

- 5 small rashers smoked bacon 1/3 tsp. garlic powder
- 1 tsp. sea salt
- 2 tsp.s paprika

- 1/3 tsp. ground black pepper 1 bell pepper, seeded and sliced
- 1 tsp. mustard
- 2 habanero peppers, halved

Cooking Instructions

Simply toss all the ingredients in a mixing dish; then, transfer them to your air fryer's basket.

Air-fry at 375 °F for 10 minutes. Serve warm.

Nutritional Value (Amount per Serving):

- Calories 122
- Fat 9 g
- Carbohydrates 0.3 g
- Protein 10 g

98. Cornbread with Pulled Pancetta

Preparation time: 24 minutes Servings: 2

Ingredients

- 2½ cups pulled Pancetta, leftover works well too 1 tsp. dried rosemary
- 1/2 tsp. chili powder
- 3 cloves garlic, peeled and pressed 1/2 recipe cornbread
- 1/2 tablespoon brown sugar
- 1/3 cup scallions, thinly sliced 1 tsp. sea salt

Cooking Instructions

Preheat a large non-stick pan over medium heat; now cook the shallots together with the garlic and the pulled bacon.

Next, add the sugar, chilli powder, rosemary and salt. Cook, stirring occasionally, until the mixture has thickened.

Preheat your air fryer to 335 ° F. Now, coat two mini loaf pans with cooking spray. Add the pulled bacon mixture and spread over the bottom with a spatula.

Spread the previously prepared cornbread batter over the spicy pulled bacon mixture.

Bake this cornbread in a preheated air fryer until a centered tester is clean, or for 18 minutes.

Nutritional Value (Amount per Serving):

- Calories 117
- Fat 9.4 g
- Carbohydrates 0.3 g
- Protein 11 g

99. Crispy Chicken Fillets

Preparation time: 10 minutes Cooking time: 15 minutes Servings: 3

Ingredients

12 ounces of chicken fillets 1 tsp. of ground black pepper 2 tbps of vegetable oil 8 tbps of breadcrumbs 4 ounces of flour 2 eggs, whisked ½ tsp. salt

Cooking Instructions

Heats Airfryer up to 330 ° F.

Add the salt, pepper and oil to the breadcrumbs then mix well.

Put the flour and egg in shallow bowls. Put the chicken in the flour, shake off the excess and then dip it in the beaten eggs and then cover evenly with the breadcrumbs pressing to make the breadcrumbs stick.

Shake off the excess and place it in the Airfryer basket.

Cook for 10 minutes and then increase the heat to 390 ° F. Finally, cook for another 5 minutes until golden brown.
Nutritional Value (Amount per Serving):
- Calories 119
- Fat 7.2 g
- Carbohydrates 0.2 g
- Protein 7.1 g

100.   Lunch Potato Salad

Preparation time: 10 minutes Cooking duration: 25 minutes Servings: 4
Ingredients:
- pound red potatoes, halved
- tbps olive oil
- Salt and black pepper to the taste
- 2 green onions, chopped
- 1 red bell pepper, chopped
- 1/3 cup lemon juice
- tbps mustard

Cooking Instructions:
On the basket of the air fryer, mix the potatoes with half of the olive oil, salt and pepper and cook at 350 ° F for 25 minutes while shaking the fryer once.
In a bowl, mix the onions with the pepper and roasted potatoes and mix.
In a small bowl, mix the lemon juice with the rest of the oil and mustard and blend very well.
Add it to the potato salad, mix well and serve for lunch.
Nutritional Value (Amount per Serving):
- Calories 120
- Fat 9 g
- Carbohydrates 0.3 g
- Protein 8.4 g

101.   Bacon and Garlic Pizzas

Preparation time: 10 minutes Cooking duration: 10 minutes Servings: 4
Ingredients:
- 4 dinner rolls, frozen
- 4 garlic cloves minced
- ½ tsp. oregano dried
- ½ tsp. garlic powder
- 1 cup ketchup
- 8 bacon slices, cooked and chopped
- 1 and ¼ cups cheddar cheese, grated
- Cooking spray

Cooking Instructions:
Place the rolls on a work surface and press them to obtain 4 ovals.
Spray each oval with cooking spray, transfer them to the air fryer and cook at 370 ° F for 2 minutes.
Spread the ketchup on each oval, divide the garlic, sprinkle with oregano and garlic powder and garnish with bacon and cheese.
Return the pizzas to your hot air fryer and cook them at 370 ° F for another 8 minutes.
Serve hot for lunch.

Nutritional Value (Amount per Serving):
- Calories 104
- Fat 9.1 g
- Carbohydrates 0.2 g
- Protein 8.5 g

102.   Stuffed Meatballs

Preparation time: 10 minutes Cooking duration: 10 minutes Servings: 4
Ingredients:
- 1/3 cup bread crumbs
- 3 tbps milk
- 1 tablespoon ketchup
- 1 egg
- ½ tsp. marjoram, dried
- Salt and black pepper to the taste
- 1 pound lean beef, ground
- 20 cheddar cheese cubes
- 1 tablespoon olive oil

Cooking Instructions:
In a bowl, mix the breadcrumbs with ketchup, milk, marjoram, salt, pepper and egg and beat well.
Add the beef, mix and form 20 meatballs with this mixture.
Shape each meatball around a cube of cheese, sprinkle with oil and rub.
Place all the meatballs in your preheated air fryer and cook at 390 ° F for 10 minutes.
Serve them for lunch with a side of salad.
Nutritional Value (Amount per Serving):
- Calories 112
- Fat 8.2 g
- Carbohydrates 0.3 g
- Protein 7.7 g

103.   Steaks and Cabbage

Preparation time: 10 minutes Cooking duration: 10 minutes Servings: 4
Ingredients:
- ½ pound sirloin steak, cut into strips
- 2 tsp.s cornstarch
- 1 tablespoon peanut oil
- 2 cups green cabbage, chopped
- 1 yellow bell pepper, chopped
- 2 green onions, chopped
- 2 garlic cloves, minced
- Salt and black pepper to the taste

Cooking Instructions:
In a bowl, mix the cabbage with salt, pepper and peanut oil, mix, transfer to air fryer basket, cook at 370 ° F for 4 minutes and transfer to bowl.
Add the steak strips to the air fryer, also add the green onions, bell pepper, garlic, salt and pepper, stir and cook for 5 minutes.
Add the cabbage on top, mix, divide into plates and serve for lunch. To enjoy!
Nutritional Value (Amount per Serving):
- Calories 111

- Fat 7.2 g
- Carbohydrates 0.3 g
- Protein 8.7 g

104. Succulent Lunch Turkey Breast

Preparation time: 10 minutes Cooking duration: 47 minutes Servings: 4

Ingredients:
- 1 big turkey breast
- 2 tsp.s olive oil
- ½ tsp. smoked paprika
- 1 tsp. thyme, dried
- ½ tsp. sage, dried
- Salt and black pepper to the taste
- 2 tbps mustard
- ¼ cup maple syrup
- 1 tablespoon margarine, soft

Cooking Instructions:

Brush the turkey breast with olive oil, season with salt, pepper, thyme, paprika and sage, rub, place in the fryer basket and fry at 350 ° F for 25 minutes.

Turn the turkey, cook for another 10 minutes, turn once more and cook for another 10 minutes.

Meanwhile, heat a pan with the margarine over medium heat, add the mustard and maple syrup, mix well, cook for a couple of minutes and remove from the heat.

Slice the turkey breast, divide it into plates and serve with the maple glaze on top.

Nutritional Value (Amount per Serving):
- Calories 140
- Fat 7.1 g
- Carbohydrates 0.3 g
- Protein 9 g

105. Creamy Chicken Stew

Preparation time: 10 minutes Cooking duration: 25 minutes Servings: 4

Ingredients:
- 1 and ½ cups canned cream of celery soup
- 6 chicken tenders
- Salt and black pepper to the taste
- 2 potatoes, chopped
- 1 bay leaf
- 1 thyme spring, chopped
- 1 tablespoon milk
- 1 egg yolk
- ½ cup heavy cream

Cooking Instructions:

In a bowl, mix chicken with cream of celery, potatoes, heavy cream, bay leaf, thyme, salt and pepper, toss, pour into your air fryer's pan and cook at 320 °F for 25 minutes. Leave your stew to cool down a bit, discard bay leaf, divide among plates and serve right away .

Nutritional Value (Amount per Serving):
- Calories 113
- Fat 9.5 g
- Carbohydrates 0.3 g
- Protein 9.4 g

106. Delicious Spicy Drumsticks

Preparation time: 2 minutes Cooking time: 18 minutes Servings: 4

Ingredients

4 chicken drumsticks 6 tsp.s of Montreal chicken spices 6 tsp.s of ground black pepper 1 tsp. of olive oil 1 tsp. of salt 6 tsp.s of chicken seasoning (your choice)

Cooking Instructions

Mix all the spices and seasonings in a bowl. Brush the chicken with olive oil.

Rub the spices on the chicken. Make sure the spices stick tightly to the chopsticks.

Heat your Airfryer at 200 ° F for 3 minutes. Place the chicken in the deep fryer and cook for 10 minutes.

Lower the heat to 150 ° F and cook again for 8 minutes.

Nutritional Value (Amount per Serving):
- Calories 113
- Fat 6.5 g
- Carbohydrates 0.3 g
- Protein 9.7 g

107. Spicy Garlic Chicken Nuggets

Preparation time: 20 minutes Cooking time: 20 minutes Servings: 2

Ingredients
- 1 eggs, whisked 2 chicken breast halves, boneless, skinless,
- ½ pound of flour 3 tbps of garlic powder 1 tablespoon of black pepper 1 tsp. of salt

Cooking Instructions

Mix the garlic, salt, pepper and flour in a deep dish. Put the beaten egg in a separate bowl.

Preheat Airfryer to 356 ° F.

Cut the chicken into small pieces and dip them in the eggs, then cover with the flour. Shake off the excess flour coating and place the chicken on a plate.

Place the chicken pieces in the airfryer and cook until golden brown for 20 minutes. Shake the chicken in half.

Nutritional Value (Amount per Serving):
- Calories 120
- Fat 8.5 g
- Carbohydrates 0.3 g
- Protein 9.1 g

108. Potato and Kale Croquettes

Preparation time: 9 minutes Servings: 6

Ingredients
- eggs, slightly beaten 1/3 cup flour
- 1/3 cup goat cheese, crumbled
- ½ tsp.s fine sea salt 4 garlic cloves, minced
- 1 cup kale, steamed
- 1/3 cup breadcrumbs 1/3tsp. red pepper flakes
- potatoes, peeled and quartered
- 1/3 tsp. dried dill weed

Cooking Instructions

First, boil the potatoes in salted water. Once the potatoes are cooked, mash them; add the black cabbage, goat cheese, minced garlic, sea salt, chilli flakes, dill and an egg;

stir to mix well.

Now, roll the mixture to form small croquettes.

Take three shallow bowls. Put the flour in the first shallow bowl.

Beat the 3 remaining eggs in the second bowl. After that, throw the breadcrumbs into the third shallow bowl.

Dip each croquette in flour; then dip them into the egg bowl; finally, wrap each croquette in breadcrumbs.

Air fry at 335 ° F for 7 minutes or until golden brown. Tate, season with seasoning and serve hot.

Nutritional Value (Amount per Serving):
- Calories 105
- Fat 7.6 g
- Carbohydrates 0.4 g
- Protein 6.3 g

109.   Italian Eggplant Sandwich

Preparation time: 10 minutes Cooking duration: 16 minutes Servings: 2

Ingredients:
- 1 eggplant, sliced
- 2 tsp.s parsley, dried
- Salt and black pepper to the taste
- ½ cup breadcrumbs
- ½ tsp. Italian seasoning
- ½ tsp. garlic powder
- ½ tsp. onion powder
- 2 tbps milk
- 4 bread slices
- Cooking spray
- ½ cup mayonnaise
- ¾ cup ketchup
- 2 cups mozzarella cheese, grated

Cooking Instructions:

Season the aubergine slices with salt and pepper, set aside for 10 minutes and then dry them well.

In a bowl, mix the parsley with the breadcrumbs, the Italian seasoning, the onion and garlic powder, the salt and the black pepper and mix.

In another bowl, mix the milk with the mayonnaise and beat well.

Brush the aubergine slices with the mayonnaise mix, dip them in the breadcrumbs, place them in the air fryer basket, sprinkle them with cooking oil and cook at 400 ° F for 15 minutes, turning after 8 minutes.

Brush each slice of bread with olive oil and arrange 2 on a work surface.

Add the mozzarella and Parmesan on each, add the slices of baked eggplant, spread ketchup and basil and garnish with the other slices of bread, greased side down.

Divide the sandwiches on plates, cut them in half and serve for lunch.

Nutritional Value (Amount per Serving):
- Calories 120
- Fat 8.1 g
- Carbohydrates 0.2 g
- Protein 8 g

110.   Onion And Parsley Turkey Rolls

Preparation time: 15 minutes Cooking time: 40 minutes Servings: 4

Ingredients

1 pound of turkey breast fillets 6 tsp.s of olive oil 1 tsp. of cinnamon 1 clove of garlic, crushed 1 small sized onion, finely chopped 1 tsp. of salt
1½ ounces of parsley, finely chopped 1½ tsp. of ground cumin ½ tsp. of ground chili

Cooking Instructions

Place the turkey fillets on a cutting board with the smaller side facing you and cut them horizontally to about 2/3 of the way. Open the slit and cut it again to form a long strip of meat.

Mix the chilli, garlic, cumin, pepper, cinnamon and salt in a large bowl. Stir in the olive oil. Remove 1 tablespoon of the mixture and set aside in a small bowl.

Add the parsley and onion to the mixture in the large bowl and mix.

Heat your deep fryer to 356 ° F.

Distribute the herb mixture over the surface of the meat and roll up well starting with the shorter end. Tie the roll with a string about an inch apart. Coat the outside of the meat rolls with the spice mixture that has been set aside.

Place in the air fryer and cook for 40 minutes.

Nutritional Value (Amount per Serving):
- Calories 109
- Fat 8.2 g
- Carbohydrates 0.3 g
- Protein 10.1 g

111.   Sweet Potatoes & Creamy Crisp Chicken Airfry

Preparation time: 15 minutes Cooking time: 40 minutes Servings: 2

Ingredients
- ¼ cup of flour, seasoned with salt and pepper 1 cup of margarinemilk 1 tsp. of garlic, finely copped 1 egg, whisked
- 2 (5-ounce) chicken breast ½ tsp. of pepper 7 ounces of breadcrumbs 2 medium sized sweet potatoes 3 tsp.s of smoked paprika 3 tsp.s of vegetable oil Salt and pepper to taste

Cooking Instructions

Place the pepper, garlic and margarine milk in the bowl of chicken breasts, cover and leave to marinate in the refrigerator overnight.

Preheat the Airfryer to 374 ° F for about 3 minutes.

Remove the marinade from the chicken and dip it in the seasoned flour, then the egg, and finally the breadcrumbs. Make sure the coating adheres tightly to the chicken.

Fry the chicken in the air fryer for 20 minutes until cooked through. Remove from the fryer.

Peel the sweet potatoes and cut them into slices, 1 cm thick. Add the oil and paprika to the chips and mix.

Place the fries in the deep fryer and fry for 20 minutes at 374 ° F. Shake at approximately 6 minute intervals. Season the fries with salt and pepper when ready.

Nutritional Value (Amount per Serving):
- Calories 105
- Fat 7.1 g
- Carbohydrates 0.2 g
- Protein 6.1 g

112. Sweet and Sour Sausage Mix

Preparation time: 10 minutes Cooking duration: 10 minutes Servings: 4

Ingredients:
- 1 pound sausages, sliced
- 1 red bell pepper, cut into strips
- ½ cup yellow onion, chopped
- 3 tbps brown sugar
- 1/3 cup ketchup
- 2 tbps mustard
- 2 tbps apple cider vinegar
- ½ cup chicken stock

Cooking Instructions:

In a bowl, mix sugar with ketchup, mustard, stock and vinegar and whisk well.

In your air fryer's pan, mix sausage slices with bell pepper, onion and sweet and sour mix, toss and cook at 350 °F for 10 minutes.

Divide into bowls and serve for lunch.

Nutritional Value (Amount per Serving):
- Calories 115
- Fat 8.4 g
- Carbohydrates 0.3 g
- Protein 7.1 g

113. Meatballs and Ketchup

Preparation time: 10 minutes Cooking duration: 15 minutes Servings: 4

Ingredients:
- 1 pound lean beef, ground
- 3 green onions, chopped
- 2 garlic cloves, minced
- 1 egg yolk
- ¼ cup bread crumbs
- Salt and black pepper to the taste
- 1 tablespoon olive oil
- 16 ounces ketchup
- 2 tbps mustard

Cooking Instructions:

In a bowl, mix the beef with onion, garlic, egg yolk, breadcrumbs, salt and pepper, mix well and form medium sized meatballs with this mixture.

Grease the meatballs with oil, put them in your air fryer and cook them at 400 ° C for 10 minutes.

In a bowl, mix the ketchup with the mustard, beat, add to the meatballs, sauté and cook at 400 ° F for another 5 minutes.

Divide the meatballs and sauce on plates and serve for lunch.

Nutritional Value (Amount per Serving):
- Calories 117
- Fat 8.7 g

- Carbohydrates 0.3 g
- Protein 7.3 g

114. Mushroom & Chicken Noodles With Glasswort And Sesame

Preparation time: 30 minutes Cooking time: 17 minutes Servings: 4

Ingredients
- 14 ounces of chicken thigh fillets, cut to pieces 14 ounces of noodles, cooked 2 cloves of garlic
- 2/3 cup of chestnut mushrooms 2/3 cup of shiitake mushrooms 1/4 cup of soy sauce 6 tsp.s of sesame oil 3 tsp.s of sesame seeds 7 ounces of glasswort 5.3 ounces of bean sprouts 1 tsp. sambal
- 1 medium sized onion, thinly sliced Krupuk

Cooking Instructions

Mix the soy sauce, garlic and sambal to form a marinade and dip the chicken pieces into it to absorb.

Add 3 teaspoons of oil to cooked noodles.

Heat the Airfryer to 392 ° F. Place the chicken pieces in the fryer basket and sprinkle with oil. Cook for 6 minutes, shaking at intervals.

Add the onion, mushrooms, glasswort and bean sprouts. Cook for another 5 minutes. Place the noodles and cook further for 5 minutes. Finally, add the krupuk at the last minute.

Remove from the airfryer and sprinkle with sesame seeds.

Nutritional Value (Amount per Serving):
- Calories 115
- Fat 8.1 g
- Carbohydrates 0.7 g
- Protein 7 g

115. Lentils Fritters

Preparation time: 10 minutes Cooking duration: 10 minutes Servings: 2

Ingredients:
- 1 cup yellow lentils, soaked in water for 1 hour and drained
- 1 hot chili pepper, chopped
- 1 inch ginger piece, grated
- ½ tsp. turmeric powder
- 1 tsp. garam masala
- 1 tsp. baking powder
- Salt and black pepper to the taste
- 2 tsp.s olive oil
- 1/3 cup water
- ½ cup cilantro, chopped
- 1 and ½ cup spinach, chopped
- 4 garlic cloves, minced
- ¾ cup red onion, chopped
- Mint chutney for serving

Cooking Instructions:

In your blender, mix the lentils with chili, ginger, turmeric, garam masala, yeast, salt, pepper, olive oil, water, coriander, spinach, onion and garlic, mix well and form medium balls with this mix.

Place them all in the preheated 400 ° F air fryer and cook for 10 minutes.

Serve the vegetarian pancakes with a side salad for lunch.

Nutritional Value (Amount per Serving):
- Calories 111
- Fat 10 g
- Carbohydrates 0.3 g
- Protein 12 g

116. Asian Popcorn Chicken

Preparation time: 30 minutes Cooking time: 15 minutes Servings: 2

Ingredients
- 1 lbs. chicken breast chicken thigh, boneless 1 clove garlic, medium, minced 1 tablespoon soy sauce 2 green onions, minced ¼ tsp. of pepper ¼ tsp. of chili pepper ¼ t tsp. of five spice ½ tsp. of sweet potato starch or corn starch 1 cup sweet potato starch/corn starch 1 egg
- ¼ cup water Breadcrumbs

Cooking Instructions

Wash the chicken and cut into cubes. Place the washed and chopped green onions and garlic in a medium bowl. Add the chilli, five-spice powder, pepper, soy sauce and starch, mixing well.

Place the chicken in the bowl and make sure the pieces are completely covered on all sides. Let the chicken marinate in the bowl for at least 30 minutes or overnight if desired.

Preheat the air fryer to 390F. Beat 1 egg with water in a ball, add starch and mix well.

Sprinkle the chicken with the starch, pressing with your hands, so that it does not fall. Place in the air fryer and cook for 12 minutes. Serve seasoned with salt and pepper.

Nutritional Value (Amount per Serving):
- Calories 100
- Fat 7 g
- Carbohydrates 0.7 g
- Protein 8 g

117. Herbal Chicken With Purple Sweet Potato

Preparation time: 5 minutes Cooking time: 22 minutes Servings: 2

Ingredients
- 1/2 portion of chicken, halved 1 tsp. olive
- 1 tablespoon herbs chicken spices, (Seahs Emperor) Handful of purple sweet potato; brushed clean and pat dry Handful of salad green

Cooking Instructions

Cut the chicken, then rinse and dry it. Marinate with olive oil and herb chicken spices for 1 hour or overnight in the refrigerator.

Place the sweet potato in the Airfryer basket, set the temperature to 350 ° F and cook for 10 minutes.

Place the marinated chicken on the Airfryer basket and cook for another 12 minutes.

During the last 4-5 minutes, check the color of the chicken to make sure it is brown, then continue cooking.

Leave the food for 1-2 minutes in the airfryer before removing it and serving it with the vegetables.

Nutritional Value (Amount per Serving):
- Calories 120
- Fat 10 g
- Carbohydrates 0.5 g
- Protein 11 g

118. Protein Egg Cups

Preparation Time: 10 minutes Cooking Time: 9 minutes Servings: 4

Ingredients:
- 3 eggs, lightly beaten 4 tomato slices
- 4 tsp cheddar cheese, shredded
- 2 bacon slices, cooked and crumbled Pepper
- Salt

Cooking Instructions:

Spray silicone muffin molds with cooking spray.

In a small bowl, beat the egg with pepper and salt.

Preheat the air fryer to 350 F.

Pour the eggs into the silicone muffin molds. Divide the cheese and bacon into the molds.

Cover each with a slice of tomato and place it in the fryer basket.

Cook for 9 minutes.

Serve and enjoy.

Nutritional Value (Amount per Serving):
1. Calories 60
2. Fat 4.4 g
3. Carbohydrates 1 g
4. Sugar 0.7 g
5. Protein 5.5 g
6. Cholesterol 121 mg

119. Zucchini Casserole

Preparation time: 10 minutes Cooking duration: 16 minutes Servings: 8

Ingredients :
- 1 cup veggie stock
- 2 tbps olive oil
- 2 sweet potatoes, peeled and cut into medium wedges
- 8 zucchinis, cut into medium wedges
- 2 yellow onions, chopped
- 1 cup coconut milk
- Salt and black pepper to the taste
- 1 tablespoon soy sauce
- ¼ tsp. thyme, dried
- ¼ tsp. rosemary, dried
- 4 tbps dill, chopped
- ½ tsp. basil, chopped

Cooking Instructions :

Heat a pan suitable for your air fryer with oil over medium heat, add onion, mix and cook for 2 minutes.

Add courgettes, thyme, rosemary, basil, potatoes, salt, pepper, broth, milk, soy sauce and dill, mix, place in the air fryer, cook at 360 °F for 14 minutes, divide between plates and serve immediately.

Nutritional Value (Amount per Serving):
- Calories 109
- Fat 8.2 g
- Carbohydrates 0.5 g
- Protein 9.7 g

120.   Corn Casserole

Preparation time: 10 minutes Cooking duration: 15 minutes Servings: 4

Ingredients:
- 2 cups corn
- 3 tbps flour
- 1 egg
- ¼ cup milk
- ½ cup light cream
- ½ cup Swiss cheese, grated
- 2 tbps margarine
- Salt and black pepper to the taste
- Cooking spray

Cooking Instructions:

In a bowl, mix the corn with the flour, egg, milk, light cream, cheese, salt, pepper and margarine and mix well.

Grease the pan of the air fryer with cooking spray, pour in the cream mixture, distribute and cook at 320 ° F for 15 minutes.

Serve hot for lunch.

Nutritional Value (Amount per Serving):
- Calories 110
- Fat 9.4 g
- Carbohydrates 0.3 g
- Protein 8.1 g

121.   Air Fried Thai Salad

Preparation time: 10 minutes Cooking duration: 5 minutes Servings: 4

Ingredients :
- 1 cup carrots, grated
- 1 cup red cabbage, shredded
- A pinch of salt and black pepper
- A handful cilantro, chopped
- 1 small cucumber, chopped
- Juice from 1 lime
- 2 tsp.s red curry paste
- 12 big shrimp, cooked, peeled and deveined

Cooking Instructions :

In a skillet suitable for yours, mix the cabbage with carrots, cucumbers and shrimp, mix, place in your air fryer and cook at 360 ° F for 5 minutes.

Add salt, pepper, coriander, lime juice and red curry paste, mix again, divide between plates and serve immediately.

Nutritional Value (Amount per Serving):
- Calories 99
- Fat 10 g
- Carbohydrates 0.5 g
- Protein 9 g

122.   Coconut and Chicken Casserole

Preparation time: 10 minutes Cooking duration: 25 minutes Servings: 4

Ingredients :
- 4 lime leaves, torn
- 1 cup veggie stock
- 1 lemongrass stalk, chopped
- 1 inch piece, grated
- 1 pound chicken breast, skinless, boneless and cut into thin strips
- 8 ounces mushrooms, chopped
- 4 Thai chilies, chopped
- 4 tbps fish sauce
- 6 ounces coconut milk
- ¼ cup lime juice
- ¼ cup cilantro, chopped
- Salt and black pepper to the taste

Cooking Instructions:

Place the broth in a pan suitable for an air fryer, bring to a boil over medium heat, add the lemongrass, ginger and lime leaves, stir and cook for 10 minutes.

Strain the soup, return to the pan, add chicken, mushrooms, milk, chillies, fish sauce, lime juice, coriander, salt and pepper, mix, place in the deep fryer and cook at 360 ° F for 15 minutes.

Divide into bowls and serve.

Nutritional Value (Amount per Serving):
- Calories 109
- Fat 8.2 g
- Carbohydrates 0.5 g
- Protein 9.7 g

123.   Easy Chicken Lunch

Preparation time: 10 minutes Cooking duration: 20 minutes Servings: 6

Ingredients :
- 1 bunch kale, chopped
- Salt and black pepper to the taste
- ¼ cup chicken stock
- 1 cup chicken, shredded
- 3 carrots, chopped
- 1 cup shiitake mushrooms, roughly sliced

Cooking Instructions :

In a blender, mix the broth with the kale, blend a few times and pour into a pan suitable for an air fryer.

Add chicken, mushrooms, carrots, salt and pepper to taste, mix, place in deep fryer and cook at 350 ° F for 18 minutes.

Nutritional Value (Amount per Serving):
- Calories 421
- Fat 41 g
- Carbohydrates 4 g
- Sugar 2.5 g
- Protein 54 g
- Cholesterol 114 mg

124. Shrimp Stuff Peppers

Preparation Time: 10 minutes Cooking Time: 6 minutes
Servings: 6
Ingredients:
- 12 baby bell peppers, cut into halves 1 tbsp olive oil
- tbsp fresh lemon juice
- ¼ cup basil pesto
- 1lb shrimp, cooked
- ½ tsp red pepper flakes, crushed 2 tbsp parsley, chopped
- Pepper Salt

Cooking Instructions:
In a bowl, mix the prawns, parsley, red pepper flakes, basil pesto, lemon juice, oil, pepper and salt.
Fill the shrimp mixture into the pepper cut in half and place it in the basket of the air fryer.
Cook at 320 F for 6 minutes.
Serve and enjoy.
Nutritional Value (Amount per Serving):
1. Calories 196
2. Fat 3.2 g
3. Carbohydrates 11 g
4. Sugar 11 g
5. Protein 12 g
6. Cholesterol 153 mg

125. Buttery Scallops

Preparation Time: 10 minutes Cooking Time: 8 minutes
Servings: 2
Ingredients:
- lb jumbo scallops
- tbsp fresh lemon juice 2 tbsp butter, melted

Cooking Instructions:
Preheat the air fryer to 400 F.
In a small bowl, mix the lemon juice and butter.
Brush the scallops with the lemon juice and butter mixture and place them in the basket of the air fryer.
Cook the scallops for 4 minutes. Turn halfway.
Brush the scallops again with the lemon butter mixture and cook for another 4 minutes. Turn halfway.
Serve and enjoy.
Nutritional Value (Amount per Serving):
- Calories 189
- Fat 13 g
- Carbohydrates 2 g
- Sugar 0.2 g
- Protein 15 g
- Cholesterol 110 mg

126. Prawn Chicken Drumettes

Preparation time: 15 minutes Cooking time: 15 minutes
Servings: 3
Ingredients
10½ ounces of chicken drumettes 1 tsp. of sesame oil 1 tsp. of ginger juice 6 tsp.s of vegetable oil ¾ tsp. of sugar 3 tsp.s of prawn paste ½ tsp. of Shaoxing wine
Cooking Instructions
Mix the sesame oil, ginger juice, sugar, shrimp paste and shaoxing wine to form the marinade. Soak the chicken in the marinade for an hour or overnight in the refrigerator.
Preheat Airfryer for 5 minutes at 356 ° F.
Lightly brush the chicken with vegetable oil and place it in a single layer in the fryer basket. Cook for 8 minutes, flip the chicken and cook for another 7 minutes until golden brown.
Nutritional Value (Amount per Serving):
- Calories 125
- Fat 6 g
- Carbohydrates 0.7 g
- Protein 9 g

127. Delicious Eggplant Hash

Preparation Time: 10 minutes Cooking Time: 14 minutes
Servings: 4
Ingredients:
- eggplant, chopped
- ¼ cup fresh mint, chopped
- ¼ cup basil, chopped 1 tsp Tabasco sauce
- ½ lb cherry tomatoes halved
- ½ cup olive oil Pepper
- Salt

Cooking Instructions:
Heat the oil in a skillet over medium-high heat.
Add the aubergines to the pan and cook for 3 minutes, stirring well and cook for another 3 minutes.
Transfer the aubergines to the pan of the air fryer.
Add the tomatoes to the same pan and cook for 1-2 minutes.
Transfer the tomatoes to the eggplant pan with the other ingredients and mix well.
Place the dish in the air fryer and cook at 320 F for 6 minutes.
Serve and enjoy.
Nutritional Value (Amount per Serving):
1. Calories 252
2. Fat 22 g
3. Carbohydrates 9 g
4. Sugar 4 g
5. Protein 4 g
6. Cholesterol 0 mg

128. Tasty And Spicy Chicken Jerks

Preparation time: 38 minutes Cooking time: 18 minutes
Servings: 5
Ingredients
- 6 tsp.s of vegetable oil 1 tsp. of white pepper 3 tsp.s of chopped fresh thyme 6 cloves of garlic, finely diced 1 tsp. of cinnamon 4 green onions, finely chopped 2½ ounces of lime juice 3 tsp.s of grated ginger 1 habanera pepper, seeded and finely chopped 1 tsp. cayenne pepper 6 tsp.s of sugar 30 chicken wings 8 tbps of red wine vinegar 6 tsp.s of soy sauce 1 tsp. of salt

Cooking Instructions
Combine all ingredients in a large bowl, making sure the chicken is well covered with the spices and seasonings. Pour into a large resealable bag and leave to marinate in

the refrigerator for 2-24 hours.

Heat the air fryer to 390 ° F.

Remove the chicken wings from the bag, discard the liquid and dry the wings with a disposable paper towel.

Place the wings in the fryer basket and fry for 18 minutes. Shake the chicken in half.

Serve with ranch dressing.

Nutritional Value (Amount per Serving):
- Calories 110
- Fat 11 g
- Carbohydrates 0.5 g
- Protein 7 g

129. Herb Carrots

Preparation Time: 10 minutes Cooking Time: 20 minutes Servings: 4

Ingredients:
- lb baby carrots, trimmed 2 tbsp fresh lime juice
- tsp herb de Provence 2 tsp olive oil
- Pepper Salt

Cooking Instructions:

Add carrots into the bowl and toss with remaining ingredients.

Transfer carrots into the air fryer basket and cook at 320 F for 20 minutes.

Serve and enjoy.

Nutritional Value (Amount per Serving):
1. Calories 65
2. Fat 2.1 g
3. Carbohydrates 9.1 g
4. Sugar 5.1 g
5. Protein 0.7 g
6. Cholesterol 0 mg

130. Sweet Potato Lunch Casserole

Preparation time: 10 minutes Cooking duration: 50 minutes Servings: 6

Ingredients :
- 3 big sweet potatoes, pricked with a fork
- 1 cup chicken stock
- Salt and black pepper to the taste
- A pinch of cayenne pepper
- ¼ tsp. nutmeg, ground
- 1/3 cup coconut cream

Cooking Instructions:

Place the sweet potatoes in the air fryer, cook them at 350 ° F for 40 minutes, cool them, peel them, coarsely chop them and transfer to a pan suitable for the air fryer.

Add broth, salt, pepper, cayenne pepper and the coconut cream, mix, place in the deep fryer and cook at 360 °F for another 10 minutes.

Divide the saucepan between bowls and serve.

Nutritional Value (Amount per Serving):
- Calories 119
- Fat 8.4 g
- Carbohydrates 0.5 g
- Protein 9.1 g

131. Tomato Mushroom Mix

Preparation Time: 10 minutes Cooking Time: 15 minutes Servings: 4

Ingredients:
- 6 oz tomatoes, chopped 2 tbsp olive oil
- ½ tsp ground nutmeg 1 onion, chopped
- 15 oz mushrooms, sliced Pepper
- Salt

Cooking Instructions:

Add all ingredients into the air fryer baking dish and mix well.

Place dish in the air fryer and cook at 380 F for 15 minutes.

Serve and enjoy.

Nutritional Value (Amount per Serving):
- Calories 101
- Fat 7.2 g
- Carbohydrates 7.4 g
- Sugar 4.3 g
- Protein 7 g
- Cholesterol 0 mg

132. Zucchini Squash Mix

Preparation Time: 10 minutes Cooking Time: 35 minutes Servings: 4

Ingredients:
- lb zucchini, sliced
- tbsp parsley, chopped
- 1 yellow squash, halved, deseeded, and chopped
  1 tbsp olive oil
- Pepper Salt

Cooking Instructions:

Add all ingredients to the large bowl and mix well.

Transfer the bowl mixture to the basket of the air fryer and cook at 400 F for 35 minutes.

Serve and enjoy.

Nutritional Value (Amount per Serving):
- Calories 42
- Fat 3.3 g
- Carbohydrates 5 g
- Sugar 2.2 g
- Protein 1.5 g
- Cholesterol 0 mg

133. Turkey Burgers

Preparation time: 10 minutes Cooking duration: 8 minutes Servings: 4

Ingredients :
- 1 pound turkey meat, ground
- 1 shallot, minced
- A drizzle of olive oil
- 1 small jalapeno pepper, minced
- 2 tsp.s lime juice
- Zest from 1 lime, grated
- Salt and black pepper to the taste
- 1 tsp. cumin, ground
- 1 tsp. sweet paprika

Guacamole for serving

Cooking Instructions :

In a bowl, mix the turkey meat with salt, pepper, cumin, paprika, shallot, jalapeño, lime juice and zest, mix well, form the burgers from this mix, drizzle with oil, place in a deep fryer. preheated air and bake at 370 ° F for 8 minutes on each side.

Divide between plates and serve with guacamole on top.

Nutritional Value (Amount per Serving):
- Calories 119
- Fat 8.2 g
- Carbohydrates 0.5 g
- Protein 9.7 g

134.   Mushroom Cheese Salad

Preparation Time: 10 minutes Cooking Time: 15 minutes Servings: 3

Ingredients:
- 10 mushrooms, halved
- tbsp fresh parsley, chopped 1 tbsp olive oil
- tbsp mozzarella cheese, grated 1 tbsp cheddar cheese, grated
- 1 tbsp dried mix herbs Pepper
- Salt

Cooking Instructions:

Add all the ingredients to the bowl and mix well.

Transfer the mixture from the bowl to the pan of the air fryer.

Place in the air fryer and cook at 380 F for 15 minutes.

Serve and enjoy.

Nutritional Value (Amount per Serving):
1. Calories 92
2. Fat 7.2 g
3. Carbohydrates 3 g
4. Sugar 1 g
5. Protein 7 g
6. Cholesterol 7 mg

135.   Crab Cheese Frittata

Preparation Time: 10 minutes Cooking Time: 14 minutes Servings: 2

Ingredients:
- 5 eggs
- ¼ tsp fresh lemon juice
- 2 tbsp fresh mint, chopped 1/3 cup goat cheese, crumbled
- ¼ cup onion, minced
- ¼ tsp pepper
- ¼ tsp salt

Cooking Instructions:

Preheat the air fryer to 325 F.

In a bowl, beat the eggs with pepper and salt. Add the other ingredients and mix well.

Spray the air fryer pan with cooking spray.

Pour the egg mixture into the prepared dish and place it in the air fryer and cook for 14 minutes.

Serve and enjoy.

Nutritional Value (Amount per Serving):
1. Calories 315

2. Fat 22 g
3. Carbohydrates 2.1 g
4. Sugar 1.5 g
5. Protein 25 g
6. Cholesterol 460 mg

136.   Greek Vegetables

Preparation Time: 10 minutes Cooking Time: 35 minutes Servings: 6

Ingredients:
- eggplant, sliced
- 4 tomatoes, quarters
- onion, chopped
- thyme sprig, chopped 1 bay leaf
- tbsp olive oil
- garlic cloves, minced 2 bell peppers, chopped 1 zucchini, sliced Pepper
- Salt

Cooking Instructions:

Add all ingredients to the pan of the air fryer and mix well.

Place the pan in the air fryer and cook at 300 F for 35 minutes.

Serve and enjoy.

Nutritional Value (Amount per Serving):
1. Calories 113
2. Fat 8 g
3. Carbohydrates 12 g
4. Sugar 8 g
5. Protein 4 g
6. Cholesterol 0 mg

137.   Broccoli Chicken Frittata

Preparation Time: 10 minutes Cooking Time: 14 minutes Servings: 2

Ingredients:
- 5 large eggs
- ¼ tsp fresh lemon juice
- 1/3 cup cheddar cheese, shredded
- ¼ cup broccoli, chopped
- ¼ cup chicken, cooked and chopped
- ¼ cup bell pepper, minced
- ¼ tsp pepper
- ¼ tsp salt

Cooking Instructions:

1. Preheat the air fryer to 325 F.
2. In a bowl, beat the eggs with pepper and salt.
3. Add the other ingredients and mix well.
4. Spray the pan of the air fryer with cooking spray.
5. Pour the egg mixture into the prepared dish and place it in the air fryer and cook for 14 minutes.
6. Serve and enjoy.

Nutritional Value (Amount per Serving):
- Calories 281
- Fat 19 g
- Carbohydrates 3.3 g
- Sugar 3 g
- Protein 25 g
- Cholesterol 490 mg

138.   Chicken and Corn Casserole

Preparation time: 10 minutes Cooking duration: 30 minutes Servings: 6

Ingredients :
- 1 cup clean chicken stock
- 2 tsp.s garlic powder
- Salt and black pepper to the taste
- 6 ounces canned coconut milk
- 1 and ½ cups green lentils
- 2 pounds chicken breasts, skinless, boneless and cubed 1/3 cup cilantro, chopped
- 3 cups corn
- 3 handfuls spinach
- 3 green onions, chopped

Cooking Instructions :

In a pan that fits your air fryer, mix stock with coconut milk, salt, pepper, garlic powder, chicken and lentils.
Add corn, green onions, cilantro and spinach, stir well, introduce in your air fryer and cook at 350 °F for 30 minutes.

Nutritional Value (Amount per Serving):
- Calories 421
- Fat 41 g
- Carbohydrates 5 g
- Sugar 2.5 g
- Protein 46 g
- Cholesterol 102 mg

139.   Creamy Cabbage

Preparation Time: 10 minutes Cooking Time: 20 minutes Servings: 4

Ingredients:
- cabbage head, shredded 1 cup heavy cream
- 4 bacon slices, chopped 1 onion, chopped Pepper
- Salt

Cooking Instructions:

Add all ingredients into the air fryer baking dish and stir well.
Place dish in the air fryer and cook at 400 F for 20 minutes.
Serve and enjoy.

Nutritional Value (Amount per Serving):
- Calories 153
- Fat 10 g
- Carbohydrates 13 g
- Sugar 7 g
- Protein 5 g
- Cholesterol 44 mg

140.   Chicken, Beans, Corn and Quinoa Casserole

Preparation time: 10 minutes Cooking duration: 30 minutes Servings: 8

- Ingredients:
- 1 cup quinoa, already cooked
- 3 cups chicken breast, cooked and shredded
- 14 ounces canned black beans
- 12 ounces corn
- ½ cup cilantro, chopped
- 6 kale leaves, chopped
- ½ cup green onions, chopped
- 1 cup clean ketchup
- 1 cup clean salsa
- 2 tsp.s chili powder
- 2 tsp.s cumin, ground
- 3 cups mozzarella cheese, shredded
- 1 tablespoon garlic powder
- Cooking spray
- 2 jalapeno peppers, chopped

Cooking Instructions:

Spray cooking spray on a pan suitable for the air fryer, add quinoa, chicken, black beans, corn, coriander, cabbage, green onions, ketchup, salsa, chili powder, cumin, garlic powder, jalapenos and mozzarella, toss into deep fryer and cook at 350 ° F for 17 minutes.
Slice and serve hot for lunch.

Nutritional Value (Amount per Serving):
- Calories 341
- Fat 36 g
- Carbohydrates 5 g
- Sugar 2.5 g
- Protein 40 g
- Cholesterol 111 mg

141.   Garlic Feta Asparagus

Preparation Time: 10 minutes Cooking Time: 15 minutes Servings: 4

Ingredients:
- 2 lbs asparagus, trimmed
- 2 tbsp fresh parsley, chopped 4 oz feta cheese, crumbled
- ½ tsp red pepper flakes
- ½ tsp dried oregano
- 3 garlic cloves, minced 1 tsp lemon zest
- ¼ cup olive oil 1 lemon juice Pepper
- Salt

Cooking Instructions:

In a bowl, whisk together the oil, oregano, chili flakes, garlic and lemon zest.
Add the asparagus, crumbled cheese, pepper and salt and mix well.
Transfer the asparagus mixture to the basket of the air fryer and cook at 350 F for 8 minutes.
Season the asparagus with the lemon juice and sprinkle with parsley.
Serve and enjoy.

Nutritional Value (Amount per Serving):
- Calories 224
- Fat 17 g
- Carbohydrates 12 g
- Sugar 5 g
- Protein 11 g
- Cholesterol 22 mg

142.   Lemon Butter Artichokes

Preparation Time: 10 minutes Cooking Time: 15 minutes
Servings: 4

Ingredients:

- 2 medium artichokes, trimmed and halved 2 tbsp fresh lemon juice
- tbsp butter, melted Pepper
- Salt

Cooking Instructions:

Place artichokes into the air fryer basket. Drizzle with butter and lemon juice and season with pepper and salt.
Cook at 380 F for 15 minutes.
Serve and enjoy.

Nutritional Value (Amount per Serving):

- Calories 53
- Fat 3.2 g
- Carbohydrates 6.2 g
- Sugar 0.8 g
- Protein 2.1 g
- Cholesterol 7 mg

143.   Chicken Meatballs

Preparation Time: 10 minutes Cooking Time: 12 minutes
Servings: 4

Ingredients:

- lb ground chicken
- 1/3 cup frozen spinach, drained and thawed 1/3 cup feta cheese, crumbled
- tsp greek seasoning
- ½ oz pork rinds, crushed Pepper
- Salt

Cooking Instructions:

Spray the basket of the air fryer with cooking spray.
Add all ingredients to the large bowl and mix until smooth.
Prepare balls of the meat mixture and place them in the basket of the air fryer and cook for 12 minutes.
Serve and enjoy.

Nutritional Value (Amount per Serving):

- Calories 261
- Fat 11 g
- Carbohydrates 1 g
- Sugar 0.5 g
- Protein 32 g
- Cholesterol 113 mg

144.   Almond Crust Chicken

Preparation Time: 10 minutes Cooking Time: 25 minutes
Servings: 2

Ingredients:

- 3 chicken breasts, skinless and boneless 1 tbsp Dijon mustard
- 2 tbsp mayonnaise
- ¼ cup almonds Pepper
- Salt

Cooking Instructions:

Add the almonds to the food processor and blend until finely ground. Transfer the almonds to a plate and set aside.

Mix mustard and mayonnaise and spread over the chicken.
Coat the chicken with the almonds and place it in the fryer basket and cook at 350 F for 25 minutes.
Serve and enjoy.

Nutritional Value (Amount per Serving):

- Calories 402
- Fat 25 g
- Carbohydrates 9 g
- Sugar 1.5 g
- Protein 47 g
- Cholesterol 124 mg

145.   Italian Chicken

Preparation Time: 10 minutes Cooking Time: 20 minutes
Servings: 4

Ingredients:

- 4 chicken thighs
- ¼ tsp onion powder
- ½ tsp garlic powder
- 2 ½ tsp dried Italian herbs 2 tbsp butter, melted

Cooking Instructions:

Brush the chicken with melted butter.
Mix the Italian herbs, onion powder and garlic powder and rub over the chicken.
Place the chicken in the basket of the air fryer and cook at 380 ° F for 20 minutes.
Serve and enjoy.

Nutritional Value (Amount per Serving):

1. Calories 320
2. Fat 12 g
3. Carbohydrates 0.4 g
4. Sugar 0.1 g
5. Protein 40 g
6. Cholesterol 142 mg

146.   Almond Pesto Salmon

Preparation Time: 10 minutes Cooking Time: 12 minutes
Servings: 2

Ingredients:

- 2 salmon fillets
- 2 tbsp butter, melted
- ¼ cup pesto
- ¼ cup almond, ground

Cooking Instructions:

Mix the pesto and almonds.
Brush the salmon fillets with melted butter and place them in the pan of the air fryer.
Top salmon fillets with pesto and almond blend.
Place dish in the air fryer and cook at 390 F for 12 minutes.
Serve and enjoy.

Nutritional Value (Amount per Serving):

- Calories 531
- Fat 44 g
- Carbohydrates 4 g
- Sugar 2.5 g
- Protein 42 g
- Cholesterol 112 mg

147. Salmon and Asparagus

Preparation time: 10 minutes Cooking duration: 23 minutes Servings: 4

Ingredients :

- 1 pound asparagus, trimmed
- 1 tablespoon olive oil
- A pinch of sweet paprika
- Salt and black pepper to the taste
- A pinch of garlic powder
- A pinch of cayenne pepper
- 1 red bell pepper, cut into halves
- 4 ounces smoked salmon

Cooking Instructions:

Place the asparagus spears and bell pepper on a lined baking sheet that fits your air fryer, add salt, pepper, garlic powder, paprika, olive oil, cayenne pepper, stir to coat, add to deep fryer , cook at 390 ° F for 8 minutes, flip and cook for an additional 8 minutes.

Add the salmon, cook for 5 minutes again, divide everything into plates and serve.

Nutritional Value (Amount per Serving):

- Calories 431
- Fat 47 g
- Carbohydrates 4 g
- Sugar 2.5 g
- Protein 44 g
- Cholesterol 112 mg

148. Chicken and Zucchini Lunch Mix

Preparation time: 10 minutes Cooking duration: 20 minutes Servings: 4

Ingredients:

- 4 zucchinis, cut with a spiralizer
- 1 pound chicken breasts, skinless, boneless and cubed
- 2 garlic cloves, minced
- 1 tsp. olive oil
- Salt and black pepper to the taste
- 2 cups cherry tomatoes, halved
- ½ cup almonds, chopped

For the pesto:

- 2 cups basil
- 2 cups kale, chopped
- 1 tablespoon lemon juice
- 1 garlic clove
- ¾ cup pine nuts
- ½ cup olive oil
- A pinch of salt

Cooking Instructions:

In your food processor, mix the basil with the black cabbage, lemon juice, garlic, pine nuts, oil and a pinch of salt, blend very well and set aside.

Heat a pan suitable for your air fryer with oil over medium heat, add the garlic, mix and cook for 1 minute.

Add the chicken, salt, pepper, mix, almonds, zucchini noodles, garlic, cherry tomatoes and pesto you made at the beginning, mix gently, place in a preheated air fryer and cook under 360 ° for 17 minutes.

Divide between plates and serve for lunch.

Nutritional Value (Amount per Serving):

- Calories 321
- Fat 46 g
- Carbohydrates 5 g
- Sugar 2.5 g
- Protein 42 g
- Cholesterol 125 mg

Optavia Lean & Green Poultry Air-Fry Recipes

149. Air Fried Philly Cheesesteak Taquitos

(Prep Time: 20 mints| Cook Time: 6-8 hours| Servings: 6)

Ingredients

- Dry Italian dressing mix: one package
- Super Soft Corn Tortillas: one pack
- Green peppers: two pieces, chopped
- One white onion, diced
- 12 cups of lean beef steak strips
- Beef stock: 2 cups
- Lettuce shredded, one cup
- Provolone cheese: ten slices
- Olive oil

Instructions

In a slow cooker, add onion, beef, broth, pepper and seasonings.

Cover and cook over low heat for 6 or 8 hours.

Heat the tortillas for two minutes in the microwave.

Allow the air fryer to preheat to 350F.

Remove the cheesesteak from the slow cooker, add 2-3 tablespoons of steak to the tortilla.

Add some cheese, roll the tortilla well and place in a deep fryer basket.

Make all the tortillas you want.

Lightly brush with olive oil

Cook for 6-8 minutes.

Flip the tortillas over and brush more oil as needed.

Serve with chopped lettuce and enjoy

Nutritional value: per serving: calories 220| carbs 22g| protein 21 |fat 16g

150. Air Fried Philly Cheesesteak Taquitos

(Prep Time: 20 mints| Cook Time: 6-8 hours| Servings: 6)

Ingredients

- Dry Italian dressing mix: one package
- Super Soft Corn Tortillas: one pack
- Green peppers: two pieces, chopped
- One white onion, diced
- 12 cups of lean beef steak strips
- Beef stock: 2 cups
- Lettuce shredded, one cup
- Provolone cheese: ten slices
- Olive oil

Instructions

In a slow cooker, add onion, beef, broth, pepper and seasonings.

Cover and cook over low heat for 6 or 8 hours.

Heat the tortillas for two minutes in the microwave.

Allow the air fryer to preheat to 350F.

Remove the cheesesteak from the slow cooker, add 2-3 tablespoons of steak to the tortilla.

Add some cheese, roll the tortilla well and place in a deep fryer basket.

Make all the tortillas you want.

Lightly brush with olive oil

Cook for 6-8 minutes.

Flip the tortillas over and brush more oil as needed.

Serve with chopped lettuce and enjoy

Nutritional value: per serving: calories 212| carbs 19g| protein 25 |fat 11g

151.   Air Fryer Chicken Wings with Buffalo Sauce

(Prep Time: 5 mints| Cook Time:25 mints| Servings: 6)

Ingredients

- Chicken drumettes & flats: 4 cups
- Salt & pepper, to taste
  Buffalo Sauce
- Hot sauce: 1/2 cup
- White vinegar: 2 tablespoons
- Melted butter: 1/2 cup
- Worcestershire sauce: 2 teaspoons
- Pinch of garlic powder

Instructions

Allow the air fryer to preheat to 380F.

Separate the wings, forming a plate and the chopsticks, discarding the tips.

Using paper towels, dry the chicken wings, sprinkle generously with salt and pepper and other seasonings of your choice.

Put them in a basket to fry and cook for about 22 minutes.

After this increase, the temperature to 400 degrees, cook for another five minutes so that the chicken skin becomes crisp.

Mix all the ingredients of the buffalo sauce and mix well.

Sprinkle the wings with homemade buffalo sauce.

Serve with the salad garnish.

Nutritional value : per serving: Cal 325| Fat: 22g| Carbs: 1.4g|Protein: 32g

152.   Orange Chicken Wings

(Prep Time: 5 mints| Cook Time: 14 mints| Servings: 2)

Ingredients

- Honey: 1 tbsp.
- Chicken Wings, Six pieces
- One orange zest and juice
- Worcestershire Sauce: 1.5 tbsp.
- Black pepper, to taste
- Herbs (sage, rosemary, oregano, parsley, basil, thyme, and mint)

Instructions

Wash and dry the chicken wings

In a bowl, add the chicken wings, pour in the zest and orange juice

Add the rest of the ingredients and rub on the chicken wings. Leave to marinate for at least half an hour.

Allow the air fryer to preheat to 180 ° C

In aluminum foil, wrap the marinated wings and put them in an air fryer and cook for 20 minutes at 180 C

After 20 minutes, remove the foil and brush the sauce over the wings and cook for another 15 minutes. Then again, brush the sauce and cook for another ten minutes.

Remove from air fryer and serve with vegetables.

Nutritional value: per serving: Calories 275 |Proteins 26g |Carbs 23g |Fat 19g |

153.   Air Fryer BBQ Chicken Wings

(Prep Time: 5 mints| Cook Time: 15 mints| Servings: 4)

Ingredients

- BBQ sauce: half cup
- Chicken wings: 4 cups
- Black pepper, to taste
- Garlic powder: 1/8 teaspoon
- Ranch
- Celery sticks

Instructions

Let the air fryer preheat to 400 degrees.

With absorbent paper, pat dry the chicken wings, rubbing the garlic powder over them. Place them in the air fryer, in an even layer.

Cook for 15 minutes, turn the wings once or twice. Cook for another 3 minutes to get crunchy skin.

Take them out of the air fryer and pour them into the barbecue sauce. mix well to coat

Serve with celery sticks, mixed greens and ranch sauce.

Nutritional value : per serving: Calories: 199kcal | Carbohydrates: 12g | Protein: 10g | Fat: 12g

154.   Air Fryer Dumplings

(Prep Time: 5 mints| Cook Time:10 mints| Servings: 3)

Ingredients

- One packet of frozen chicken, vegetable, or pork dumplings
- Salad greens: one cup
- Dipping sauce
- Maple syrup: 1/8 cup
- Soy sauce: 1/4 cup
- Red pepper flakes: Pinch
- Garlic powder: 1/2 tsp.
- Rice vinegar: 1/2 tsp.
- Water: 1/4 cup

Instructions

Allow the air fryer to preheat to 370 degrees for four minutes.

Place the gnocchi in the basket of the air fryer in a single layer and spray with oil.

Fry in the air for five minutes, turn the basket, sprinkle

with a little more oil.

Leave to cook for another six minutes.

Meanwhile combine all the dipping sauce ingredients in a bowl and mix well.

Remove the gnocco and serve with the vegetables.

Nutritional value : per serving: Cal 222|FAT: 9g |Carbs: 21g |Protein: 16g

155.   Sriracha-Honey Chicken Wings

(Prep Time: 30 mints| Cook Time:15 min| Servings: 2)

Ingredients

*   Soy sauce: 1 and 1/2 tablespoons
*   Chicken wings: 4 cups
*   Sriracha sauce: 2 tablespoons
*   Butter: 1 tablespoon
*   Half cup honey
*   Juice of half lime
*   Scallion's cilantro, and chives for garnish

Instructions

Let the air fryer preheat to 360 degrees F.

Place the chicken wings in the basket of an air fryer, cook for half an hour, flip the wings every seven minutes and cook thoroughly.

Meanwhile, in a saucepan, add all the sauce ingredients and simmer for three minutes.

Remove the chicken wings and cover them well with the sauce.

Garnish with the shallot. Serve with microgreen salad.

Nutritional value: per serving: Calories 217 |Proteins 19g |Carbs 11g|Fat 12g |

156.   Air Fryer Grilled Chicken Recipe

(Prep Time: 30 mints| Cook Time:20 mints| Servings: 3)

Ingredients

*   Chicken tenders: 4 cups
    Marinade
*   Honey: 2 Tbsp.
*   Olive oil: 1/4 cup
*   White vinegar: 2 Tbsp.
*   Water: 2 Tbsp.
*   Half teaspoon salt
*   Garlic powder: 1 tsp.
*   Half teaspoon of paprika
*   Onion powder: 1 tsp.
*   Half teaspoon crushed red pepper

Instructions

In a bowl, add all the ingredients of the marinade and mix well.

Then add the chicken mix to coat. Cover with cling film and leave to marinate in the refrigerator for half an hour.

Place the chicken tenders in the basket of the air fryer in an even layer.

Cook for 3 minutes at 390 F. Flip the tenders and cook for another five minutes or until the chicken is completely cooked.

Serve with the salad garnish.

Nutritional value : per serving: calories 233|fat 12g| protein 25 g| carbs 13g

157.   Air Fryer Nashville Hot Chicken with Spinach Salad

(Prep Time: 30 mints| Cook Time:25 mints| Servings: 8)

Ingredients

*   Buttermilk: 2 cups
*   Chicken thighs(bone-in): 8
*   Cayenne pepper: 1 tsp.
*   Hot sauce: 1/4 cup
*   Garlic powder: 2 Tbsp.
*   Salt: 1 tsp.
*   Low-fat butter: 1/2 cup
*   Flour: 2 cups
*   Black pepper: 1 tsp.
*   Old bay: 1 tsp.
*   Paprika: 1 tsp.

Instructions

In a bowl, add the hot sauce and buttermilk, mix well, then add the chicken pieces.

Leave to marinate in the refrigerator for 1 to 24 hours.

In a bowl, add the garlic powder, flour, salt, black pepper, paprika, cayenne pepper, and old bay leaf. Mix well.

Always cook the chicken in a single layer, in the air fryer

Remove the chicken from the buttermilk, cover it with the flour. Let the chicken rest on a wire rack for 15 minutes before placing it in the air fryer.

Place the breaded chicken in the air fryer, leaving space between the pieces.

Cook for 25 minutes, at 390 F. after the first half, remove the basket and spray the chicken with olive oil

This step is optional. Mix two tablespoons. Spicy sauce with melted butter. Brush the cooked crispy chicken with it.

Serve with the spinach salad.

Nutritional value : per serving: calories 339|Fat 21g|Carbs 17g|protein 21g

158.   Low Carb Parmesan Chicken Meat balls

(Prep Time: 10 mints| Cook Time:12 mints| Servings: 20)

Ingredients

*   Pork rinds: half cup, ground
*   Ground chicken: 4 cups
*   Parmesan cheese: half cup grated
*   Kosher salt: 1 tsp.
*   Garlic powder: 1 tsp.
*   One egg beaten
*   Paprika: 1 tsp.
*   Pepper: half tsp.
    Breading
*   Pork rinds: half cup ground

Instructions

Let the air fryer preheat to 400 ° F.

Add the cheese, chicken, egg, pepper, half a cup of pork rinds, garlic, salt and paprika into a large mixing ball. Mix well into a dough, form 1-and-a-half-inch balls.

Coat the meatballs with the pork rinds (minced).

The oil sprays the air frying basket and adds the meatballs

in an even layer.

Cook for 12 minutes at 400 ° F, turning once halfway through cooking.

Serve with salad.

Nutritional value : per serving: Cal 250| fat 11 g| carbs 13.1 g| protein 18.9 g

159. Teriyaki Chicken Drumsticks with Salad Greens

(Prep Time: 30 mints| Cook Time:20 mints| Servings: 6)

Ingredients

- Six chicken drumsticks
- Teriyaki sauce: one cup
- Salad greens: one cup
- Sesame seeds and chopped green onion, for garnish

Instructions

Let the air fryer preheat to 360 ° F.

Pour the teriyaki sauce into a large zip lock bag, add the chicken legs.

Mix them so well coated. Leave to marinate for half an hour.

Place the chopsticks in a single layer in the basket of the air fryer, leave to cook for 20 minutes.

Shake the basket several times for even cooking.

Top with green onions, sesame seeds and serve with the salad garnish.

Nutritional value : per serving: Calories: 166kcal | Carbohydrates: 9g | Protein: 13g | Fat: 8g |

160. Air Fryer Italian Sausage & Vegetables

(Prep Time: 5 mints| Cook Time:14 mints| Servings: 4)

Ingredients

- One bell pepper
- Italian Sausage: 4 pieces spicy or sweet
- One small onion
- 1/4 cup of mushrooms

Instructions

Let the air fryer preheat at 400 F for three minutes.

Put the Italian sausage in a single layer in the fryer basket and cook for six minutes.

Slice the vegetables while cooking the sausages.

After six minutes, reduce the temperature to 360 F. Flip the sausage in half. Add the mushrooms, onions and peppers to the basket around the sausage.

Cook at 360 degrees for 8 minutes. After 4 minutes, stir around the sausage and vegetables.

With an instant-read thermometer, the temperature of the sausage should be 160 F.

Cook more for a few minutes if the temperature is not 160F.

Remove the vegetables and sausage and serve hot with brown rice.

Nutritional value : per serving: calories 299| fat: 23g| carbs 11g|Protein: 15g

161. Air-Fried Buttermilk Chicken

(Prep Time: 30 mints| Cook Time:20 mints| Servings: 6)

Ingredients

- Chicken thighs: 4 cups skin-on, bone-in Marinade
- Buttermilk: 2 cups
- Black pepper: 2 tsp.
- Cayenne pepper: 1 tsp.
- Salt: 2 tsp.
  Seasoned Flour
- B aking powder: 1 tbsp.
- All-purpose flour: 2 cups
- Paprika powder: 1 tbsp.
- Salt: 1 tsp.
- Garlic powder: 1 tbsp.

Instructions

Let the air warm up to 180 C.

With a paper towel, dry the chicken legs.

In a bowl, add the paprika, black pepper, mix the salt well, then add the chicken pieces. Add the buttermilk and coat the chicken well. Leave to marinate for at least 6 hours.

In another bowl, add the yeast, salt, flour, pepper and paprika. Place the chicken pieces one at a time and cover them with the dressing.

Spray oil on the chicken pieces and put the breaded chicken skin upward in the fryer basket in one layer, cook for 8 minutes, then turn the chicken pieces for another ten minutes

Remove and serve with salad.

Nutritional value : per serving: Cal 217|fat 19 g| protein 19g|carbs 13 g

162. Air Fried Empanadas

(Prep Time: 10 mints| Cook Time:20 mints| Servings: 2)

Ingredients

- Square gyoza wrappers: eight pieces
- Olive oil: 1 tablespoon
- White onion: 1/4 cup, finely diced
- Mushrooms: 1/4 cup, finely diced
- Half cup lean ground beef
- Chopped garlic: 2 teaspoons
- Paprika: 1/4 teaspoon
- Ground cumin: 1/4 teaspoon
- Six green olives, diced
- Ground cinnamon: 1/8 teaspoon
- Diced tomatoes: half cup
- One egg, lightly beaten

Instructions

In a skillet, over medium heat, add the oil, onions and beef and cook for 3 minutes, until the beef turns brown.

Add the mushrooms and cook for six minutes until they begin to brown. Then add the paprika, cinnamon, olives, cumin and garlic and cook for 3 minutes or more.

Add the chopped tomatoes and cook for one minute. Turn off the heat; let it cool for five minutes.

Place the gyoza wrappers on a flat surface add a spoon and a half. of beef stuffing in each wrapper. Brush the edges with water or egg, fold the wrappers, pinch the edges.

Place four empanadas in an even layer in a deep fryer bas-

ket and cook for 7 minutes at 400 ° F until golden brown. Serve with sauce and salad.
Nutritional value : per serving Calories 333 |Fat 17g |Protein 19g |Carbohydrate 13.9g

163.   Air Fryer Cornish Hen
(Prep Time: 5 mints| Cook Time:25 mints| Servings: 3)
Ingredients
- One Cornish hen
- Salt & black pepper, to taste
- Olive oil spray
- Paprika, ¼ tbsp.
Instructions
- Mix all the spices and rub the spices all over the Cornish hen.
- Spray the basket of the air fryer with olive oil.
- Put the Cornish hen in an air fryer.
- Bake for 25 minutes at 390 F. flip after half time.
- Serve with a mixed green salad.
Nutritional value: per serving: Calories: 310 | Protein: 23g | Fat: 23g | carbs: 25 g

164.   Air Fryer Chicken & Broccoli
(Prep Time: 10 mints| Cook Time:15 mints| Servings: 4)
Ingredients
- Olive oil: 2 Tablespoons
- Chicken breast: 4 cups, bone and skinless (cut into cubes)
- Half medium onion, roughly sliced
- Low sodium soy sauce: 1 Tbsp.
- Garlic powder: half teaspoon
- Rice vinegar: 2 teaspoons
- Broccoli: 1-2 cups, cut into florets
- Hot sauce: 2 teaspoons
- Fresh minced ginger: 1 Tbsp.
- Sesame seed oil: 1 teaspoon
- Salt & black pepper, to taste
Instructions
- In a bowl, add the chicken breast, onion and broccoli. Combine them well.
- In another bowl, add the ginger, oil, sesame oil, rice vinegar, hot sauce, garlic powder and soy sauce, mixing well. Then add the broccoli, chicken and onions to the marinade.
- Sprinkle the chicken well with the sauces. And let it rest in the refrigerator for 15 minutes
- Place the chicken mixture in an even layer in the basket of the air fryer and cook for 16-20 minutes, at 380 F. in the middle, gently toss the basket and cook the chicken evenly
- Add another five minutes if needed.
- Add salt and pepper if necessary.
- serve hot with lemon wedges
Nutritional value: per serving: Calories 199| Fat 6g |Carbohydrates 5g |Protein 23g

165.   Air Fry Rib-Eye Steak
(Prep Time: 5 mints| Cook Time: 14 mints| Servings: 2)
Ingredients

- Lean rib eye steaks: 2, medium size
- Salt & freshly ground black pepper, to taste
Instructions
Allow the air to fry to preheat to 400 F. Dry the steaks with paper towels.
Use any mixture of spices or just salt and pepper on steaks. Generously on both sides of the steak.
Place the steaks in the basket of the air fryer. Cook according to the rarity you want.
Or cook for 14 minutes and flip after half the time.
Remove from the air fryer and let it rest for about 5 minutes.
Serve with green micro salad.
Nutritional value : per serving: Calories: 475kcal | Protein: 41g | Fat: 32g | carbs: 21 g

166.   Teriyaki Chicken Drumsticks with Salad Greens
(Prep Time: 30 mints| Cook Time:20 mints| Servings: 6)
Ingredients
- Six chicken drumsticks
- Teriyaki sauce: one cup
- Salad greens: one cup
- Sesame seeds and chopped green onion, for garnish
Instructions
Let the air fryer preheat to 360 ° F.
Pour the teriyaki sauce into a large zip lock bag, add the chicken legs.Mix them so well coated. Leave to marinate for half an hour.
Place the chopsticks in a single layer in the basket of the air fryer, leave to cook for 20 minutes.
Shake the basket several times for even cooking.
Top with green onions, sesame seeds and serve with the salad garnish.
Nutritional value : per serving: Calories: 161kcal | Carbohydrates: 9g | Protein: 17g | Fat: 9g |

167.   Air Fryer Ravioli
(Prep Time: 10 mints| Cook Time:10 mints| Servings: 6)
Ingredients
- Olive oil: 1 teaspoon
- Italian-style bread crumbs: 2 cups
- Homemade marinara sauce
- Cheese ravioli with cooked chicken: 12 pieces
- Parmesan cheese: 1/4 cup
- Buttermilk: 1 cup
Instructions
Add cheese and chicken to dumpling wrappers, and with water seal the edges.
Then coat the ravioli with buttermilk.
In a bowl, add the olive oil and breadcrumbs, mix well and add the ravioli to the mixture
Place the breaded ravioli in the basket of the air fryer on baking paper.
Cook for five minutes at 200 ° F
Serve with salad and marinara dipping sauce.

Nutritional Value: per serving: Calories 215 |Proteins 13g |Carbs 13g |Fat 18g

168. Crispy Korean Air Fried Chicken Wings

(Prep Time: 10 mints| Cook Time: 30 mints| Servings: 4)

Ingredients

- Chicken wings: 4 cups
- Onion powder: 1 tsp
- Corn starch : ¾ cup
- Garlic powder : 1 tsp
- Salt: ½ tsp

Korean Air Fried Chicken Sauce

- Soy sauce : 1 Tbsp.
- Korean chili paste: 2 Tbsp.
- Honey : 3 Tbsp.
- Ginger minced: 1 tsp
- Garlic minced: 1 tsp
- Brown sugar : 2 Tbsp.
- Half tsp. salt

Instructions

Wash and dry the chicken wings, in a bowl, add ½ teaspoon of salt, onion powder,

and the garlic powder then add the chicken wings and cover them well

Then cover the wings with corn starch. And put them in the air fryer.

Let the wings cook at 390 F for half an hour. Rotate every ten minutes.

Korean Sauce

In a saucepan, over medium heat, add all the ingredients, boil and simmer for five minutes. Turn off the heat

Add the cooked wings to the sauce and coat well.

Serve with steamed vegetables.

Nutritional value : per serving: Calories: 343 | Carbohydrates: 22g | Protein: 21g | Fat: 17g |

169. Air Fryer Chicken Cheese Quesadilla

(Prep Time: 4 mints| Cook Time: 7 mints| Servings: 4)

Ingredients

- Precooked chicken: one cup, diced
- Tortillas: 2 pieces
- Low-fat cheese: one cup (shredded)

Instructions

Spray some oil in the air basket and place a tortilla on it.

Add the cooked chicken and the cheese on top.

Add the second tortilla above. Place a metal grill on top.

Cook for 6 minutes at 370 degrees, turn it in half so that it cooks evenly.

Slice and serve with salad

Nutritional value : per serving: Calories: 161kcal | Carbohydrates: 7g | Protein: 13g | Fat: 7g |

170. Lemon Rosemary Chicken

(Prep Time: 30 mints| Cook Time:20 mints| Servings: 2)

Ingredients

For marinade

- Chicken: 2 and ½ cups
- Ginger: 1 tsp, minced
- Olive oil: 1/2 tbsp.
- Soy sauce: 1 tbsp.

For the sauce

- Half lemon
- Honey: 3 tbsp.
- Oyster sauce: 1 tbsp.
- Fresh rosemary: half cup, chopped

Instructions

In a large bowl, add the marinade ingredients with the chicken and mix well.

Store in the refrigerator for at least half an hour.

Leave the oven to preheat to 200 ° C for three minutes.

Place the marinated chicken in the air fryer in a single layer. And cook for 6 minutes at 200 degrees.

In the meantime, combine all the sauce ingredients in a bowl and mix well except the lemon wedges.

Generously brush the sauce over the half cooked chicken and add the lemon juice.

Cook for another 13 minutes at 200 C. Turn the chicken in half. Let the chicken brown evenly.

Serve with a micro vegetable salad.

Nutrition Value: per serving: Calories 318 |Proteins 23g |Carbs 9g|Fat 11 g |

171. Air Fried Maple Chicken Thighs

(Prep Time: 10 mints| Cook Time:25mints| Servings: 4)

Ingredient

- One egg
- Buttermilk: 1 cup
- Maple syrup: half cup
- Chicken thighs: 4 pieces
- Granulated garlic: 1 tsp.

Dry Mix

- Granulated garlic: half tsp.
- All-purpose flour: half cup
- Salt: one tbsp.
- Sweet paprika: one tsp.
- Smoked paprika: half tsp.
- Tapioca flour: ¼ cup
- Cayenne pepper: ¼ teaspoon
- Granulated onion: one tsp.
- Black pepper: ¼ teaspoon
- Honey powder: half tsp.

Instructions

In a zip lock bag, add the egg, a teaspoon. of granulated garlic, buttermilk and maple syrup, add the chicken legs and leave to marinate for an hour or more in the refrigerator

In a bowl, add the sweet paprika, the tapioca flour, the granulated onion, half a teaspoon. of granulated garlic, flour, cayenne pepper, salt, pepper, honey powder and smoked paprika mix well.

Allow the air fry to preheat to 380 F.

Coat the marinated chicken thighs in the dry spice mixture, shake off the excess.

Place the chicken skin face down in the air fryer

Leave to cook for 12 minutes. Flip the thighs in half and cook for another 13 minutes.

Serve with salad.

Nutritional value : per serving: 419.4 calories| protein 21.3g| carbohydrates 22.8g| fat 14.4g

172.   General Tso's Chicken

(Prep Time: 5 mints| Cook Time:25 mints| Servings: 4)

Ingredients

- Chicken thighs: 8 cups boneless, skinless (cubed)
- 3 green onions, roughly chopped
- Corn starch : 2 tsp
- Vegetable oil: 1 Tbsp.
- Rice vinegar: 2 Tbsp.
- Six red chilies, dried
- Potato starch: 1/3 cup
- Garlic minced: 2 tsp
- Brown suga r : 3/4 cup
- Chicken broth : half cup
- Ginger minced: 1 tsp
- Soy sauc e : half cup
- Sesame oil: 1 tsp
- Salt, to taste
- Cup water: 1/4

Instructions

Allow the air fryer to preheat to 400 F.

In a bowl, add the potato starch and the chicken legs, cover them well. Add the chicken legs to the air fryer in an even layer and cook for 25 minutes.

Shake the basket of the air fryer every 5-7 minutes.

Meanwhile, heat the olive oil in a skillet over medium heat and add the garlic, ginger, dried chillies and green onions, cook for one minute, until the onions have softened.

Mix the soy sauce, sesame oil, chicken broth, a pinch of salt, brown sugar, rice vinegar and mix well. Boil and cook for three minutes.

Then add the fried chicken in sauce and cover well.

Incorporate the cornstarch mixture (with water), cook for one minute.

Serve with boiled vegetables and enjoy.

Nutritional value : per serving: Calories: 420|fat 22 g| protein 21 g| carbs 22.1 g|

173.   Air Fryer Spicy Chicken & Vegetables

(Prep Time: 20 mints| Cook Time:30 mints| Servings: 2)

Ingredients

Spiced Chicken

- Chicken breasts: 2 skinless, boneless
- Onion powder: half tsp.
- Olive oil: 1/2 Tbsp.
- Chili powder: 1 tsp.
- Cumin: 1/4 tsp.
- Paprika: half tsp.

- Salt: half tsp.
- Garlic powder: half tsp.
- Pepper: half tsp.

Vegetables

- Carrots: 2-3 large
- Onion: one red
- Olive oil: 1/2 Tbsp.
- Chopped scallions
- Pinch of salt

Instructions

Allow the air fryer to preheat to 325 F

In a large bowl, add all the spices for the chicken and make a spice mix. Then add the chicken breasts with half a spoon. of olive oil and cover well. Set it aside.

Cut the vegetables according to your preferences. Cut the onions into layers and separate each layer, coat all the vegetables with half a spoon. of olive oil and salt

Put the vegetables in the air fryer first, then add the chicken on top - Cook for at least 35 minutes or more. Flip the chicken in half and discard the vegetables.

Serve hot.

Nutritional value : per serving: Calories: 334cal | Carbohydrates: 31g | Protein: 25g | Fat: 13g |

174.   Air-Fried Chicken Pie

(Prep Time: 10 mints| Cook Time: 30 mints| Servings: 2)

Ingredients

- Puff pastry: 2 sheets
- Chicken thighs: 2 pieces, cut into cubes
- One small onion, chopped
- Small potatoes: 2, chopped
- Mushrooms: 1/4 cup
- Light soya sauce
- One carrot, chopped
- Black pepper, to taste
- Worcestershire sauce: to taste
- Salt, to taste
- Italian mixed dried herbs
- Garlic powder: a pinch
- Plain flour: 2 tbsp.
- Milk, as required
- Melted butter

Instructions

In a bowl, add the light soy sauce and pepper, add the chicken cubes and cover well.

In a pan over medium heat, sauté the carrot, potatoes and onion. Add some water if needed to cook the vegetables.

Add the chicken cubes and mushrooms and cook them too.

Mix black pepper, salt, Worcestershire sauce, garlic powder and dried herbs.

When the chicken is cooked, add a little flour and mix well.

Add the milk and let the vegetables cook until tender.

Put a piece of puff pastry in the pan of the air fryer, make holes with a fork.

Add the cooked chicken filling on top and the eggs and puff pastry on top

holes. Cut the excess dough. Glaze with spray oil or melted butter

Air fry at 180 ° F, for six mints or until golden brown.

Serve with microgreens.
Nutritional value : per serving: calories 221|protein 22g|fat 20 g| carbs 15g

175. Air Fried Tom Yum Chicken Wings
(Prep Time: 30 mints| Cook Time:20 mints| Servings: 3)
Ingredients
- Tom Yum Paste: 2 tbsp.
- 8 Chicken Wings
- Water: 1 tbsp.
- COATING
- Corn flour: 2 tbsp.
- Baking Powder: half teaspoon
- Tapioca Starch: 2 tbsp.

Instructions
Mix the Tom Yum paste with the water in a small bowl.
Add the chicken wings to the tom yum mix, coat well and refrigerate the marinade for four hours.
Allow the air fryer to preheat to 180 ° C.
In a bowl, mix the tapioca starch, baking powder and corn-meal and mix well. Coat the chicken in the flour mixture. Spray the oil on the chicken.
Place the chicken in the air fryer in an even layer and cook for 10-12 minutes
Turn them once and cook for more 5.8 mines
Remove from the deep fryer and serve with salad and lemon wedges
Nutritional value: per serving: Calories 323 |Proteins 25g |Carbs 19g|Fat 15g |Fiber 7g

176. Smothered Chicken Thighs
(Prep Time: 30 mints| Cook Time:30 mints| Servings: 4)
Ingredients
- 8-ounce of chicken thighs
- 1 tsp paprika
- One pinch salt
- Mushrooms: half cup
- Onions, roughly sliced

Instructions
Allow the air fryer to preheat to 400F
Chicken legs seasoned with paprika, salt and pepper on both sides.
Place the thighs in the air fryer and cook for 20 minutes.
Meanwhile, sauté the mushrooms and onion.
Remove the legs from the deep fryer and serve with sauteed mushrooms and onions.
And serve with chopped shallots and a side of salad
Nutritional value : per serving: Kcal 459| Fat: 30g| Net Carbs: 2.4g|Protein: 41g

1.36 Garlic Parmesan Chicken Tenders
(Prep Time: 5 mints| Cook Time:12 mints| Servings: 4)
Ingredients
- One egg
- Eight raw chicken tenders
- Water: 2 tablespoons
- Olive oil

To coat
- Panko breadcrumbs: 1 cup
- Half tsp of salt
- Black Pepper: 1/4 teaspoon
- Garlic powder: 1 teaspoon
- Onion powder: 1/2 teaspoon
- Parmesan cheese: 1/4 cup
- any dipping Sauce

Instructions
Add all the ingredients for the coating to a large bowl
In another bowl, mix the water and egg.
Dip the chicken into the egg mixture and then into the mixture for topping.
Place the offerings in the air frying basket in a single layer.
Spray with light olive oil
Cook at 400 degrees for 12 minutes. Flip the chicken in half.
Serve with salad and enjoy.
Nutritional value : per serving: Calories: 227kcal | Carbohydrates: 11g | Protein: 25g | Fat: 8g |

177. Air Fryer Beef Steak Kabobs with Vegetables
(Prep Time: 30 mints| Cook Time:10 mints| Servings: 4)
Ingredients
- Soy sauce: 2 tbsp.
- Lean beef chuck ribs: 4 cups, cut into one-inch pieces
- Low-fat sour cream: 1/3 cup
- Half onion
- 8 skewers: 6 inch
- One bell peppers

Instructions
In a bowl, add the soy sauce and sour cream, mix well. Add the pieces of lean beef, cover well and leave to marinate for half an hour or more.
Cut the onion and bell pepper into one-inch pieces. Soak the skewers in water for ten minutes.
Add onions, peppers and beef on skewers; alternatively, sprinkle with black pepper
Cook for 10 minutes, in a preheated air fryer at 400F, turn halfway.
• Serve with yogurt sauce.
Nutritional Value: per serving: Calories 273 |Proteins 22g |Carbs 16g|Fat 11g |

178. Air Fried Steak with Asparagus Bundles
(Prep Time: 20 mints| Cook Time:30 mints| Servings: 2)
Ingredients
- Olive oil spray
- Flank steak (2 pounds)- cut into 6 pieces
- Kosher salt and black pepper
- Two cloves of minced garlic
- Asparagus: 4 cups
- Tamari sauce: half cup
- Three bell peppers: sliced thinly
- Beef broth: 1/3 cup

- 1 Tbsp. of unsalted butter
- Balsamic vinegar: 1/4 cup

Instructions

Sprinkle the steak with salt and pepper and rub.

In a zip lock bag, add the garlic and Tamari sauce, then add the steak, mix well and seal the bag.

Leave to marinate for one hour overnight.

Similarly, place the peppers and asparagus in the center of the steak.

Roll the steak around the vegetables and secure it tightly with toothpicks.

Preheat the air fryer.

Spray the steak with olive oil spray. And put the steaks in the air fryer.

Bake for 15 minutes at 400 degrees or higher until steaks are cooked through

Remove the steak from the deep fryer and let it rest for five minutes

Remove the steak wads and let them rest for 5 minutes before serving / slicing.

Meanwhile, add the butter, balsamic vinegar and broth over medium heat. Mix well and reduce by half. Add salt and pepper to taste.

Pour over the steaks before serving.

Nutritional value: per serving: Calories 475 |Proteins 24g |Carbs 23g |Fat 12g |

179.   Lemon-Garlic Chicken Thighs

(Prep Time: 2 hours' mints| Cook Time: 35 mints| Servings: 4)

Ingredients

- Lemon juice ¼ cup
- 1 Tbsp. olive oil
- 1 tsp mustard
- Cloves of garlic
- ¼ tsp salt
- tsp black pepper
- Chicken thighs
- Lemon wedges

Instructions

In a bowl, whisk together the olive oil, lemon juice, Dijon mustard, garlic, salt and pepper.

Place the chicken legs in a large resealable plastic bag. Pour the marinade over the chicken and the sealed bag, making sure all parts of the chicken are covered. Leave to cool for at least 2 hours.

Preheat a pan to 175 ° C (360 ° F).

Remove the chicken with the towels from the marinade and pat dry.

Place the chicken pieces in the basket of the air fryer, if necessary, cook them in batches.

Fry until the chicken is no longer pink on the bone and the sauce runs evenly, 22 to 24 mins. When serving, spread a lemon wedge on each piece.

Nutritional value : per serving: Cal 251|Fat: 19.6g| Carbs: 3.1g| Protein: 18.4g

180.   Chicken Fajitas

(Prep Time: 10 mints| Cook Time:20 mints| Servings: 6)

Ingredients

- Chicken breasts: 4 cups, cut into thin strips
- Bell peppers, sliced
- Salt: half tsp.
- Cumin: 1 tsp.
- Garlic powder: 1/4 tsp
- Chili powder: half tsp.
- Lime juice: 1 tbsp.

Instructions

In a bowl, add the seasonings, chicken and lime juice and mix well.

Then add the sliced peppers and cover well.

Spray the air fryer with olive oil.

Place the chicken and peppers and cook for 15 minutes at 400 F. Invert halfway through cooking.

Serve with lemon wedges and enjoy.

Nutritional value : per serving: Calories 147 |Proteins 20g |Carbs 7g|Fat 7g |Fiber 7g

181.   Crumbed Chicken Tenderloins

(Prep Time: 10 mints| Cook Time:12 mints| Servings: 4)

Ingredients

- Eight chicken tenderloins
- Olive oil: 2 tablespoons
- One egg whisked
- 1/4 cup breadcrumbs

Instructions

Allow the air fryer to heat up to 350 F.

In a large bowl, add the breadcrumbs and oil, mix well to form a crumbly mixture

Dip the chicken fillet in the beaten egg and cover it with the breadcrumbs.

Place the breaded chicken in the air fryer and cook at 350 ° F for 12 minutes or more.

Remove from the air fryer and serve with the salad garnish.

Nutritional value: per serving: Calories 204|Proteins 22g |Carbs 15g |Fat 11g |

182.   Mexican-Style Air Fryer Stuffed Chicken Breasts

(Prep Time: 20 mints| Cook Time:10 mints| Servings: 2)

Ingredients

- Olive oil: 2 teaspoons
- One chicken breast (skinless, boneless)
- Chili powder: 4 tsp., divided
- Chipotle flakes: 2 tsp.
- Half bell pepper, sliced
- Mexican oregano: 2 tsp.
- Salt and pepper, to taste
- Ground cumin: 4 tsp., divided
- Half juice of a lime
- Half onion, sliced
- One jalapeno pepper, sliced

Instructions

In a bowl, add two teaspoons of cumin and two teaspoons. of chilli powder, mix well

Allow the air fryer to preheat to 400 F.

Pound the chicken breast until 1/4 inch thick.

In a bowl, mix the remaining chili powder, chipotle flakes, salt, oregano, remaining cumin and pepper. Rub this spice mix all over the chicken.

Place half of the pepper, jalapeño and onion in half of the breast. Roll the chicken around and secure it with large toothpicks.

Add the olive oil on the breast rolls and cover in the cumin and chilli mixture.

Add the chicken breast to the deep fryer and cook for six minutes.

Flip the breast rolls and cook for another five minutes until the temperature of the chicken reaches 165 F.

Pour the lime juice over the breast rolls and serve hot.

Nutritional value : per serving: 189.3 calories| protein 15.8g | carbohydrates 17.2g |fat 7.5g

183.   Herb-Marinated Chicken Thighs

(Prep Time: 30 mints| Cook Time:10 mints| Servings: 4)

Ingredients

- Chicken thighs: 8 skin-on, bone-in,
- Lemon juice: 2 Tablespoon
- Onion powder: half teaspoon
- Garlic powder: 2 teaspoon
- Spike Seasoning: 1 teaspoon.
- Olive oil: 1/4 cup
- Dried basil: 1 teaspoon
- Dried oregano: half teaspoon.
- Black Pepper: 1/4 tsp.

Instructions

In a bowl, add the dried oregano, olive oil, lemon juice, dried sage, garlic powder, spicy seasoning, onion powder, dried basil, black pepper.

In a zip lock bag, add the spice mixture and chicken and mix well.

Marinate the chicken in the refrigerator for at least six hours or more.

Preheat the air fryer to 360 ° F.

Place the chicken in the basket of the air fryer, cook for six to eight minutes, flip the chicken over and cook for another six minutes.

Until the internal temperature of the chicken reaches 165F.

Remove from air fryer and serve with microgreens.

Nutritional value : per serving: Cal 106|Fat: 7g| Carbs 1.4g|Protein 5g

184.   Air Fryer Meatloaf

(Prep Time: 10 mints| Cook Time:40 mints| Servings: 8)

Ingredients

- Ground lean beef: 4 cups
- Bread crumbs: 1 cup (soft and fresh)
- Chopped mushrooms: ½ cup
- Cloves of minced garlic
- Shredded carrots: ½ cup

- Beef broth: ¼ cup
- Chopped onions: ½ cup
- Two eggs beaten
- Ketchup: 3 Tbsp.
- Worcestershire sauce: 1 Tbsp.
- Dijon mustard: 1 Tbsp.

For Glaze
- Honey: ¼ cup
- Ketchup: half cup
- Dijon mustard: 2 tsp

Instructions

In a large bowl, add the meat broth and breadcrumbs, mix well. And set it aside in a food processor, add the garlic, onions, mushrooms and carrots and whisk over high heat until finely chopped.

In a separate bowl, add the soaked breadcrumbs, Dijon mustard, Worcestershire

sauce, eggs, lean ground beef, ketchup and salt. With your hands, combine well and turn it into a loaf.

Allow the air fryer to preheat to 390 F.

Place the meatloaf in the air fryer and cook for 45 minutes.

Meanwhile, add the Dijon mustard, ketchup and brown sugar to a bowl and mix. Glaze this mix on the meatloaf when there are five minutes left.

Let the meatloaf rest for ten minutes before serving.

Nutritional value: per serving: Calories 337 |Proteins 18g |Carbs 14g|Fat 8.9 g |

185.   Beef Schnitzel (Air Fried)

(Prep Time: 10 mints| Cook Time:15 mints| Servings: 1)

Ingredients

- One lean beef schnitzel
- Olive oil: 2 tablespoon
- Breadcrumbs: ¼ cup
- One egg
- One lemon, to serve

Instructions

Allow the air fryer to heat up to 180 C.

In a large bowl, add the breadcrumbs and oil, mix well to form a crumbly mixture

Dip the beef steak in the beaten egg and cover it with the breadcrumbs.

Place the breaded meat in the air fryer and cook at 180 ° C for 15 minutes or more until cooked through.

Remove from the air fryer and serve with the salad and lemon garnish.

Nutrition Value: per serving: Calories 347 |Proteins 22g |Carbs 11g |Fat 13g |Fiber 8g

186.   Air Fryer Rotisserie Chicken

(Prep Time: 5 mints| Cook Time: 60 mints| Servings: 6)

Ingredients

- Paprika : 1 tsp.
- One chicken
- Dried basil: 1 tsp.
- Onion powder: 1/2 tsp.
- Dried oregano: 1 tsp.

- Pepper: half tsp.
- Salt : 1 and 1/2 tsp.
- Chopped cilantro and scallions

Instructions

Allow the air fryer to preheat to 360 ° F.

In a bowl, add all the spices and rub all over the chicken.

Place the chicken in the air fryer and let it cook at 360 degrees for half an hour or more if necessary.

Serve with salad and garnish with scallions and coriander.

Nutritional value : per serving: Calories: 399kcal | Carbohydrates: 1.2g | Protein: 31g | Fat: 25g

187. Air Fryer Hamburger

(Prep Time: 5 mints| Cook Time:13 mints| Servings: 4)

Ingredients

- Buns:4
- Lean ground beef chuck: 4 cups
- Salt , to taste
- Slices of any cheese: 4 slices
- Black Pepper, to taste

Instructions

Allow the air fryer to preheat to 350 F.

In a bowl, add the lean ground beef, pepper and salt. Mix well and form meatballs.

Put them in the air fryer in one layer, cook for 6 minutes, turn them in half. A minute before removing the meatballs add the cheese on top.

When the cheese is melted, remove it from the air fryer.

Add ketchup, any toppings to your sandwiches, add tomatoes, lettuce and meatballs.

Serve hot.

Nutritional value : per serving: Calories: 522kcal | Carbohydrates: 21g | Protein: 34g | Fat: 31g |

188. Air Fryer Blackened Chicken Breast

(Prep Time: 10 mints| Cook Time:20 mints| Servings: 2)

Ingredients

- Paprika: 2 teaspoons
- Ground thyme: 1 teaspoon
- Cumin: 1 teaspoon
- Cayenne pepper: half tsp.
- Onion powder: half tsp.
- Black Pepper: half tsp.
- Salt: ¼ teaspoon
- Vegetable oil: 2 teaspoons
- Pieces of chicken breast halves (without bones and skin)

Instructions

In a mixing bowl, add the onion powder, salt, cumin, paprika, black pepper, thyme and cayenne pepper. Mix it well.

Pour the oil over the chicken and rub. Dip each piece of chicken in the blackening spice mixture on both sides.

Let it sit for five minutes while the air fryer is preheating.

Preheat it for five minutes at 360F.

Place the chicken in the air fryer and let it cook for ten minutes. Turn and then cook for another ten minutes.

After that, let it rest for five minutes, then slice and serve with the green part

Nutritional value : per serving: 437.1 calories| protein 76.4g| carbohydrates 3.9g| fat 8.5g

189. Air Fried Spicy Chicken Wings

(Prep Time: 30 mints| Cook Time:20 mints| Servings: 2)

Ingredients

- Honey: 1 tbsp.
- Chicken Wings: 6 pcs
- Cloves of minced Garlic
- Worcestershire Sauce: 2 tbsp.
- Chili Flakes: 1 tsp.
- Salt & pepper, to taste
- Cooking Spray

Instructions

Wash and dry the chicken wings.

In a bowl, mix the chili flakes, salt, Worcestershire sauce, pepper and honey. Mix well and add the chicken wings and leave to marinate for at least an hour.

Drizzle the marinated chicken wings with olive oil

Place the chicken wings in the basket of the air fryer and cook for 8 minutes at 160 C.

Turn halfway and cook for more than four minutes.

Serve with air-fried courgettes.

Nutritional value: per serving: Calories 310 |Proteins 26g |Carbs 13 g |Fat 16g |

190. Lemon Pepper Chicken

(Prep Time: 3 mints| Cook Time:15 mints| Servings: 2)

Ingredients

- Two Lemons rind, juice, and zest
- One Chicken Breast
- Minced Garlic: 1 Tsp
- Black Peppercorns: 2 tbsp.
- Chicken Seasoning: 1 Tbsp.
- Salt & pepper, to taste

Instructions

Let the air fryer preheat to 350 ° F.

In a large aluminum foil, add all the seasonings along with the lemon zest.

Add salt and pepper to the chicken and rub the seasonings all over the chicken breast.

Place the chicken in aluminum foil. And fold it tightly.

Flatten the chicken inside the foil with a rolling pin

Put it in the air fryer and cook at 350 ° F for 15 minutes.

Serve hot.

Nutritional value : per serving: Calories: 149 | Carbohydrates: 26g | Protein: 11g | Fat: 3g

191. Mixed Vegetables with Chicken

(Prep Time: 20 mints| Cook Time:20 mints| Servings: 2)

Ingredients

- 1/2 onion diced
- Chicken breast: 4 cups, cubed pieces
- Half zucchini chopped
- Italian seasoning: 1 tablespoon
- Bell pepper chopped: 1/2 cup
- Clove of garlic pressed

- Broccoli florets: 1/2 cup
- Olive oil: 2 tablespoons
- Half teaspoon of chili powder, garlic powder, pepper, salt,

Instructions

Let the air fryer heat up to 400 F and cut the vegetables into cubes

In a bowl, add the seasoning, oil and add the vegetables, chicken and mix well

Place chicken and vegetables in the air fryer and cook for ten minutes, stir halfway through cooking, cook in batches.

Make sure the vegetables are charred and the chicken is cooked.

Serve hot.

Nutritional value : per serving: :| Calories: 237kcal | Carbohydrates: 9g | Protein: 22g | Fat: 11g |

192. Air Fryer Sesame Chicken Breast

(Prep Time: 5 mints| Cook Time:30 mints| Servings: 2)

Ingredients

- Sesame oil: 2 Tbsp.
- Chicken breasts: 2 pieces boneless and skin-on
- Black Pepper: 1/2 tsp
- Onions powder: 1 Tbsp.
- Sweet paprika: 1 Tbsp.
- Salt: 1 tsp
- Cayenne pepper: 1/4 tsp
- Granulated garlic: 1 Tbsp.

Instructions

Pour sesame oil all over the chicken and rub, then sprinkle with all the spices, pepper and salt

Sprinkle the chicken well with the spices.

Place the chicken breasts in the air fryer, skin side up. Make sure you leave space between the chicken pieces.

Cook for 20 minutes, at 380F. After 20 minutes, flip the chicken and cook for another ten minutes.

Remove from the air fryer and let it rest for five minutes.

Serve with air-fried vegetables.

Nutritional value: per serving: Calories 245 |Proteins 22g |Carbs 13g |Fat 21g |

193. Mushroom Oatmeal

(Prep time: 10 min| Cooking time: 20 min| Servings: 4)

Ingredients

- One small yellow onion, chopped
- 1 cup steel-cut oats
- 1 Garlic cloves, minced
- 2 Tablespoons butter
- ½ cup of water
- One and a half cup of canned chicken stock
- Thyme springs, chopped
- 2 Tablespoons extra virgin olive oil
- ½ cup gouda cheese, grated
- 1 cup mushroom, sliced
- Salt and black pepper to taste

Instructions

Heat a skillet over medium heat that fits your fryer with

butter, add

onions and garlic, stir and cook for 4 minutes.

Add the oats, sugar, salt, pepper, broth and thyme, mix, place in the air fryer and cook for 16 minutes at 360 ° F.

Meanwhile, prepare a pan over medium heat with the olive oil, add the mushrooms, cook for 3 minutes, add the oatmeal and cheese, beat, divide into bowls and serve for breakfast.

Enjoy.

Nutritional value: per serving: calories 281|fat 6g| fiber 7g|-carbs 23g| protein 17g

194. Air Fryer Chicken Parmesan

(Prep Time: 20 mints| Cook Time:30 mints| Servings: 4)

Ingredients

- Whole wheat seasoned breadcrumbs: 6 tbsp.
- Chicken breast: 2 pieces, make four thinner cutlets
- Mozzarella cheese: 6 tbsp. (reduced fat)
- Parmesan cheese: 2 tbsp. (grated)
- Marinara: 1/2 cup
- One tbsp. melted butter
- Olive oil

Instructions

Allow the air fryer to preheat to 360 F for three minutes.

In a bowl, add the Parmesan and breadcrumbs, mix well.

Pour the melted butter over the chicken and cover it with the Parmesan mixture. Eliminate excess.

Place the chicken in the air fryer and drizzle with oil.

Cook for six minutes, flip the chicken. Add the grated cheese and sauce on top and cook for another three minutes.

Serve with microgreens.

Nutritional value : per serving: Calories: 257kcal| Carbohydrates: 13g|Protein: 32.5g| Fat: 9.8g

195. Air Fryer No Breading Chicken Breast

(Prep Time: 10 mints| Cook Time:20 mints| Servings: 2)

Ingredients

- Olive oil spray
- Chicken breasts: 4 (boneless)
- Onion powder: 3/4 teaspoon
- Salt: ¼ cup
- Smoked paprika: half tsp.
- 1/8 tsp. of cayenne pepper
- Garlic powder: 3/4 teaspoon
- Dried parsley: half tsp.

Instructions

In a large bowl, add six cups of hot water, add salt (1/4 cup) and mix to dissolve.

Place the chicken breasts in hot salted water and let them cool for almost 2 hours.

Remove from water and pat dry.

In a bowl, add all the spices with ¾ tsp. of salt. Sprinkle the oil all over the chicken and rub the spice mixture all over the chicken.

Let the air fryer heat up to 380F.

Place the chicken in the air fryer and cook for ten minutes.

Turn halfway and serve with green salad.
Nutritional value : per serving: Calories: 218kcal|Carbohydrates: 1g| Protein: 37g| Fat: 4.1g

196. Crispy Parmesan Buttermilk Chicken Tenders

(Prep Time: 10 mints| Cook Time:18 mints| Servings: 4)

Ingredients

- Half cup of all-purpose flour
- Buttermilk: 3/4 cup
- Chicken breasts: 2, boneless, skinless
- Kosher salt: 3/4 teaspoon, divided
- Grated Parmesan cheese: 1/4 cup
- Black Pepper: 3/4 teaspoon, divided
- Worcestershire sauce: 1 and 1/2 teaspoons, divided
- Smoked paprika: half teaspoon, divided
- Oil spray
- Whole wheat breadcrumbs: 1 and 1/2 cups
- One large egg

Instructions

Cut the chicken into slices.
In a bowl, add the buttermilk and Worcestershire sauce (half), salt and half
paprika and pepper. Add this mix in a zip lock bag with chicken tenders and let it marinate for six hours or more.
In a bowl, add the melted butter and breadcrumbs, Parmesan and combine well
Beat the egg with the remaining Worcestershire sauce.
In another bowl, add the smoked paprika, pepper, flour and salt.
Coat the offerings in the flour mixture, then again in the egg, then in the breadcrumb mixture.
Allow the air fryer to preheat to 400 F. Place the breaded offerings in the air fryer basket in an even layer.
Cook at 400 F for 13-15 minutes, turn the chicken over after half the time.
Serve with sauces and microgreens
Nutritional value : per serving: Calories: 254kcal| Carbohydrates: 11g|Protein: 33.5g| Fat: 9.1g

197. Air Fryer Southwest Chicken

(Prep Time: 20 mints| Cook Time:30 mints| Servings: 4)

Ingredients

- Avocado oil: one tbsp.
- Four cups of boneless, skinless, chicken breast
- Chili powder: half tsp.
- Salt, to taste
- Cumin: half tsp.
- Onion powder: 1/4 tsp.
- Lime juice: two tbsp.
- Garlic powder: 1/4 tsp

Instructions

In a zip lock bag, add the chicken, oil and lime juice.
Add all the spices to a bowl and rub all the chicken into the zip lock bag.
Leave to marinate in the fridge for ten minutes or more.
Take the chicken out of the zip lock bag and place it in the air fryer.
Cook for 25 minutes at 400 F, turning the chicken in half until the internal temperature reaches 165 degrees.
Nutritional value : per serving: Calories: 161kcal|Carbohydrates: 1.3g|Protein: 22g|Fat: 6g

198. Air- Fried Grilled BBQ Chicken

(Prep Time: 10 mints| Cook Time: 12 mints| Servings: 2)

Ingredients

- Chicken Steaks: 2 pieces
- Sea salt: 1 tsp.
- 1 tsp. olive oil
- Freshly ground Black Pepper: 1/2 teaspoon Blue Cheese &Butter
- Blue Cheese: 1/ 4 cup
- 1/2 cup of butter (at room temperature)

Instructions

While preparing the steak, the most important thing is to let the meat rest
temperature for 30 minutes, for the minimum.
Start the recipe by letting the air fryer heat up. To prepare any type of steak, you must always preheat the air fryer. Therefore, the meat will come out fine, so turn on the air fryer at 400 F for 5 minutes.
Rub the steak with butter or herb-flavored olive oil and sprinkle with sea salt and black pepper.
Place the stakes for 6 minutes in the air fryer, then turn them again for almost 6 minutes.
Again, let the steak rest for at least 5 minutes, then slice it. The steaks will continue to cook, even when cooked.
Combine only the butter and blue cheese in a small mixing bowl to make the cheese. You can serve the steak however you like.
Put the butter in a film and roll it up well, it looks like a roll, keep it in the refrigerator and cut a few pieces for each portion.
Nutritional value: per serving: Calories 202 |Proteins 23g |Carbs 2g|Fat 6g |

199. Bell Peppers Frittata

(Prep time: 10 min| Cooking time: 20 min| Servings: 4)

Ingredients

- 2 Tablespoons olive oil
- 2 cups chicken sausage, casings removed and chopped
- One sweet onion, chopped
- 1 red bell pepper, chopped
- 1 orange bell pepper, chopped
- 1 green bell pepper, chopped
- Salt and black pepper to taste
- 8 eggs, whisked
- ½ cup mozzarella cheese, shredded
- 2 teaspoons oregano, chopped

Instructions

Add 1 tablespoon of oil to the air fryer, add bacon, heat to 320 degrees F and sauté for 1 minute.
Remove the remaining butter, onion, red pepper, orange and white, mix and simmer for another 2 minutes.

Stir and cook for 15 minutes, add the oregano, salt, pepper and eggs.

Add the mozzarella, leave the omelette aside for a couple of minutes, divide and serve between plates.

Enjoy.

Nutritional value: per serving: calories 210, fat 2g, fiber 5g, carbs 8g, protein 11g

200. Green Bean Casserole

(Prep time: 10 min| Cook Time: 15 min | Serves 4)

Ingredients

- 4 tablespoons unsalted butter
- 1/4 cup diced yellow onion
- 1/2 cup chopped white mushrooms
- 1/2 cup heavy whipping cream
- ¼ cup low-fat cream cheese
- 1/2 cup chicken broth
- 1/4 teaspoon xanthan gum
- 4 cups fresh green beans, edges trimmed
- 1 tbsp. of pork rinds, finely ground

Instructions

Melt the butter in a medium saucepan over low heat. Saute the onion and mushrooms for about 3–5 minutes, before they become soft and fragrant.

Apply whipped cream, cream cheese and broth to the saucepan. Beat easily first. Bring to a boil, then reduce to a simmer. Sprinkle the xanthan gum into the pan and cook.

Cut the green beans into 2 "chunks and place them in a 4-cup circular baking dish. Pour over the sauce mixture and stir until cooked. Cover the bowl with the ground pork rinds.

Set the temperature to 320 ° F and change the timer for 15 minutes.

Top when fully cooked, browned and fork with tender green beans. Serve soft.

Nutritional value: per serving: calories: 261|protein: 4.6 g| fiber: 3.6 g| net carbohydrates: 6.5 g| fat: 25.4 g| |

Optavia Lean & Green Turkey Air-fry recipes

201. Air-Fried Turkey Breast with Maple Mustard Glaze

(Prep Time: 10 mints| Cook Time:55 mints| Servings: 6)

Ingredients

- Whole turkey breast: 5 pounds
- Olive oil: 2 tsp.
- Maple syrup: 1/4 cup
- Dried sage: half tsp.
- Smoked paprika: half tsp.
- Dried thyme: one tsp.
- Salt: one tsp.
- Freshly ground black pepper: half tsp.
- Dijon mustard: 2 tbsp.

Instructions

Allow the air fryer to preheat to 350 F

Rub the olive oil all over the turkey breast

In a bowl, mix salt, sage, pepper, thyme and paprika. Mix well and coat the turkey with this spicy sauce.

Place the turkey in an air fryer, cook for 25 minutes at 350ºF. Flip the turkey over and cook for another 12 minutes. Turn again and cook for another ten minutes. With an instant read thermometer, the internal temperature should reach 165ºF.

Meanwhile, in a saucepan, mix the mustard, maple syrup and with a teaspoon. of butter.

Brush this glaze all over the turkey when cooked.

Cook for another five minutes. Slice and serve with green salad.

Nutritional value : per serving: Cal 390 | Fat: 25 g| Carbs: 20g | Protein: 55g

202. Air Fryer Turkey Breast

(Prep Time: 5 mints| Cook Time:55 mints| Servings: 10)

Ingredients

- Turkey breast: 4 pounds, ribs removed, bone with skin
- Olive oil: 1 tablespoon
- Salt: 2 teaspoons
- Dry turkey seasoning (without salt): half tsp.

Instructions

Rub half a spoon. Of olive oil on the turkey breast. Sprinkle salt, turkey seasoning on both sides of the turkey breast with half a tablespoon. Of olive oil.

Allow the air fryer to preheat to 350 F. Place the turkey skin face down in the air fryer and cook for 20 minutes, until the turkey temperature reaches 160 F for half an hour to 40 minutes.

Let it rest for ten minutes before slicing.

Serve with green salad.

Nutritional value : per serving: Calories: 236kcal| Protein: 31.5g|Fat: 12g|carbs 20 g

203. Air Fryer Turkey Breast Tenderloin

(Prep Time: 5 mints| Cook Time:25 mints| Servings: 3)

Ingredients

- Turkey breast tenderloin: one-piece
- Thyme: half tsp.
- Sage: half tsp.
- Paprika: half tsp.
- Pink salt: half tsp.
- Freshly ground black pepper: half tsp.

Instructions

Allow the air fryer to preheat to 350 F

In a bowl, mix all the spices and herbs, rub all over the turkey.

Spray oil on the air fryer basket. Put the turkey in the air fryer and let it cook at 350 F for 25 minutes, flip it in half.

Serve with green micro salad.

Nutritional value : per serving: Calories: 152kcal | Carbohydrates: 1g | Protein: 11g | Fat: 1g |

204.   Juicy Turkey Burgers with Zucchini

(Prep Time: 10 mints| Cook Time:10 mints| Servings: 5)

Ingredients

- Gluten-free breadcrumbs: 1/4 cup(seasoned)
- Grated zucchini: 1 cup
- Red onion: 1 tbsp. (grated)
- Lean ground turkey: 4 cups
- One clove of minced garlic
- 1 tsp of kosher salt and fresh pepper

Instructions

In a bowl, combine the zucchini (removed the moisture with a paper towel), ground turkey, garlic, salt, onion, pepper, breadcrumbs. Mix well

With his hands he makes five patties. But not too often.

Allow the air fryer to preheat to 375 F

Place in a single layer air fryer and cook for 7 minutes or more. Until completely cooked and browned.

Put in buns with ketchup and lettuce and enjoy.

Nutritional value per serving: Calories: 166kcal|Carbohydrates: 4.1g| Protein: 16g|Fat: 6g|

205.   Air Fryer Turkey Fajitas Platter

(Prep Time: 5 mints| Cook Time:20 mints| Servings: 2)

Ingredients

- Cooked Turkey Breast: 1/4 cup
- Six Tortilla Wraps
- One Avocado
- One Yellow Pepper
- One Red Pepper
- Half Red Onion
- Soft Cheese: 5 Tbsp.
- Mexican Seasoning: 2 Tbsp.
- Cumin: 1 Tsp
- Kosher salt& Pepper
- Cajun Spice: 3 Tbsp.
- Fresh Coriander

Instructions

Chop the avocado and slice the vegetables.

Cut the turkey breast into small cubes.

In a bowl, add the onions, turkey, soft cheese and peppers along with the seasonings. Mix it well.

Place it in foil and the air fryer.

Cook for 20 minutes at 400 ° F.

Serve hot.

Nutritional value per serving: Calories: 389kcal | Carbohydrates: 81g | Protein: 32g | Fat: 31g |

Optavia Lean & Green Low Budget Recipes

206.   Air Fryer Sweet & Sour Chicken

(Prep Time: 5 mints| Cook Time: 10 mints| Servings: 2)

Ingredients

Chicken

- 4 cups chicken breasts /thighs: cut into one-inch pieces
- Cornstarch: 2 tablespoons

Sweet & Sour Sauce

- Cornstarch: 2 tablespoons
- Pineapple juice: 1 cup

- Water: 2 tablespoons
- Honey: half cup
- Soy sauce: 1 tablespoon
- Rice wine vinegar: 3 tablespoons
- Ground ginger: 1/4 teaspoon

Optional

- 1/4 cup pineapple chunks
- 3-4 drops of red food coloring (for traditional orange look)

Instructions

Let the air fryer preheat to 400 degrees.

Coat the chicken with cornstarch until it is completely covered.

Place the chicken in the air fryer and cook for 7.9 minutes. Remove from the air fryer

Meanwhile, in a saucepan, add the pineapple juice, ginger, brown sugar, soy sauce and rice wine vinegar and cook. Let it simmer for five minutes.

Prepare a cornstarch paste and add the sauce. Let it simmer for a minute.

Cover the cooked chicken pieces and serve with steamed vegetables

Nutritional value : per serving: Cal 309|Fat: 9g| Carbs 15g|Protein 24g

207.   Crispy Korean Air Fried Chicken Wings

(Prep Time: 10 mints| Cook Time: 30 mints| Servings: 4)

Ingredients

- Chicken wings: 4 cups
- Onion powder: 1 tsp
- Corn starch : ¾ cup
- Garlic powder : 1 tsp
- Salt: ½ tsp

Korean Air Fried Chicken Sauce

- Soy sauce : 1 Tbsp.
- Korean chili paste: 2 Tbsp.
- Honey: 3 Tbsp.
- Ginger minced: 1 tsp
- Garlic minced: 1 tsp
- Brown sugar : 2 Tbsp.
- Half tsp. salt

Instructions

Wash and dry the chicken wings, in a bowl, add ½ teaspoon of salt, onion powder and garlic powder, then add the chicken wings and coat them well

Then cover the wings with corn starch. And put them in the air fryer.

Let the wings cook at 390 F for half an hour. Rotate every ten minutes.

Korean Sauce

In a saucepan, over medium heat, add all the ingredients, boil and simmer for five minutes. Turn off the heat

Add the cooked wings to the sauce and coat well.

Serve with steamed vegetables.

Nutritional value : per serving: Calories: 348 | Carbohydrates: 22g | Protein: 21g | Fat: 18g |

208. Low Carb Air-Fried Calzones

(Prep Time: 15 mints| Cook Time:27 mints| Servings: 2)

Ingredients

- Cooked chicken breast: 1/3 cup(shredded)
- One teaspoon olive oil
- Spinach leaves(baby): 3 cups
- Whole-wheat pizza dough, freshly prepared
- Marinara sauce: 1/3 cup(lower-sodium)
- Diced red onion:1/4 cup
- Skim mozzarella cheese: 6 Tbsp.
- Cooking spray

Instructions

In a medium skillet, over medium heat, add the oil, onions. Brown until soft. Then add the spinach leaves, cook until wilted. Turn off the heat and add the chicken and the marinara sauce.

Cut the pasta into two pieces.

Add 1/4 of the spinach mixture to each piece of circular dough.

Add the skimmed grated cheese on top. Fold the dough and fold the edges.

Spray the trousers with cooking spray.

Put the breeches in the air fryer. Bake for 12 minutes, at 325 ° F, until the batter is light brown. Flip the calzone over and cook for another eight minutes.

Nutritional value: per serving: Calories 368|Fat 14g | Protein 20g |Carbohydrate 14g

209. Air Fryer Personal Mini Pizza

(Prep Time: 2 mints| Cook Time:5 mints| Servings: 1)

Ingredients

- Sliced olives: 1/4 cup
- One pita bread
- One tomato
- Shredded cheese: 1/2 cup

Instructions

Allow the air fryer to preheat to 350 F

Place the pita on a plate. Add the cheese, tomato slices and olives.

Cook for five minutes at 350 F

Remove the pizza from the air fryer.

Slice it and enjoy it

Nutritional value per serving: Calories: 349kcal | Carbohydrates: 33g | Protein: 16g | Fat: 15g |

210. Air Fried Cheesy Chicken Omelet

(Prep Time: 5 mints| Cook Time: 18 mints| Servings: 2)

Ingredients

- Cooked Chicken Breast: half cup(diced)divided
- Four eggs
- Onion powder: 1/4 tsp, divided
- Salt: 1/2 tsp., divided
- Pepper: 1/4 tsp., divided
- Shredded cheese: 2 tbsp. divided
- Granulated garlic: 1/4 tsp, divided

Instructions

Take two molds, grease with olive oil.

Add two eggs to each mold. Add the cheese with the dressing.

Blend to combine. Add 1/4 cup of cooked chicken on top.

Cook for 14-18 minutes, in the air fryer at 330 ° F, or until cooked through.

Nutritional value: per serving: Calories 175 |Proteins 24g |Carbs 11g |Fat 6g |

211. Low Carb Chicken Tenders

(Prep Time: 10 mints| Cook Time:20 mints| Servings: 3)

Ingredients

- Chicken tenderloins: 4 cups
- Eggs: one
- Superfine Almond Flour: ½ cup
- Powdered Parmesan cheese: ½ cup
- Kosher Sea salt: ½ teaspoon
- (1-teaspoon) freshly ground black pepper
- (1/2 teaspoon) Cajun seasoning,

Instructions

In a saucer, pour the beaten egg.

Mix all ingredients in a cheese zip lock bag. Freshly ground almond flour, black pepper and kosher salt and other seasonings.

Spray the air fryer with spray oil.

To avoid lumpy fingers with breading and eggs. Use different hands for the egg and breading. Dip each tender in egg and then bread until all are breaded.

Using a fork to place one tender at a time. Carry it in the zip-lock bag and shake it hard. make sure all offerings are coated in almond blend

Use the fork to take out the tender and place it in the basket of the air fryer.

Spray oil on tenders.

Bake for 12 minutes at 350 ° F, or before 160 ° F registers inside. Increase the temperature to 400 ° F to shade the surface for 3 minutes.

Serve with sauce.

Nutritional value: per serving: Calories 288 |Proteins 22g |Carbs 5g|Fat 11g |Fiber 7g

212. Air-Fried Tortilla Hawaiian Pizza

(Prep Time: 10 mints| Cook Time:20 mints| Servings: 1)

Ingredients

- Mozzarella Cheese
- Tortilla wrap
- Tomato sauce: 1 tbsp.
- Toppings
- Cooked chicken shredded or hotdog: 2 tbsp.
- Pineapple pieces: 3 tbsp.
- Ham: half slice, cut into pieces
- Cheese slice cut into pieces

Instructions

Place the tortilla on a plate, add the tomato sauce and distribute it.

Add some shredded mozzarella, garnish. Top with slices of cheese

Place in the air fryer and cook for five to ten minutes at 320 C.

Take it out of the air fryer and slice it. Serve hot with baby spinach.

Nutritional value : per serving: Calories 172 |Proteins 24g |Carbs 12g |Fat 16g |

213. 5-Ingredient Air Fryer Lemon Chicken

(Prep Time: 5 mints| Cook Time:15 mints| Servings: 4)

Ingredients

- Whole-wheat crumbs: 1 and 1/2 cups
- Six pieces of chicken tenderloins
- Two eggs
- Two half lemons and lemon slices
- Kosher salt to taste

Instructions

On a plate, beat the eggs.

On a separate plate, add the breadcrumbs

With the egg, cover the chicken and pass it in the bread-crumbs.

Add the breaded chicken to the air fryer

Cook for 14 minutes at 400 F, flip the chicken in half.

Remove from the air fryer and squeeze the lemon juice and sprinkle with kosher salt and serve with lemon slices.

Nutritional value : per serving: Cal 245| Fat: 14g| Net Carbs: 11g|Protein: 23g

214. Air Fryer Buffalo Cauliflower

(Prep Time: 5 mints| Cook Time:15 mints| Servings: 4)

Ingredients

- Homemade buffalo sauce: 1/2 cup
- One head of cauliflower, cut bite-size pieces
- Butter melted: 1 tablespoon
- Olive oil
- Kosher salt & pepper, to taste

Instructions

Spray cooking oil on the basket of the air fryer.

In a bowl, add the buffalo sauce, melted butter, pepper and salt. Mix well.

Place the cauliflower pieces in the air fryer and sprinkle over the olive oil. Cook at 400 F for 7 minutes.

Remove the cauliflower from the air fryer and add it to the sauce. Sprinkle the cauliflower well.

Return the sauce-coated cauliflower to the air fryer.

Bake at 400 F, for 7-8 minutes or until crisp.

Remove from air fryer and serve with leaner protein.

Nutritional value : per serving: Calories 111kcal | Carbohydrates 5g | Protein 5g | Fat 8g

215. Air Fryer Popcorn Chicken

(Prep Time: 10 mints| Cook Time:20 mints| Servings: 2)

Ingredients

For Marinade

- 8 cups, chicken tenders, cut into bite-size pieces
- Freshly ground black pepper: 1/2 tsp
- Almond milk : 2 cups
- Salt: 1 tsp
- paprika: 1/2 tsp

Dry Mix

- Salt: 3 tsp
- Flour: 3 cups
- Paprika: 2 tsp
- Oil spray
- Freshly ground black pepper: 2 tsp

Instructions

In a bowl, add all the ingredients of the marinade and the chicken. Mix well and place it in a zip lock bag and in the refrigerator for a minimum of two hours, or six hours.

In a large bowl, add all the dry ingredients.

Cover the marinated chicken with the dry mixture. In the marinade again then for the second time in the dry mixture.

Spray the basket of the air fryer with olive oil and arrange the breaded chicken pieces in a single layer. Spray the oil on the chicken pieces as well.

Cook at 370 degrees for 10 minutes, turning halfway.

Serve immediately with salad or dipping sauce.

Nutritional value: per serving: Calories 330 |Proteins 22g |Carbs 12g |Fat 15g |

216. Air Fryer Chicken Wings with Buffalo Sauce

(Prep Time: 5 mints| Cook Time:25 mints| Servings: 6)

Ingredients

- Chicken drumettes & flats: 4 cups
- Salt & pepper, to taste

Buffalo Sauce

- Hot sauce: 1/2 cup
- White vinegar: 2 tablespoons
- Melted butter: 1/2 cup
- Worcestershire sauce: 2 teaspoons
- Pinch of garlic powder

Instructions

Allow the air fryer to preheat to 380F.

Separate the wings, forming a plate and the chopsticks, discarding the tips.

Using paper towels, dry the chicken wings, sprinkle generously with salt and pepper and other seasonings of your choice.

Put them in a basket to fry and cook for about 22 minutes.

After this increase, the temperature to 400 degrees, cook for another five minutes so that the chicken skin becomes crisp.

Mix all the ingredients of the buffalo sauce and mix well.

Sprinkle the wings with homemade buffalo sauce.

Serve with the salad garnish.

Nutritional value : per serving: Cal 319| Fat: 22g| Carbs: 1g|Protein: 32g

217. Tasty Kale & Celery Crackers

(Prep time: 10 min| Cooking time: 20 min| Servings: 6)

Ingredients

- One cups flax seed, ground
- 1 cups flax seed, soaked overnight and drained
- 2 bunches kale, chopped
- 1 bunch basil, chopped

- ½ bunch celery, chopped
- 2 garlic cloves, minced
- 1/3 cup olive oil

Instructions

Mix ground flaxseed with celery, kale, basil and garlic in the food
processor and mix well.

Add the oil and soaked flax seeds, then mix again, sprinkle into the air fryer pan, crack the medium crackers, and cook for 20 minutes at 380 degrees F.

Serve as an appetizer and divide into cups.

Enjoy

Nutritional Value: per serving: calories 133|fat 1g| fiber 4g| carbs 7g| Protein 2g

218. Air Fryer Cornish Hen

(Prep Time: 5 mints| Cook Time:25 mints| Servings: 3)

Ingredients

- One Cornish hen
- Salt & black pepper, to taste
- Olive oil spray
- Paprika, ¼ tbsp.

Instructions

Mix all the spices and rub the spices all over the Cornish hen.

Spray the basket of the air fryer with olive oil.

Put the Cornish hen in an air fryer.

Bake for 25 minutes at 390 F. flip after half time.

Serve with a mixed green salad.

Nutritional value: per serving: Calories: 310 | Protein: 23g | Fat: 20g | carbs: 23 g

219. Air Fryer Party Meatballs

(Prep Time: 5 mints| Cook Time:15 mints| Servings: 4)

Ingredients

- Worcester Sauce: 21/2 Tbsp.
- Lean Mince Beef: 4 cups
- Dry Mustard: half tsp.
- Tabasco: 1 Tbsp.
- Brown Sugar; half cup
- Vinegar: ¼ Cup
- Tomato Ketchup: ¾ Cup
- Lemon Juice: 1 Tbsp.
- Three crushed Gingersnaps

Instructions

Add all the seasoning ingredients to a large bowl and mix well.

Then add the minced meat and mix well.

With your hands, turn them into medium-sized balls.

Place them in the air fryer and cook at 375F for 15 minutes, until done.

Remove and add some sticks before serving.

Nutritional value: per serving: Calories: 373kcal | Carbohydrates: 23g | Protein: 21g | Fat: 15g

220. Air-Fried Chicken Pie

(Prep Time: 10 mints| Cook Time: 30 mints| Servings: 2)

Ingredients

- Puff pastry: 2 sheets
- Chicken thighs: 2 pieces, cut into cubes
- One small onion, chopped
- Small potatoes: 2, chopped
- Mushrooms: 1/4 cup
- Light soya sauce
- One carrot, chopped
- Black pepper, to taste
- Worcestershire sauce: to taste
- Salt, to taste
- Italian mixed dried herbs
- Garlic powder: a pinch
- Plain flour: 2 tbsp.
- Milk, as required
- Melted butter

Instructions

In a bowl, add the light soy sauce and pepper, add the chicken cubes and cover well.

In a pan over medium heat, sauté the carrot, potatoes and onion. Add some water if needed to cook the vegetables.

Add the chicken cubes and mushrooms and cook them too.

Mix black pepper, salt, Worcestershire sauce, garlic powder and dried herbs.

When the chicken is cooked, add a little flour and mix well.

Add the milk and let the vegetables cook until tender.

Put a piece of puff pastry in the pan of the air fryer, make holes with a fork.

Add the cooked chicken filling on top and the eggs and puff pastry with holes on top. Cut the excess dough. Glaze with spray oil or melted butter

Air fry at 180 ° F, for six mints or until golden brown.

Serve with microgreens.

Nutritional value : per serving: calories 244|protein 22g|fat 19 g| carbs 15g

221. Air Fryer Italian Sausage & Vegetables

(Prep Time: 5 mints| Cook Time:14 mints| Servings: 4)

Ingredients

- One bell pepper
- Italian Sausage: 4 pieces spicy or sweet
- One small onion
- 1/4 cup of mushrooms

Instructions

Let the air fryer preheat at 400 F for three minutes.

Put the Italian sausage in a single layer in the fryer basket and cook for six minutes.

Slice the vegetables while cooking the sausages.

After six minutes, reduce the temperature to 360 F. Flip the sausage in half. Add the mushrooms, onions and peppers to the basket around the sausage.

Cook at 360 degrees for 8 minutes. After 4 minutes, stir around the sausage and vegetables.

With an instant-read thermometer, the temperature of the sausage should be 160 F.

Cook more for a few minutes if the temperature is not 160F. Remove the vegetables and sausage and serve hot with brown rice.

Nutritional value : per serving: calories 281| fat: 20g| carbs 11g|Protein: 14g

222.   Air Fryer Chicken Nuggets
(Prep Time: 15 mints| Cook Time:15 mints| Servings: 4)
Ingredients
- Olive oil spray
- Skinless boneless: 2 chicken breasts, cut into bite pieces
- Half tsp. of kosher salt& freshly ground black pepper, to taste
- Grated parmesan cheese: 2 tablespoons
- Italian seasoned breadcrumbs: 6 tablespoons (whole wheat)
- Whole wheat breadcrumbs: 2 tablespoons
- olive oil: 2 teaspoons

Instructions
Let the air fryer preheat for 8 minutes, at 400 F
In a large bowl, add the panko, parmesan and breadcrumbs and mix well.
Sprinkle kosher salt and pepper on chicken and olive oil, mix well.
Take a few pieces of chicken, dip them in the breadcrumb mixture.
Place these pieces in an air fryer and sprinkle with olive oil.
Cook for 8 minutes, turning halfway through cooking
Have fun with black cabbage chips.
Nutritional value : per serving: Calories: 183kcal, Carbohydrates: 7g, Protein: 22g, Fat: 5.5g

223.   Air-Fried Buttermilk Chicken
(Prep Time: 30 mints| Cook Time:20 mints| Servings: 6)
Ingredients
- Chicken thighs: 4 cups skin-on, bone-in
   Marinade
- Buttermilk: 2 cups
- Black pepper: 2 tsp.
- Cayenne pepper: 1 tsp.
- Salt: 2 tsp.

Seasoned Flour
- Baking powder: 1 tbsp.
- All-purpose flour: 2 cups
- Paprika powder: 1 tbsp.
- Salt: 1 tsp.
- Garlic powder: 1 tbsp.

Instructions
Let the air warm up to 350 F.
With a paper towel, dry the chicken legs.
In a bowl, add the paprika, black pepper, mix the salt well, then add the chicken pieces. Add the buttermilk and coat the chicken well. Leave to marinate for at least 6 hours.
In another bowl, add the yeast, salt, flour, pepper and paprika. Place the chicken pieces one at a time and cover them with the dressing.
Spray oil on the chicken pieces and put the breaded chick-

en skin upward in the fryer basket in one layer, cook for 8 minutes, then turn the chicken pieces for another ten minutes
Remove and serve with salad.
Nutritional value : per serving: Cal 212|fat 15 g| protein 21g|carbs 13 g

224.   Air Fryer Low Carb Chicken Bites
(Prep Time: 10 mints| Cook Time:10 mints| Servings: 3)
Ingredients
- Chicken breast: 2 cups
- Kosher salt& pepper to taste
- Smashed potatoes: one cup
- Scallions: ¼ cup
- One Egg beat
- Whole wheat breadcrumbs: 1 cup

Instructions
Boil the chicken until soft.
Chop the chicken with the help of a fork.
Add the mashed potatoes and shallots to the shredded chicken. Season with kosher salt and pepper.
Sprinkle with the egg and then in the breadcrumbs.
Place in the air fryer and cook for 8 minutes at 380F. Or until golden brown.
Serve hot.
Nutritional value : per serving: Calories: 244|protein 21g| carbs 16g|fat 8 g

225.   Air Fried Empanadas
(Prep Time: 10 mints| Cook Time:20 mints| Servings: 2)
Ingredients
- Square gyoza wrappers: eight pieces
- Olive oil: 1 tablespoon
- White onion: 1/4 cup, finely diced
- Mushrooms: 1/4 cup, finely diced
- Half cup lean ground beef
- Chopped garlic: 2 teaspoons
- Paprika: 1/4 teaspoon
- Ground cumin: 1/4 teaspoon
- Six green olives, diced
- Ground cinnamon: 1/8 teaspoon
- Diced tomatoes: half cup
- One egg, lightly beaten

Instructions
In a skillet, over medium heat, add the oil, onions and beef and cook for 3 minutes, until the beef turns brown.
Add the mushrooms and cook for six minutes until they begin to brown. Then add the paprika, cinnamon, olives, cumin and garlic and cook for 3 minutes or more.
Add the chopped tomatoes and cook for one minute. Turn off the heat; let it cool for five minutes.
Place the gyoza wrappers on a flat surface add a spoon and a half. of beef stuffing in each wrapper. Brush the edges with water or egg, fold the wrappers, pinch the edges.
Place four empanadas in an even layer in a deep fryer basket and cook for 7 minutes at 400 ° F until golden brown.
Serve with sauce and salad.
Nutritional value : per serving Calories 333 |Fat 17g |Protein 18g |Carbohydrate 12.9g

1.14 Air Fryer BBQ Chicken Wings

(Prep Time: 5 mints| Cook Time: 15 mints| Servings: 4)

Ingredients

- BBQ sauce: half cup
- Chicken wings: 4 cups
- Black pepper, to taste
- Garlic powder: 1/8 teaspoon
- Ranch
- Celery sticks

Instructions

Let the air fryer preheat to 400 degrees.

With absorbent paper, pat dry the chicken wings, rubbing the garlic powder over them. Place them in the air fryer, in an even layer.

Cook for 15 minutes, turn the wings once or twice. Cook for another 3 minutes to get crunchy skin.

Take them out of the air fryer and pour them into the barbecue sauce. mix well to coat

Serve with celery sticks, mixed greens and ranch sauce.

Nutritional value : per serving: Calories: 187kcal | Carbohydrates: 15g | Protein: 10g | Fat: 10g

226. Crumbed Chicken Tenderloins

(Prep Time: 10 mints| Cook Time:12 mints| Servings: 4)

Ingredients

- Eight chicken tenderloins
- Olive oil: 2 tablespoons
- One egg whisked
- 1/4 cup breadcrumbs

Instructions

Allow the air fryer to heat up to 350 F.

In a large bowl, add the breadcrumbs and oil, mix well to form a crumbly mixture

Dip the chicken fillet in the beaten egg and cover it with the breadcrumbs.

Place the breaded chicken in the air fryer and cook at 350 ° F for 12 minutes or more.

Remove from the air fryer and serve with the salad garnish.

Nutritional value: per serving: Calories 209|Proteins 22g |Carbs 15g |Fat 10g |

227. Cheesy Cauliflower Tots

(Prep Time: 15 mints| Cook Time:12 mints| Servings: 4)

Ingredients

- 1 large head cauliflower
- 1 cup shredded mozzarella cheese
- 1/2 cup grated Parmesan cheese
- 1 large egg
- 1/4 teaspoon garlic powder
- 1/4 teaspoon dried parsley
- 1/8 teaspoon onion powder

Instructions

Fill a large pot with 2 cups of water on the stove and place a steamer in the oven. Put the bath to boil.

Break the blooming cauliflower and place it on a steaming pot: cover the pot and lid.

Let the cauliflower cook for 7 minutes until the fork is tender. Put the gauze or clean tea towel from the steamer basket and let it cool.

Push on the sink to remove as much moisture as possible. If not all the moisture is removed, the mixture will be too soft to form small ones.

Squeeze until smooth with a blade.

In a large bowl, place the cauliflower and add the mozzarella, parmesan, egg, garlic powder, parsley and onion powder. Remove until well combined. The blend should be smooth but easy to shape.

Take 2 tablespoons of the mixture and roll the mixture into a tot shape. Repeat with the leftover mixture. Place the basket in the air fryer.

Set the temperature to 320 ° F and set the timer for 12 minutes.

Turn the tots halfway through the cooking period.

The cauliflowers should be golden brown when fully cooked. Serve hot.

Nutritional Value: per serving: calories: 171| protein 15.5g|fiber 5.0g| carbohydrates: 6.6 g |fat: 9.5 g|

228. Air Fry Rib-Eye Steak

(Prep Time: 5 mints| Cook Time: 14 mints| Servings: 2)

Ingredients

- Lean rib eye steaks: 2, medium size
- Salt & freshly ground black pepper, to taste

Instructions

Allow the air to fry to preheat to 400 F. Dry the steaks with paper towels.

Use any mixture of spices or just salt and pepper on steaks. Generously on both sides of the steak.

Place the steaks in the basket of the air fryer. Cook according to the rarity you want. Or cook for 14 minutes and flip after half the time.

Remove from the air fryer and let it rest for about 5 minutes.

Serve with green micro salad.

Nutritional value : per serving: Calories: 476kcal | Protein: 42g | Fat: 33g | carbs: 21 g

229. Beef Schnitzel

(Prep Time: 10 mints| Cook Time:15 mints| Servings: 1)

Ingredients

- One lean beef schnitzel
- Olive oil: 2 tablespoon
- Breadcrumbs: ¼ cup
- One egg
- One lemon, to serve

Instructions

Let the air fryer heat up to 180 C.

In a large bowl, add the breadcrumbs and oil, mix well to form a crumbly mixture

Dip the beef steak in the beaten egg and cover it with the breadcrumbs.

Place the breaded meat in the air fryer and cook at 180 ° C for 15 minutes or more until cooked through.

Remove from the air fryer and serve with the salad and

lemon garnish.

Nutrition Value: per serving: Calories 350 |Proteins 24g |Carbs 15g |Fat 13g |Fiber 7g

230. Air Fryer Chicken Cheese Quesadilla
(Prep Time: 4 mints| Cook Time: 7 mints| Servings: 4)

Ingredients

- Precooked chicken: one cup, diced
- Tortillas: 2 pieces
- Low-fat cheese: one cup (shredded)

Instructions

Spray some oil in the air basket and place a tortilla on it.

Add the cooked chicken and the cheese on top.

Add the second tortilla above. Place a metal grill on top.

Cook for 6 minutes at 370 degrees, turn it in half so that it cooks evenly.

Slice and serve with salad

Nutritional value : per serving: Calories: 177kcal | Carbohydrates: 6g | Protein: 13g | Fat: 8g |

231. Air Fried Tom Yum Chicken Wings
(Prep Time: 30 mints| Cook Time:20 mints| Servings: 3)

Ingredients

- Tom Yum Paste: 2 tbsp.
- 8 Chicken Wings
- Water: 1 tbsp.
  COATING
- Corn flour: 2 tbsp.
- Baking Powder: half teaspoon
- Tapioca Starch: 2 tbsp.

Instructions

Mix the Tom Yum paste with the water in a small bowl.

Add the chicken wings to the tom yum mix, coat well and refrigerate the marinade for four hours.

Allow the air fryer to preheat to 180 ° C.

In a bowl, mix the tapioca starch, baking powder and cornmeal and mix well. Coat the chicken in the flour mixture. Spray the oil on the chicken.

Place the chicken in the air fryer in an even layer and cook for 10-12 minutes

Turn them once and cook for more 5.8 mines

Remove from the deep fryer and serve with salad and lemon wedges

Nutritional value: per serving: Calories 323 |Proteins 24g |Carbs 19g|Fat 16g |Fiber 6g

232. Sriracha-Honey Chicken Wings
(Prep Time: 30 mints| Cook Time:15 mints| Servings: 2)

Ingredients

- Soy sauce: 1 and 1/2 tablespoons
- Chicken wings: 4 cups
- Sriracha sauce: 2 tablespoons
- Butter: 1 tablespoon
- Half cup honey
- Juice of half lime
- Scallion's cilantro, and chives for garnish

Instructions

Let the air fryer preheat to 360 degrees F.

Place the chicken wings in the basket of an air fryer, cook for half an hour, flip the wings every seven minutes and cook thoroughly.

Meanwhile, in a saucepan, add all the sauce ingredients and simmer for three minutes.

Remove the chicken wings and cover them well with the sauce.

Garnish with the shallot. Serve with microgreen salad.

Nutritional value: per serving: Calories 217 |Proteins 22g |Carbs 13g|Fat 13g |

233. Air Fryer Ravioli
(Prep Time: 10 mints| Cook Time:10 mints| Servings: 6)

Ingredients

- Olive oil: 1 teaspoon
- Italian-style bread crumbs: 2 cups
- Homemade marinara sauce
- Cheese ravioli with cooked chicken: 12 pieces
- Parmesan cheese: 1/4 cup
- Buttermilk: 1 cup

Instructions

Add the cheese and chicken to the gnocchi wrappers and seal the edges with water.

Then coat the ravioli with buttermilk.

In a bowl, add the olive oil and breadcrumbs, mix well and add the ravioli to the mixture

Place the breaded ravioli in the basket of the air fryer on baking paper.

Cook for five minutes at 200 ° F

Serve with salad and marinara dipping sauce.

Nutritional Value: per serving: Calories 228 |Proteins 14g |Carbs 13g |Fat 11g

234. Air Fryer Dumplings
(Prep Time: 5 mints| Cook Time:10 mints| Servings: 3)

Ingredients

- One packet of frozen chicken, vegetable, or pork dumplings
- Salad greens: one cup
- Dipping sauce
- Maple syrup: 1/8 cup
- Soy sauce: 1/4 cup
- Red pepper flakes: Pinch
- Garlic powder: 1/2 tsp.
- Rice vinegar: 1/2 tsp.
- Water: 1/4 cup

Instructions

Allow the air fryer to preheat to 370 degrees for four minutes.

Place the gnocchi in the basket of the air fryer in a single layer and spray with oil.

Fry in the air for five minutes, turn the basket, sprinkle with a little more oil.

Leave to cook for another six minutes.

Meanwhile combine all the dipping sauce ingredients in a bowl and mix well.

• Remove the gnocco and serve with the vegetables.
Nutritional value : per serving: Cal 223|Fat: 9g |Carbs: 23g |Protein: 16g

235.   Air Fryer Grilled Chicken Recipe
(Prep Time: 30 mints| Cook Time:20 mints| Servings: 3)
Ingredients
• Chicken tenders: 4 cups
Marinade
• Honey: 2 Tbsp.
• Olive oil: 1/4 cup
• White vinegar: 2 Tbsp.
• Water: 2 Tbsp.
• Half teaspoon salt
• Garlic powder: 1 tsp.
• Half teaspoon of paprika
• Onion powder: 1 tsp.
• Half teaspoon crushed red pepper

Instructions
In a bowl, add all the ingredients of the marinade and mix well.

Then add the chicken mix to coat. Cover with cling film and leave to marinate in the refrigerator for half an hour.

• Place the chicken tenders in the basket of the air fryer in an even layer.

Cook for 3 minutes at 390 F. Flip the tenders and cook for another five minutes or until the chicken is completely cooked.

Serve with the salad garnish.

Nutritional value : per serving: calories 235|fat 15g| protein 23 g| carbs 10g

236.   Orange Chicken Wings
(Prep Time: 5 mints| Cook Time: 14 mints| Servings: 2)
Ingredients
• Honey: 1 tbsp.
• Chicken Wings, Six pieces
• One orange zest and juice
• Worcestershire Sauce: 1.5 tbsp.
• Black pepper, to taste
• Herbs (sage, rosemary, oregano, parsley, basil, thyme, and mint)

Instructions
Wash and dry the chicken wings

In a bowl, add the chicken wings, pour in the zest and orange juice

Add the rest of the ingredients and rub on the chicken wings. Leave to marinate for at least half an hour.

Allow the air fryer to preheat to 350 ° F

In aluminum foil, wrap the marinated wings and put them in an air fryer and cook for 20 minutes at 350 C

After 20 minutes, remove the foil and brush the sauce over the wings and cook for another 15 minutes. Then again, brush the sauce and cook for another ten minutes.

Remove from air fryer and serve with vegetables.

Nutritional value: per serving: Calories 279 |Proteins 25g |Carbs 21g |Fat 15g |

237.   Air Fryer Nashville Hot Chicken with Spinach Salad
(Prep Time: 30 mints| Cook Time:25 mints| Servings: 8)
Ingredients
• Buttermilk: 2 cups
• Chicken thighs(bone-in): 8
• Cayenne pepper: 1 tsp.
• Hot sauce: 1/4 cup
• Garlic powder: 2 Tbsp.
• Salt: 1 tsp.
• Low-fat butter: 1/2 cup
• Flour: 2 cups
• Black pepper: 1 tsp.
• Old bay: 1 tsp.
• Paprika: 1 tsp.

Instructions
In a bowl, add the hot sauce and buttermilk, mix well, then add the chicken pieces.

Leave to marinate in the refrigerator for 1 to 24 hours.

In a bowl, add the garlic powder, flour, salt, black pepper, paprika, cayenne pepper, and old bay leaf. Mix well.

Always cook the chicken in a single layer, in the air fryer

Remove the chicken from the buttermilk, cover it with the flour. Let the chicken rest on a wire rack for 15 minutes before placing it in the air fryer.

Place the breaded chicken in the air fryer, leaving space between the pieces.

Cook for 25 minutes, at 390 F. after the first half, remove the basket and spray the chicken with olive oil

This step is optional. Mix two tablespoons. Spicy sauce with melted butter. Brush the cooked crispy chicken with it.

Serve with the spinach salad.

Nutritional value : per serving: calories 350|Fat 25g|Carbs 14g|protein 23g

238.   Lemon Rosemary Chicken
(Prep Time: 30 mints| Cook Time:20 mints| Servings: 2)
Ingredients
For marinade
• Chicken: 2 and ½ cups
• Ginger: 1 tsp, minced
• Olive oil: 1/2 tbsp.
• Soy sauce: 1 tbsp.
For the sauce
• Half lemon
• Honey: 3 tbsp.
• Oyster sauce: 1 tbsp.
• Fresh rosemary: half cup, chopped

Instructions
In a large bowl, add the marinade ingredients with the chicken and mix well.

Store in the refrigerator for at least half an hour.

Leave the oven to preheat to 200 ° C for three minutes.

Place the marinated chicken in the air fryer in a single layer. And cook for 6 minutes at 200 degrees.

In the meantime, combine all the sauce ingredients in a bowl and mix well except the lemon wedges.

Generously brush the sauce over the half cooked chicken and add the lemon juice.

Cook for another 13 minutes at 200 C. Turn the chicken in half. Let the chicken brown evenly.

Serve with a micro vegetable salad.

Nutrition Value: per serving: Calories 328 |Proteins 27g |Carbs 6g|Fat 12 g |

239. Low Carb Parmesan Chicken Meat balls

(Prep Time: 10 mints| Cook Time:12 mints| Servings: 20)

Ingredients

- Pork rinds: half cup, ground
- Ground chicken: 4 cups
- Parmesan cheese: half cup grated
- Kosher salt: 1 tsp.
- Garlic powder: 1 tsp.
- One egg beaten
- Paprika: 1 tsp.
- Pepper: half tsp.

Breading
- Pork rinds: half cup ground

Instructions

Let the air fryer preheat to 400 ° F.

Add the cheese, chicken, egg, pepper, half a cup of pork rinds, garlic, salt and paprika into a large mixing ball. Mix well into a dough, form 1-and-a-half-inch balls.

Coat the meatballs with the pork rinds (minced).

The oil sprays the air frying basket and adds the meatballs in an even layer.

Cook for 12 minutes at 400 ° F, turning once halfway through cooking.

Serve with salad.

Nutritional value : per serving: Cal 244| fat 12 g| carbs 11.1 g| protein 17.9 g

240. Air Fryer Chicken & Broccoli

(Prep Time: 10 mints| Cook Time:15 mints| Servings: 4)

Ingredients

- Olive oil: 2 Tablespoons
- Chicken breast: 4 cups, bone and skinless (cut into cubes)
- Half medium onion, roughly sliced
- Low sodium soy sauce: 1 Tbsp.
- Garlic powder: half teaspoon
- Rice vinegar: 2 teaspoons
- Broccoli: 1-2 cups, cut into florets
- Hot sauce: 2 teaspoons
- Fresh minced ginger: 1 Tbsp.
- Sesame seed oil: 1 teaspoon
- Salt & black pepper, to taste

Instructions

In a bowl, add the chicken breast, onion and broccoli. Combine them well.

In another bowl, add the ginger, oil, sesame oil, rice vinegar, hot sauce, garlic powder and soy sauce, mixing well. Then add the broccoli, chicken and onions to the marinade.

Sprinkle the chicken well with the sauces. And let it rest in

the refrigerator for 15 minutes

Place the chicken mixture in an even layer in the basket of the air fryer and cook for 16-20 minutes, at 380 F. in the middle, gently toss the basket and cook the chicken evenly

Add another five minutes if needed.

Add salt and pepper if necessary.

serve hot with lemon wedges

Nutritional value: per serving: Calories 199|Fat 7g | Carbohydrates 6g | Protein 23g

241. Mexican-Style Air Fryer Stuffed Chicken Breasts

(Prep Time: 20 mints| Cook Time:10 mints| Servings: 2)

Ingredients

- Olive oil: 2 teaspoons
- One chicken breast (skinless, boneless)
- Chili powder: 4 tsp., divided
- Chipotle flakes: 2 tsp.
- Half bell pepper, sliced
- Mexican oregano: 2 tsp.
- Salt and pepper, to taste
- Ground cumin: 4 tsp., divided
- Half juice of a lime
- Half onion, sliced
- One jalapeno pepper, sliced

Instructions

In a bowl, add two teaspoons of cumin and two teaspoons. of chilli powder, mix well

Allow the air fryer to preheat to 400 F.

Pound the chicken breast until 1/4 inch thick.

In a bowl, mix the remaining chili powder, chipotle flakes, salt, oregano, remaining cumin and pepper. Rub this spice mix all over the chicken.

Place half of the pepper, jalapeño and onion in half of the breast. Roll the chicken around and secure it with large toothpicks.

Add the olive oil to the breast rolls and cover them with the cumin and chilli mixture.

Add the chicken breast to the deep fryer and cook for six minutes.

Flip the breast rolls and cook for another five minutes until the temperature of the chicken reaches 165 F.

Pour the lime juice over the breast rolls and serve hot.

Nutritional value : per serving: 195.3 calories| protein 14.8g | carbohydrates 15.2g |fat 8.5g

242. Air Fryer Spicy Chicken & Vegetables

(Prep Time: 20 mints| Cook Time:30 mints| Servings: 2)

Ingredients

Spiced Chicken
- Chicken breasts: 2 skinless, boneless
- Onion powder: half tsp.
- Olive oil: 1/2 Tbsp.
- Chili powder: 1 tsp.
- Cumin: 1/4 tsp.
- Paprika: half tsp.

- Salt: half tsp.
- Garlic powder: half tsp.
- Pepper: half tsp.

Vegetables
- Carrots: 2-3 large
- Onion: one red
- Olive oil: 1/2 Tbsp.
- Chopped scallions
- Pinch of salt

Instructions

Allow the air fryer to preheat to 325 F

In a large bowl, add all the spices for the chicken and make a spice mix. Then add the chicken breasts with half a spoon. of olive oil and cover well. Set it aside.

Cut the vegetables according to your preferences. Cut the onions into layers and separate each layer, coat all the vegetables with half a spoon. of olive oil and salt

Put the vegetables in the air fryer first, then add the chicken on top - Cook for at least 35 minutes or more. Flip the chicken in half and discard the vegetables.

Serve hot.

Nutritional value : per serving: Calories: 354cal | Carbohydrates: 31g | Protein: 25g | Fat: 10g |

243.   Air Fryer Meatloaf

(Prep Time: 10 mints| Cook Time:40 mints| Servings: 8)

Ingredients

- Ground lean beef: 4 cups
- Bread crumbs: 1 cup (soft and fresh)
- Chopped mushrooms: ½ cup
- Cloves of minced garlic
- Shredded carrots: ½ cup
- Beef broth: ¼ cup
- Chopped onions: ½ cup
- Two eggs beaten
- Ketchup: 3 Tbsp.
- Worcestershire sauce: 1 Tbsp.
- Dijon mustard: 1 Tbsp.

For Glaze
- Honey: ¼ cup
- Ketchup: half cup
- Dijon mustard: 2 tsp

Instructions

In a large bowl, add the meat broth and breadcrumbs, mix well. And set it aside in a food processor, add the garlic, onions, mushrooms and carrots and whisk over high heat until finely chopped.

In a separate bowl, add the soaked breadcrumbs, Dijon mustard, Worcestershire sauce, eggs, lean ground beef, ketchup, and salt. With your hands, combine well and turn it into a loaf.

Allow the air fryer to preheat to 390 F.

Place the meatloaf in the air fryer and cook for 45 minutes.

Meanwhile, add the Dijon mustard, ketchup and brown sugar to a bowl and mix. Glaze this mix on the meatloaf when there are five minutes left.

Let the meatloaf rest for ten minutes before serving.

Nutritional value: per serving: Calories 320 |Proteins 17g |Carbs 14g|Fat 9.2 g |

244.   General Tso's Chicken

(Prep Time: 5 mints| Cook Time:25 mints| Servings: 4)

Ingredients

- Chicken thighs: 8 cups boneless, skinless (cubed)
- 3 green onions, roughly chopped
- Corn starch : 2 tsp
- Vegetable oil: 1 Tbsp.
- Rice vinegar: 2 Tbsp.
- Six red chilies, dried
- Potato starch: 1/3 cup
- Garlic minced: 2 tsp
- Brown sugar : 3/4 cup
- Chicken broth : half cup
- Ginger minced: 1 tsp
- Soy sauce : half cup
- Sesame oil: 1 tsp
- Salt, to taste
- Cup water: 1/4

Instructions

Allow the air fryer to preheat to 400 F.

In a bowl, add the potato starch and the chicken legs, cover them well. Add the chicken legs to the air fryer in an even layer and cook for 25 minutes.

Shake the basket of the air fryer every 5-7 minutes.

Meanwhile, heat the olive oil in a skillet over medium heat and add the garlic, ginger, dried chillies and green onions, cook for one minute, until the onions have softened.

Mix the soy sauce, sesame oil, chicken broth, a pinch of salt, brown sugar, rice vinegar and mix well. Boil and cook for three minutes.

Then add the fried chicken in sauce and cover well.

Incorporate the cornstarch mixture (with water), cook for one minute.

• Serve with boiled vegetables and enjoy.

Nutritional value : per serving: Calories: 439|fat 21 g| protein 25 g| carbs 22.1 g|

245.   Air Fryer No Breading Chicken Breast

(Prep Time: 10 mints| Cook Time:20 mints| Servings: 2)

Ingredients

- Olive oil spray
- Chicken breasts: 4 (boneless)
- Onion powder: 3/4 teaspoon
- Salt: ¼ cup
- Smoked paprika: half tsp.
- 1/8 tsp. of cayenne pepper
- Garlic powder: 3/4 teaspoon
- Dried parsley: half tsp.

Instructions

In a large bowl, add six cups of hot water, add salt (1/4 cup) and mix to dissolve.

Place the chicken breasts in hot salted water and let them cool for almost 2 hours.

Remove from water and pat dry.

In a bowl, add all the spices with ¾ tsp. of salt. Sprinkle the oil all over the chicken and rub the spice mixture all over the chicken.

Let the air fryer heat up to 380F.

Place the chicken in the air fryer and cook for ten minutes. Turn halfway and serve with green salad.

Nutritional value : per serving: Calories: 208kcal|Carbohydrates: 1g| Protein: 39g| Fat: 4.5g

246. Air Fried Steak with Asparagus Bundles

(Prep Time: 20 mints| Cook Time:30 mints| Servings: 2)

Ingredients

- Olive oil spray
- Flank steak (2 pounds)- cut into 6 pieces
- Kosher salt and black pepper
- Two cloves of minced garlic
- Asparagus: 4 cups
- Tamari sauce: half cup
- Three bell peppers: sliced thinly
- Beef broth: 1/3 cup
- 1 Tbsp. of unsalted butter
- Balsamic vinegar: 1/4 cup

Instructions

Sprinkle the steak with salt and pepper and rub.

In a zip lock bag, add the garlic and Tamari sauce, then add the steak, mix well and seal the bag.

Leave to marinate for one hour overnight.

Similarly, place the peppers and asparagus in the center of the steak.

Roll the steak around the vegetables and secure it tightly with toothpicks.

Preheat the air fryer.

Spray the steak with olive oil spray. And put the steaks in the air fryer.

Bake for 15 minutes at 400 degrees or higher until steaks are cooked through

Remove the steak from the deep fryer and let it rest for five minutes

Remove the steak wads and let them rest for 5 minutes before serving / slicing.

Meanwhile, add the butter, balsamic vinegar and broth over medium heat. Mix well and reduce by half. Add salt and pepper to taste.

Pour over the steaks before serving.

Nutritional value : per serving: Calories 480 |Proteins 24g |Carbs 22g |Fat 13g |

247. Air Fryer Beef Steak Kabobs with Vegetables

(Prep Time: 30 mints| Cook Time:10 mints| Servings: 4)

Ingredients

- Soy sauce: 2 tbsp.
- Lean beef chuck ribs: 4 cups, cut into one-inch pieces
- Low-fat sour cream: 1/3 cup
- Half onion
- 8 skewers: 6 inch
- One bell peppers

Instructions

In a bowl, add the soy sauce and sour cream, mix well. Add the pieces of lean beef, cover well and leave to marinate for half an hour or more.

Cut the onion and bell pepper into one-inch pieces. Soak the skewers in water for ten minutes.

Add onions, peppers and beef on skewers; alternatively, sprinkle with black pepper

Cook for 10 minutes, in a preheated air fryer at 400F, turn halfway.

Serve with yogurt sauce.

Nutritional Value: per serving: Calories 271 |Proteins 21g |Carbs 14g|Fat 11g |

248. Low Carb Air-Fried Calzones

(Prep Time: 15 mints| Cook Time:27 mints| Servings: 2)

Ingredients

- Cooked chicken breast: 1/3 cup(shredded)
- One teaspoon olive oil
- Spinach leaves(baby): 3 cups
- Whole-wheat pizza dough, freshly prepared
- Marinara sauce: 1/3 cup(lower-sodium)
- Diced red onion:1/4 cup
- Skim mozzarella cheese: 6 Tbsp.
- Cooking spray

Instructions

In a medium skillet, over medium heat, add the oil, onions. Brown until soft. Then add the spinach leaves, cook until wilted. Turn off the heat and add the chicken and the marinara sauce.

Cut the pasta into two pieces.

Add 1/4 of the spinach mixture to each piece of circular dough.

Add the skimmed grated cheese on top. Fold the dough and fold the edges.

Spray the trousers with cooking spray.

Put the breeches in the air fryer. Bake for 12 minutes, at 325 ° F, until the batter is light brown. Flip the calzone over and cook for another eight minutes.

Nutritional value: per serving: Calories 348|Fat 12g | Protein 21g |Carbohydrate 18g

249. Air Fried Maple Chicken Thighs

(Prep Time: 10 mints| Cook Time:25mints| Servings: 4)

Ingredient

- One egg
- Buttermilk: 1 cup
- Maple syrup: half cup
- Chicken thighs: 4 pieces
- Granulated garlic: 1 tsp.

Dry Mix

- Granulated garlic: half tsp.
- All-purpose flour: half cup
- Salt: one tbsp.
- Sweet paprika: one tsp.
- Smoked paprika: half tsp.
- Tapioca flour: ¼ cup
- Cayenne pepper: ¼ teaspoon

- Granulated onion: one tsp.
- Black pepper: ¼ teaspoon
- Honey powder: half tsp.

Instructions

In a zip lock bag, add the egg, a teaspoon. of granulated garlic, buttermilk and maple syrup, add the chicken legs and leave to marinate for an hour or more in the refrigerator

In a bowl, add the sweet paprika, the tapioca flour, the granulated onion, half a teaspoon. of granulated garlic, flour, cayenne pepper, salt, pepper, honey powder and smoked paprika mix well.

Allow the air fry to preheat to 380 F.

Coat the marinated chicken thighs in the dry spice mixture, shake off the excess.

Place the chicken skin face down in the air fryer

Leave to cook for 12 minutes. Flip the thighs in half and cook for another 13 minutes.

Serve with salad.

Nutritional value : per serving: 420calories| protein 25.3g| carbohydrates 21.8g| fat 15.4g

250.   Air Fryer Hamburger

(Prep Time: 5 mints| Cook Time:13 mints| Servings: 4)

Ingredients

- Buns:4
- Lean ground beef chuck: 4 cups
- Salt , to taste
- Slices of any cheese: 4 slices
- Black Pepper, to taste

Instructions

Allow the air fryer to preheat to 350 F.

In a bowl, add the lean ground beef, pepper and salt. Mix well and form meatballs.

Put them in the air fryer in one layer, cook for 6 minutes, turn them in half. A minute before removing the meatballs add the cheese on top.

When the cheese is melted, remove it from the air fryer.

Add ketchup, any toppings to your sandwiches, add tomatoes, lettuce and meatballs.

Serve hot.

Nutritional value : per serving: Calories: 540kcal | Carbohydrates: 21g | Protein: 33g | Fat: 31g |

251.   Air Fryer Personal Mini Pizza

(Prep Time: 2 mints| Cook Time:5 mints| Servings: 1)

Ingredients

- Sliced olives: 1/4 cup
- One pita bread
- One tomato
- Shredded cheese: 1/2 cup

Instructions

Allow the air fryer to preheat to 350 F

Place the pita on a plate. Add the cheese, tomato slices and olives.

Cook for five minutes at 350 F

Remove the pizza from the air fryer.

Slice it and enjoy it

Nutritional value : per serving: Calories: 354kcal | Carbohydrates: 34g | Protein: 19g | Fat: 15g |

252.   Smothered Chicken Thighs

(Prep Time: 30 mints| Cook Time:30 mints| Servings: 4)

Ingredients

- 8-ounce of chicken thighs
- 1 tsp paprika
- One pinch salt
- Mushrooms: half cup
- Onions, roughly sliced

Instructions

Allow the air fryer to preheat to 400F

The chicken legs season with paprika, salt and pepper on both sides.

Place the thighs in the air fryer and cook for 20 minutes.

Meanwhile, sauté the mushrooms and onion.

Remove the legs from the deep fryer and serve with sauteed mushrooms and onions.

And serve with chopped shallots and a side of salad

Nutritional value : per serving: Kcal 470.3| Fat: 35g| Net Carbs: 4.4g|Protein: 42.5g

253.   Herb-Marinated Chicken Thighs

(Prep Time: 30 mints| Cook Time:10 mints| Servings: 4)

Ingredients

- Chicken thighs: 8 skin-on, bone-in,
- Lemon juice: 2 Tablespoon
- Onion powder: half teaspoon
- Garlic powder: 2 teaspoon
- Spike Seasoning: 1 teaspoon.
- Olive oil: 1/4 cup
- Dried basil: 1 teaspoon
- Dried oregano: half teaspoon.
- Black Pepper: 1/4 tsp.

Instructions

In a bowl, add the dried oregano, olive oil, lemon juice, dried sage, garlic powder, spicy seasoning, onion powder, dried basil, black pepper.

In a zip lock bag, add the spice mixture and chicken and mix well.

Marinate the chicken in the refrigerator for at least six hours or more.

Preheat the air fryer to 360 ° F.

Place the chicken in the basket of the air fryer, cook for six to eight minutes, flip the chicken over and cook for another six minutes.

Until the internal temperature of the chicken reaches 165F.

Remove from air fryer and serve with microgreens.

Nutritional value : per serving: Cal 100|Fat: 9g| Carbs 1g|Protein 4g

254.   Air Fried Spicy Chicken Wings

(Prep Time: 30 mints| Cook Time:20 mints| Servings: 2)

Ingredients

- Honey: 1 tbsp.
- Chicken Wings: 6 pcs

- Cloves of minced Garlic
- Worcestershire Sauce: 2 tbsp.
- Chili Flakes: 1 tsp.
- Salt & pepper, to taste
- Cooking Spray

Instructions

Wash and dry the chicken wings.

In a bowl, mix the chili flakes, salt, Worcestershire sauce, pepper and honey. Mix well and add the chicken wings and leave to marinate for at least an hour.

Drizzle the marinated chicken wings with olive oil

Place the chicken wings in the basket of the air fryer and cook for 8 minutes at 160 C.

Turn halfway and cook for more than four minutes.

Serve with air-fried courgettes.

Nutritional value: per serving: Calories 320 |Proteins 25g |Carbs 12 g |Fat 15g |

255.   Air Fryer Rotisserie Chicken

(Prep Time: 5 mints| Cook Time: 60 mints| Servings: 6)

Ingredients

- Paprika : 1 tsp.
- One chicken
- Dried basil: 1 tsp.
- Onion powder: 1/2 tsp.
- Dried oregano: 1 tsp.
- Pepper: half tsp.
- Salt : 1 and 1/2 tsp.
- Chopped cilantro and scallions

Instructions

Allow the air fryer to preheat to 360 ° F.

In a bowl, add all the spices and rub all over the chicken.

Place the chicken in the air fryer and let it cook at 360 degrees for half an hour or more if necessary.

Serve with salad and garnish with scallions and coriander.

Nutritional value : per serving: Calories: 381kcal | Carbohydrates: 1g | Protein: 32g | Fat: 25g

256.   Lemon-Garlic Chicken Thighs

(Prep Time: 2 hours' mints| Cook Time: 35 mints| Servings: 4)

Ingredients

- Lemon juice ¼ cup
- 1 Tbsp. olive oil
- 1 tsp mustard
- Cloves of garlic
- ¼ tsp salt
- 1tsp black pepper
- Chicken thighs
- Lemon wedges

Instructions

In a bowl, whisk together the olive oil, lemon juice, Dijon mustard, garlic, salt and pepper.

Place the chicken legs in a large resealable plastic bag. Pour the marinade over the chicken and the sealed bag, making sure all parts of the chicken are covered. Leave to cool for at least 2 hours.

Preheat a pan to 175 ° C (360 ° F).

Remove the chicken with the towels from the marinade and pat dry.

Place the chicken pieces in the basket of the air fryer, if necessary, cook them in batches.

Fry until the chicken is no longer pink on the bone and the sauce is uniform, 22 to 24 minutes. Just before serving, spread a lemon wedge over each piece.

Nutritional value : per serving: Cal 268|Fat: 19.6g| Carbs: 3.2g| Protein: 17.4g

257.   Air Fryer Popcorn Chicken

(Prep Time: 10 mints| Cook Time:20 mints| Servings: 2)

Ingredients

For Marinade

- 8 cups, chicken tenders, cut into bite-size pieces
- Freshly ground black pepper: 1/2 tsp
- Almond milk : 2 cups
- Salt: 1 tsp
- paprika: 1/2 tsp

Dry Mix

- Salt: 3 tsp
- Flour: 3 cups
- Paprika: 2 tsp
- Oil spray
- Freshly ground black pepper: 2 tsp

Instructions

In a bowl, add all the ingredients of the marinade and the chicken. Mix well and place it in a zip lock bag and in the refrigerator for a minimum of two hours, or six hours.

In a large bowl, add all the dry ingredients.

Cover the marinated chicken with the dry mixture. In the marinade again then for the second time in the dry mixture.

Spray the basket of the air fryer with olive oil and arrange the breaded chicken pieces in a single layer. Spray the oil on the chicken pieces as well.

Cook at 370 degrees for 10 minutes, turning halfway.

Serve immediately with salad or dipping sauce.

Nutritional value: per serving: Calories 340 |Proteins 20g |Carbs 14g |Fat 10g |

258.   Garlic Parmesan Chicken Tenders

(Prep Time: 5 mints| Cook Time:12 mints| Servings: 4)

Ingredients

- One egg
- Eight raw chicken tenders
- Water: 2 tablespoons
- Olive oil

To coat

- Panko breadcrumbs: 1 cup
- Half tsp of salt
- Black Pepper: 1/4 teaspoon
- Garlic powder: 1 teaspoon
- Onion powder: 1/2 teaspoon
- Parmesan cheese: 1/4 cup
- any dipping Sauce

Instructions

Add all the ingredients for the coating to a large bowl

In another bowl, mix the water and egg.

Dip the chicken into the egg mixture and then into the mixture for topping.

Place the offerings in the air frying basket in a single layer.

Spray with light olive oil

Cook at 400 degrees for 12 minutes. Flip the chicken in half.

Serve with salad and enjoy.

Nutritional value : per serving: Calories: 220kcal | Carbohydrates: 13g | Protein: 27g | Fat: 6g |

259. Air Fryer Blackened Chicken Breast

(Prep Time: 10 mints| Cook Time:20 mints| Servings: 2)

Ingredients

• Paprika: 2 teaspoons
• Ground thyme: 1 teaspoon
• Cumin: 1 teaspoon
• Cayenne pepper: half tsp.
• Onion powder: half tsp.
• Black Pepper: half tsp.
• Salt: ¼ teaspoon
• Vegetable oil: 2 teaspoons
• Pieces of chicken breast halves (without bones and skin)

Instructions

In a mixing bowl, add onion powder, salt, cumin, paprika, black pepper, thyme, and cayenne pepper. Mix it well.

Drizzle oil over chicken and rub. Dip each piece of chicken in blackening spice blend on both sides.

Let it rest for five minutes while the air fryer is preheating.

Preheat it for five minutes at 360F.

Put the chicken in the air fryer and let it cook for ten minutes. Flip and then cook for another ten minutes.

After, let it sit for five minutes, then slice and serve with the side of green

Nutritional value : per serving: 432.1 calories| protein 79.4g| carbohydrates 3.2g| fat 9.5g

260. Air Fryer Southwest Chicken

(Prep Time: 20 mints| Cook Time:30 mints| Servings: 4)

Ingredients

• Avocado oil: one tbsp.
• Four cups of boneless, skinless, chicken breast
• Chili powder: half tsp.
• Salt, to taste
• Cumin: half tsp.
• Onion powder: 1/4 tsp.
• Lime juice: two tbsp.
• Garlic powder: 1/4 tsp

Instructions

In a zip lock bag, add the chicken, oil and lime juice.

Add all the spices to a bowl and rub all the chicken into the zip lock bag.

Leave to marinate in the fridge for ten minutes or more.

Take the chicken out of the zip lock bag and place it in the air fryer. Cook for 25 minutes at 400 F, turning the chicken in half until the internal temperature reaches 165 degrees.

Nutritional value : per serving: Calories: 165kcal|Carbohydrates: 1g|Protein: 24g|Fat: 6g

261. Air Fryer Sesame Chicken Breast

(Prep Time: 5 mints| Cook Time:30 mints| Servings: 2)

Ingredients

• Sesame oil: 2 Tbsp.
• Chicken breasts: 2 pieces boneless and skin-on
• Black Pepper: 1/2 tsp
• Onions powder: 1 Tbsp.
• Sweet paprika: 1 Tbsp.
• Salt: 1 tsp
• Cayenne pepper: 1/4 tsp
• Granulated garlic: 1 Tbsp.

Instructions

Pour sesame oil all over the chicken and rub, then sprinkle with all the spices, pepper and salt

Sprinkle the chicken well with the spices.

Place the chicken breasts in the air fryer, skin side up. Make sure you leave space between the chicken pieces.

Cook for 20 minutes, at 380F. After 20 minutes, flip the chicken and cook for another ten minutes.

Remove from the air fryer and let it rest for five minutes.

Serve with air-fried vegetables.

Nutritional value: per serving: Calories 250 |Proteins 20g |Carbs 14g |Fat 20g |

262. Chicken Fajitas

(Prep Time: 10 mints| Cook Time:20 mints| Servings: 6)

Ingredients

• Chicken breasts: 4 cups, cut into thin strips
• Bell peppers, sliced
• Salt: half tsp.
• Cumin: 1 tsp.
• Garlic powder: 1/4 tsp
• Chili powder: half tsp.
• Lime juice: 1 tbsp.

Instructions

In a bowl, add the seasonings, chicken and lime juice and mix well.

Then add the sliced peppers and cover well.

Spray the air fryer with olive oil.

Place the chicken and peppers and cook for 15 minutes at 400 F. Invert halfway through cooking.

Serve with lemon wedges and enjoy.

Nutritional value : per serving: Calories 140 |Proteins 22g |Carbs 6g|Fat 5g |Fiber 7g

263. Air Fryer Chicken Parmesan

(Prep Time: 20 mints| Cook Time:30 mints| Servings: 4)

Ingredients

• Whole wheat seasoned breadcrumbs: 6 tbsp.
• Chicken breast: 2 pieces, make four thinner cutlets
• Mozzarella cheese: 6 tbsp. (reduced fat)
• Parmesan cheese: 2 tbsp. (grated)
• Marinara: 1/2 cup
• One tbsp. melted butter
• Olive oil

Instructions

Allow the air fryer to preheat to 360 F for three minutes.

In a bowl, add the Parmesan and breadcrumbs, mix well.

Pour the melted butter over the chicken and cover it with the Parmesan mixture. Eliminate excess.

Place the chicken in the air fryer and drizzle with oil.

Cook for six minutes, flip the chicken. Add the grated cheese and sauce on top and cook for another three minutes.

Serve with microgreens.

Nutritional value : per serving: Calories: 251kcal| Carbohydrates: 14g|Protein: 31.5g| Fat: 9.5g

264. Mixed Vegetables with Chicken

(Prep Time: 20 mints| Cook Time:20 mints| Servings: 2)

Ingredients

- 1/2 onion diced
- Chicken breast: 4 cups, cubed pieces
- Half zucchini chopped
- Italian seasoning: 1 tablespoon
- Bell pepper chopped: 1/2 cup
- Clove of garlic pressed
- Broccoli florets: 1/2 cup
- Olive oil: 2 tablespoons
- Half teaspoon of chili powder, garlic powder, pepper, salt,

Instructions

Let the air fryer heat up to 400 F and cut the vegetables into cubes

In a bowl, add the seasoning, oil and add the vegetables, chicken and mix well

Place chicken and vegetables in the air fryer and cook for ten minutes, stir halfway through cooking, cook in batches.

Make sure the vegetables are charred and the chicken is cooked.

Serve hot.

Nutritional value : per serving: :| Calories: 230kcal | Carbohydrates: 8g | Protein: 26g | Fat: 10g |

265. Lemon Pepper Chicken

(Prep Time: 3 mints| Cook Time:15 mints| Servings: 2)

Ingredients

- Two Lemons rind, juice, and zest
- One Chicken Breast
- Minced Garlic: 1 Tsp
- Black Peppercorns: 2 tbsp.
- Chicken Seasoning: 1 Tbsp.
- Salt & pepper, to taste

Instructions

Let the air fryer preheat to 180 ° C.

In a large aluminum foil, add all the seasonings along with the lemon zest.

Add salt and pepper to the chicken and rub the seasonings all over the chicken breast.

Place the chicken in aluminum foil. And fold it tightly.

Flatten the chicken inside the foil with a rolling pin

Put it in the air fryer and cook at 180 ° C for 15 minutes.

Serve hot.

Nutritional value : per serving: Calories: 140 | Carbohydrates: 24g | Protein: 13g | Fat: 2g

266. Crispy Parmesan Buttermilk Chicken Tenders

(Prep Time: 10 mints| Cook Time:18 mints| Servings: 4)

Ingredients

- Half cup of all-purpose flour
- Buttermilk: 3/4 cup
- Chicken breasts: 2, boneless, skinless
- Kosher salt: 3/4 teaspoon, divided
- Grated Parmesan cheese: 1/4 cup
- Black Pepper: 3/4 teaspoon, divided
- Worcestershire sauce: 1 and 1/2 teaspoons, divided
- Smoked paprika: half teaspoon, divided
- Oil spray
- Whole wheat breadcrumbs: 1 and 1/2 cups
- One large egg

Instructions

Cut the chicken into slices.

In a bowl, add the buttermilk and Worcestershire sauce (half), the salt and half the paprika and pepper. Add this mix in a zip lock bag with chicken tenders and let it marinate for six hours or more.

In a bowl, add the melted butter and breadcrumbs, Parmesan and combine well

Beat the egg with the remaining Worcestershire sauce.

In another bowl, add the smoked paprika, pepper, flour and salt.

Coat the offerings in the flour mixture, then again in the egg, then in the breadcrumb mixture.

Allow the air fryer to preheat to 400 F. Place the breaded offerings in the air fryer basket in an even layer.

Cook at 400 F for 13-15 minutes, turn the chicken over after half the time.

Serve with sauces and microgreens

Nutritional value : per serving: Calories 350|Fat 14g|Carbohydrates 12g|Protein 23g

267. Air- Fried Grilled BBQ Chicken

(Prep Time: 10 mints| Cook Time: 12 mints| Servings: 2)

Ingredients

- Chicken Steaks: 2 pieces
- Sea salt: 1 tsp.
- 1 tsp. olive oil
- Freshly ground Black Pepper: 1/2 teaspoon

Blue Cheese &Butter

- Blue Cheese: 1/ 4 cup
- 1/2 cup of butter (at room temperature)

Instructions

While preparing the steak, the most important thing is to let the meat sit at room temperature for 30 minutes, for a minimum.

Start the recipe by letting the air fryer heat up. To prepare any type of steak, you must always preheat the air fryer. Therefore, the meat will come out fine, so turn on the air fryer at 400 F for 5 minutes.

Rub the steak with butter or herb-flavored olive oil and

sprinkle with sea salt and black pepper.

Place the stakes for 6 minutes in the air fryer, then turn them again for almost 6 minutes.

Again, let the steak rest for at least 5 minutes, then slice it. The steaks will continue to cook, even when cooked.

Combine only the butter and blue cheese in a small mixing bowl to make the cheese. You can serve the steak however you like.

Put the butter in a film and roll it up well, it looks like a roll, keep it in the refrigerator and cut a few pieces for each portion.

Nutritional value : per serving: Calories 200 |Proteins 20g |Carbs 2g|Fat 5g |

268.   Air Fryer Buffalo Cauliflower
(Prep Time: 5 mints| Cook Time:15 mints| Servings: 4)
Ingredients
- Homemade buffalo sauce: 1/2 cup
- One head of cauliflower, cut bite-size pieces
- Butter melted: 1 tablespoon
- Olive oil
- Kosher salt & pepper, to taste

Instructions

Spray cooking oil on the basket of the air fryer.

In a bowl, add the buffalo sauce, melted butter, pepper and salt. Mix well.

Place the cauliflower pieces in the air fryer and sprinkle over the olive oil. Cook at 400 F for 7 minutes.

Remove the cauliflower from the air fryer and add it to the sauce. Sprinkle the cauliflower well.

Return the sauce-coated cauliflower to the air fryer.

Bake at 400 F, for 7-8 minutes or until crisp.

Remove from air fryer and serve with leaner protein.

Nutritional value : per serving: Calories 101kcal | Carbohydrates 4g | Protein 3g | Fat: 7g

269.   Mushroom Oatmeal
(Prep time: 10 min| Cooking time: 20 min| Servings: 4)
Ingredients
- One small yellow onion, chopped
- 1 cup steel-cut oats
- 1 Garlic cloves, minced
- 2 Tablespoons butter
- ½ cup of water
- One and a half cup of canned chicken stock
- Thyme springs, chopped
- 2 Tablespoons extra virgin olive oil
- ½ cup gouda cheese, grated
- 1 cup mushroom, sliced
- Salt and black pepper to taste

Instructions

Heat a skillet over medium heat that fits your fryer with butter, add the onions and garlic, stir and cook for 4 minutes.

Add the oats, sugar, salt, pepper, broth and thyme, mix, place in the air fryer and cook for 16 minutes at 360 ° F.

Meanwhile, prepare a pan over medium heat with the olive oil, add the mushrooms, cook for 3 minutes, add the

oatmeal and cheese, beat, divide into bowls and serve for breakfast.

Enjoy.

Nutritional value: per serving: calories 284|fat 8g| fiber 8g|-carbs 20g| protein 17g

270.   Green Bean Casserole
(Prep time: 10 min| Cook Time: 15 min | Serves 4)
Ingredients
- 4 tablespoons unsalted butter
- 1/4 cup diced yellow onion
- 1/2 cup chopped white mushrooms
- 1/2 cup heavy whipping cream
- ¼ cup low-fat cream cheese
- 1/2 cup chicken broth
- 1/4 teaspoon xanthan gum
- 4 cups fresh green beans, edges trimmed
- 1 tbsp. of pork rinds, finely ground

Instructions

Melt the butter in a medium saucepan over low heat. Saute the onion and mushrooms for about 3–5 minutes, before they become soft and fragrant.

Apply whipped cream, cream cheese and broth to the saucepan. Beat easily first. Bring to a boil, then reduce to a simmer. Sprinkle the xanthan gum into the pan and cook.

Cut the green beans into 2 "chunks and place them in a 4-cup circular baking dish. Pour over the sauce mixture and stir until cooked. Cover the bowl with the ground pork rinds.

Set the temperature to 320 ° F and change the timer for 15 minutes.

Top when fully cooked, browned and fork with tender green beans. Serve soft.

Nutritional value : per serving: calories: 267|protein: 3.6 g| fiber: 3.2 g| net carbohydrates: 6.5 g| fat: 23.4 g| |

271.   Bell Peppers Frittata
(Prep time: 10 min| Cooking time: 20 min| Servings: 4)
Ingredients
- 2 Tablespoons olive oil
- 2 cups chicken sausage, casings removed and chopped
- One sweet onion, chopped
- 1 red bell pepper, chopped
- 1 orange bell pepper, chopped
- 1 green bell pepper, chopped
- Salt and black pepper to taste
- 8 eggs, whisked
- ½ cup mozzarella cheese, shredded
- 2 teaspoons oregano, chopped

Instructions

Add 1 tablespoon of oil to the air fryer, add bacon, heat to 320 degrees F and sauté for 1 minute.

Remove the remaining butter, onion, red pepper, orange and white, mix and simmer for another 2 minutes.

Stir and cook for 15 minutes, add the oregano, salt, pepper and eggs.

Add the mozzarella, leave the omelette aside for a couple of

minutes, divide and serve between plates.
To enjoy.
Nutritional value: per serving: calories 212, fat 4g, fiber 6g, carbs 8g, protein 12g

272. Air Fryer Sweet & Sour Chicken
(Prep Time: 5 mints| Cook Time: 10 mints| Servings: 2)

Ingredients
Chicken
- 4 cups chicken breasts /thighs: cut into one-inch pieces
- Cornstarch: 2 tablespoons

Sweet & Sour Sauce
- Cornstarch: 2 tablespoons
- Pineapple juice: 1 cup
- Water: 2 tablespoons
- Honey: half cup
- Soy sauce: 1 tablespoon
- Rice wine vinegar: 3 tablespoons
- Ground ginger: 1/4 teaspoon

Optional
- 1/4 cup pineapple chunks
- 3-4 drops of red food coloring (for traditional orange look)

Instructions
Let the air fryer preheat to 400 degrees.
Coat the chicken with cornstarch until it is completely covered.
Place the chicken in the air fryer and cook for 7.9 minutes. Remove from the air fryer
Meanwhile, in a saucepan, add the pineapple juice, ginger, brown sugar, soy sauce and rice wine vinegar and cook. Let it simmer for five minutes.
Prepare a cornstarch paste and add the sauce. Let it simmer for a minute.
Cover the cooked chicken pieces and serve with steamed vegetables
Nutritional value : per serving: Cal 302|Fat: 8g| Carbs 18g|Protein 22g

273. Tasty Kale & Celery Crackers
(Prep time: 10 min| Cooking time: 20 min| Servings: 6)

Ingredients
- One cups flax seed, ground
- 1 cups flax seed, soaked overnight and drained
- 2 bunches kale, chopped
- 1 bunch basil, chopped
- ½ bunch celery, chopped
- 2 garlic cloves, minced
- 1/3 cup olive oil

Instructions
Mix the ground flaxseed with celery, kale, basil and garlic in the food processor and mix well.
• Add the oil and soaked flax seeds, then mix again, sprinkle into the air fryer pan, crack the medium crackers, and cook for 20 minutes at 380 degrees F.
Serve as an appetizer and divide into cups.
Enjoy

Nutritional Value: per serving: calories 143|fat 1g| fiber 2g| carbs 8g| Protein 4g
Optavia Lean & Green Pork Air-fry Recipes

274. Low Carb Pork Dumplings with Dipping Sauce
(Prep Time: 30 mints| Cook Time:20 mints| Servings: 6)

Ingredients
- 18 dumpling wrappers
- One teaspoon olive oil
- Bok choy: 4 cups(chopped)
- Rice vinegar: 2 tablespoons
- Diced ginger: 1 tablespoon
- Crushed red pepper: 1/4 teaspoon
- Diced garlic: 1 tablespoon
- Lean ground pork: half cup
- Cooking spray
- Lite soy sauce: 2 teaspoons
- Honey: half tsp.
- Toasted sesame oil: 1 teaspoon
- Finely chopped scallions

Instructions
In a large skillet, heat the olive oil, add the bok choy, cook for 6 minutes and add the garlic, ginger and cook for one minute. Transfer this mixture to a paper towel and pat dry any excess oil
In a bowl, add the mixture of bok choy, chopped chili and lean ground pork and mix well.
Place a gnocchi wrap on a plate and add a spoon. to fill half of the wrapper. With water, seal the edges and fold them.
Spray air fryer basket with air, add dumplings into air fryer basket and cook at 375 F for 12 minutes or until golden brown.
Meanwhile, to make the sauce, combine the sesame oil, rice vinegar, shallot, soy sauce and honey in a mixing bowl.
Serve the gnocchi with the sauce.
Nutritional value : per serving: Calories 140| Fat 5g |Protein 12g |Carbohydrate 9g|

275. Gluten-Free Air Fryer Chicken Fried Brown Rice
(Prep Time: 10 mints| Cook Time:20 mints| Servings: 2)

Ingredients
- Olive Oil Cooking Spray
- Chicken Breast: 1 Cup, Diced & Cooked &
- White Onion: 1/4 cup chopped
- Celery: 1/4 Cup chopped
- Cooked brown rice: 4 Cups
- Carrots: 1/4 cup chopped

Instructions
Place the foil on the air fryer basket, make sure to leave room for airflow, roll up on the sides
Spray the film with olive oil. Mix all the ingredients.
On top of the foil, add all the ingredients to the air fryer basket.
Give a splash of olive oil on the mixture.
Cook for five minutes at 390 ° F.

Open the air fryer and give the mixture a spin cook for another five minutes at 390 ° F.
Remove from air fryer and serve hot.
Nutritional value : per serving: Cal 350|Fat: 6g|Carbs 20g|Protein 22g

276. Air Fryer Cheesy Pork Chops
(Prep Time: 5mints| Cook Time:8 mints| Servings: 2)
Ingredients
- 4 lean pork chops
- Salt: half tsp.
- Garlic powder: half tsp.
- Shredded cheese: 4 tbsp.
- Chopped cilantro

Instructions
Let the air fryer preheat to 350 degrees.
With garlic, coriander and salt, rub the pork chops. Put the air fryer on. Let it cook for four minutes. Flip them over and cook for another two minutes.
Add the cheese on top and cook for another two minutes or until the cheese has melted.
Serve with salad.
Nutritional value : per serving: Calories: 467kcal | Protein: 61g | Fat: 22g | Saturated Fat: 8g |

277. Air Fryer Pork Chop & Broccoli
(Prep Time: 20 mints| Cook Time:20 mints| Servings: 2)
Ingredients
- Broccoli florets: 2 cups
- Bone-in pork chop: 2 pieces
- Paprika: half tsp.
- Avocado oil: 2 tbsp.
- Garlic powder: half tsp.
- Onion powder: half tsp.
- Two cloves of crushed garlic
- Salt: 1 teaspoon divided

Instructions
Let the air fryer preheat to 350 degrees. Spray the basket with cooking oil
Add a spoon. Oil, onion powder, half a teaspoon. of salt, garlic powder and paprika in a bowl mix well, rub this spice mixture on the sides of the pork chop
Add the pork chops to the fryer basket and cook for five minutes
Meanwhile, add a teaspoon. oil, garlic, half a teaspoon of salt and broccoli in a bowl and coat them well
Turn the pork chop and add the broccoli, let it cook for another five minutes.
Remove from air fryer and serve.
Nutritional value : per serving: Calories 483|Total Fat 20g|Carbohydrates 12g|protein 23 g

278. Mustard Glazed Air Fryer Pork Tenderloin
(Prep Time: 10 mints| Cook Time:18 mints| Servings: 4)
Ingredients
- Yellow mustard: ¼ cup

- One pork tenderloin
- Salt: ¼ tsp
- Honey: 3 Tbsp.
- Freshly ground black pepper: ⊠ tsp
- Minced garlic: 1 Tbsp.
- Dried rosemary: 1 tsp
- Italian seasoning: 1 tsp

Instructions
Using a knife, cut the top of the pork tenderloin. Add the garlic (minced) into the cuts. Then sprinkle with kosher salt and pepper.
In a bowl, add the honey, mustard, rosemary, and Italian seasoning mixture until well blended. Rub this mustard mix all over the pork.
Leave to marinate in the refrigerator for at least two hours.
Place the pork tenderloin in the basket of the air fryer. Cook for 18-20 minutes at 400 F. With an instant read thermometer the internal temperature of the pig should be 145 F.
Remove from air fryer and serve with a side of salad.
Nutritional value : per serving: Calories: 390 | Carbohydrates: 11g | Protein: 59g | Fat: 11g |

279. Air Fryer Pork Taquitos
(Prep Time: 10 mints| Cook Time:20 mints| Servings: 10)
Ingredients
- Pork tenderloin: 3 cups, cooked & shredded
- Cooking spray
- Shredded mozzarella: 2 and 1/2 cups, fat-free
- 10 small tortillas
- Salsa for dipping
- One juice of a lime

Instructions
Allow the air fryer to preheat to 380 F.
Add the lime juice to the pork and mix well
With a damp towel over the tortilla, microwave for ten seconds to soften it
Add the pork filling and cheese on top, in a tortilla, roll the tortilla tightly
Place the tortillas on a greased baking sheet
Sprinkle oil on the tortillas. Bake for 7-10 minutes or until the tortillas are golden, turn them halfway.
Serve with salad.
Nutritional value : per serving: Cal 253 |Fat: 18g| Carbs: 10g| Protein: 20g|

280. Pork Rind Nachos
(Prep time: 5 min| Cooking Time: 5 min| Serves 2)
Ingredients
- 2 tbsp. of pork rinds
- 1/4 cup shredded cooked chicken
- 1/2 cup shredded Monterey jack cheese
- 1/4 cup sliced pickled jalapeños
- 1/4 cup guacamole
- 1/4 cup full-fat sour cream

Instructions
Place the pork rinds in a 6-inch round pan. Fill with grilled chicken and Monterey jack cheese. Place the pan in the basket with the air fryer.

Set the temperature to 370 ° F and set the timer for 5 minutes or until the cheese has melted.
Eat immediately with jalapeños, guacamole, and sour cream.
Nutritional value : per serving: calories 295 |protein: 30.1 g| fiber: 1.2 g| net carbohydrates: 1.8 g |fat: 27.5 g| carbohydrates: 3.0 g |

281. Air Fried Jamaican Jerk Pork Recipe
(Prep Time: 10 mints| Cook Time:20 mints| Servings: 4)
Ingredients
• 　　　Pork, cut into three-inch pieces
• 　　　Jerk paste : ¼ cup
Instructions
Rub the jerk dough on all the pork pieces.
Leave to marinate for at least four hours in the refrigerator. Or for longer.
Allow the air fryer to preheat to 390 F. Spray with olive oil
Before placing in the air fryer, allow the meat to rest for 20 minutes at room temperature.
Cook for 20 minutes at 390 ° F in the air fryer, turn halfway.
Remove from air fryer and let sit for ten minutes before slicing.
Serve with microgreens.
Nutritional value : per serving: Calories: 234kcal | Protein: 31g | Fat: 9g |carbs 12 g

282. Air Fryer Whole Wheat Crusted Pork Chops
(Prep Time: 10 mints| Cook Time:12 mints| Servings: 4)
Ingredients
• 　　　Whole-wheat breadcrumbs: 1 cup
• 　　　Salt: ¼ teaspoon
• 　　　Pork chops: 2-4 pieces (center cut and boneless)
• 　　　Chili powder: half teaspoon
• 　　　Parmesan cheese: 1 tablespoon
• 　　　Paprika: 1½ teaspoons
• 　　　One egg beaten
• 　　　Onion powder: half teaspoon
• 　　　Granulated garlic: half teaspoon
• 　　　Pepper, to taste
Instructions
Allow the air fryer to preheat to 400 F.
rub kosher salt on each side of the pork chops, let it rest
Add the beaten egg to a large bowl
Add the parmesan, breadcrumbs, garlic, pepper, paprika, chilli powder and onion powder to a bowl and mix well
Dip the pork chop in the egg and then in the breadcrumbs
Put it in the air fryer and spray it with oil.
Leave to cook for 12 minutes at 400 F. turn it upside down, halfway through cooking. Cook for another six minutes.
Serve with salad.
Nutritional value : per serving: 425 calories|20 g fat| 5 g fiber|31 g protein| Carbs 19 g
Optavia Lean & Green Seafood Air-fry Recipes

283. Air Fryer Scallops with Tomato Cream Sauce
(Prep Time: 5 mints| Cook Time:10 mints| Servings: 2)
Ingredients
• 　　　Sea scallops eight jumbo
• 　　　Tomato Paste: 1 tbsp.
• 　　　Chopped fresh basil one tablespoon
• 　　　3/4 cup of low-fat Whipping Cream
• 　　　Kosher salt half teaspoon
• 　　　Ground Freshly black pepper half teaspoon
• 　　　Minced garlic 1 teaspoon
• 　　　Frozen Spinach, thawed half cup
• 　　　Oil Spray
Instructions
Take a seven-inch (heat-resistant) pan and add the spinach in a single layer on the bottom
Rub the olive oil on both sides of the scallops, season with salt and kosher pepper.
over the spinach, place the seasoned scallops
Place the pan in the air fryer and cook for ten minutes at 350F, until the scallops are cooked through and the internal temperature reaches 135F.
Serve immediately.
Nutritional value : per serving: Calories: 259kcal | Carbohydrates: 6g | Protein: 19g | Fat: 13g |

284. Shrimp Spring Rolls
(Prep Time: 10 mints| Cook Time:25 mints| Servings: 4)
Ingredients
• 　　　Deveined raw shrimp: half cup chopped(peeled)
• 　　　Olive oil: 2 and 1/2 tbsp.
• 　　　Matchstick carrots: 1 cup
• 　　　Slices of red bell pepper: 1 cup
• 　　　Red pepper: 1/4 teaspoon(crushed)
• 　　　Slices of snow peas: 3/4 cup
• 　　　Shredded cabbage: 2 cups
• 　　　Lime juice: 1 tablespoon
• 　　　Sweet chili sauce: half cup
• 　　　Fish sauce: 2 teaspoons
• 　　　Eight spring roll(wrappers)
Instructions
In a pan, add one and a half tablespoons. of olive, until it smokes lightly. Mix the pepper, cabbage, carrots and cook for two minutes. Turn off the heat, take out into a baking dish and let it cool for five minutes.
In a bowl, add the prawns, lime juice, cabbage mixture, chopped red pepper, fish sauce, and snow peas. Mix well
Arrange the spring rolls on a plate. Add 1/4 cup of the filling to the center of each wrapper. Fold firmly with water. Brush the olive oil over the folded buns.
Place the spring rolls in the basket of the air fryer and cook for 6-7 minutes at 390 ° F until golden and crisp.
It can be served with sweet chilli sauce.
Nutritional value : per serving: Calories 180 |Fat 9g| Protein 17g |Carbohydrate 9g

285. Air Fryer Southern Style Catfish with Green Beans

(Prep Time: 10 mints| Cook Time:20 mints| Servings: 2)

Ingredients

- Catfish fillets: 2 pieces
- Green beans: half cup, trimmed
- Honey: 2 teaspoon
- Freshly ground black pepper and salt, to taste divided
- Crushed red pepper: half tsp.
- Flour: 1/4 cup
- One egg, lightly beaten
- Dill pickle relish: 3/4 teaspoon
- Apple cider vinegar: half tsp
- 1/3 cup whole-wheat breadcrumbs
- Mayonnaise: 2 tablespoons
- Dill
- Lemon wedges

Instructions

In a bowl, add the green beans, sprinkle them with cooking oil. Sprinkle with chopped red pepper, 1/8 teaspoon kosher salt and half a teaspoon. Of honey and cook in the air fryer at 400 F until soft and golden, for 12 minutes. Remove from the fryer and cover with aluminum foil

Meanwhile, sprinkle the catfish with flour. Then pass it in the egg to cover, then in the breadcrumbs. Place the fish in an air fryer basket and drizzle with cooking oil.

Bake for 8 minutes, at 400ºF, until cooked and golden.

Sprinkle with pepper and salt. Meanwhile, mix the vinegar, dill, dressing, mayonnaise, and honey in a bowl. Serve the sauce with fish and green beans.

Nutritional value : per serving: Cal 243| fat 18 g| Carbs 18 g| Protein 33 g

286. Easy Shrimp PO' Boy

(Prep Time: 20 mints| Cook Time:10 mints| Servings: 4)

Ingredients

- Iceberg lettuce: 2 cups shredded
- Shrimp:4 cups, deveined
- Buttermilk: 1/4 cup
- Fish Fry Coating : 1/2 cup
- Creole Seasoning : 1 teaspoon
- Eight slices of tomato

Remoulade Sauce

- Creole Seasoning : half tsp.
- Mayo : half cup(reduced-fat)
- Half lemon's juice
- Dijon mustard: 1 tsp
- Worcestershire: 1 tsp
- Minced garlic: one tsp.
- One green onion chopped
- Hot sauce: one tsp

Instructions

Remoulade Sauce

Mix all ingredients in a bowl. Chill in Refrigerator.

Shrimp

In a zip lock bag, add the buttermilk and creole dressing with shrimp and mix well, marinate for half an hour.

With cooking oil, spray the basket of the air fryer. Place the shrimp in the basket of the air fryer.

Sprinkle the shrimp with olive oil.

Cook at 400 F for five minutes. Flip the shrimp and cook for another five minutes.

Add the remoulade sauce on the wholemeal bread. Then add the tomato slices and the lettuce on top, then the shrimp. Enjoy

Nutritional value per serving: 247 Kcal| total fat 19.3g |carbohydrates 15.6g | protein 24.7g

287. Shrimp Scampi

(Prep Time: 5 mints| Cook Time:10 mints| Servings: 2)

Ingredients

- Raw Shrimp: 4 cups
- Lemon Juice: 1 tablespoon
- Chopped fresh basil
- Red Pepper Flakes: 2 teaspoons
- Butter: 2.5 tablespoons
- Chopped chives
- Chicken Stock: 2 tablespoons
- Minced Garlic: 1 tablespoon

Instructions

Let the air fryer preheat with a metal skillet to 330 ° F

In the hot pan, add the garlic, the red pepper flakes and half the butter. Let it cook for two minutes.

Add the butter, prawns, chicken stock, minced garlic, chives, lemon juice and basil to the pan. Let it cook for five minutes. Dip the shrimp in the melted butter.

Remove from the air fryer and let it rest for one minute.

Add the fresh basil leaves and chives and serve.

Nutritional value : per serving: 287 Kcal |total fat 5.5g |carbohydrates 7.5g | protein 18g

288. Quick & Easy Air Fryer Salmon

(Prep Time: 5 mints| Cook Time:12 mints| Servings: 4)

Ingredients

- Lemon pepper seasoning : 2 teaspoons
- Salmon: 4 cups
- Olive oil : one tablespoon
- Seafood seasoning :2 teaspoons
- Half lemon's juice
- Garlic powder:1 teaspoon
- Kosher salt to taste

Instructions

In a bowl, add a spoon. of olive oil and half lemon juice.

Pour this mixture over the salmon and rub. Leave the skin on the salmon. It will come off when cooked.

Rub the salmon with kosher salt and spices.

Place the parchment paper in the basket of the air fryer. Put the salmon in the air fryer.

Cook at 360 degrees for ten minutes. Cook until the internal temperature of the salmon reaches 140 F.

Let the salmon rest for five minutes before serving.

Serve with salad and lemon wedges.

Nutritional value : per serving: 132 Cal| total fat 7.4g |carbohydrates 12 g| protein 22.1g

289. Air Fryer Sushi Roll

(Prep Time: 1 hour 30 mints| Cook Time:10 mints| Servings: 3)

Ingredients

For the Kale Salad

- Rice vinegar: half teaspoon
- Chopped kale: one and a 1/2 cups
- Garlic powder:1/8 teaspoon
- Sesame seeds: 1 tablespoon
- Toasted sesame oil: 3/4 teaspoon
- Ground ginger: 1/4 teaspoon
- Soy sauce: 3/4 teaspoon
- Sushi Rolls
- Half avocado - sliced
- Cooked Sushi Rice - cooled
- Whole wheat breadcrumbs: half cup
- Sushi: 3 sheets

Instructions

Make the Kale Salad

In a bowl, add vinegar, garlic powder, kale, soy sauce, sesame oil, and ground ginger. With your hands, mix with sesame seeds and set it aside.

Sushi Rolls

Place a sheet of sushi on a flat surface. With damp fingertips, add a spoonful of rice and spread it on the pastry. Cover the paper with the rice, leaving a half-inch space at one end.

Add the kale salad with avocado slices. Roll up sushi, use water if needed.

Add the breadcrumbs to a bowl. Coat the sushi roll with Sriracha Mayo, then in the breadcrumbs.

Add the rolls to the air fryer. Cook for ten minutes at 390 ° F, shake the basket in half.

Take them out of the fryer and let them cool, then cut them with a sharp knife.

Serve with soy sauce.

Nutritional value per serving: Calories: 369cal| Fat: 13.9g|Carbohydrates: 15g|Protein: 26.3g

290. Air Fryer Garlic-Lime Shrimp Kebabs

(Prep Time: 5 mints| Cook Time:18 mints| Servings: 2)

Ingredients

- One lime
- Raw shrimp: 1 cup
- Salt: 1/8 teaspoon
- 1 clove of garlic
- Freshly ground black pepper

Instructions

Leave the wooden skewers to soak in water for 20 minutes.

Allow the air fryer to preheat to 350F.

In a bowl, mix the prawns, minced garlic, lime juice, kosher salt and pepper

Add the prawns on the skewers.

Place the skewers in the air fryer and cook for 8 minutes. Turn halfway.

Top with cilantro and your favorite sauce.

Nutritional value : per serving: Calories: 76kcal | Carbohydrates: 4g | Protein: 13g |fat 9 g

291. Air Fryer Parmesan Shrimp

(Prep Time: 5 mints| Cook Time:10 mints| Servings: 4)

Ingredients

- Olive oil: 2 tablespoons
- Jumbo cooked shrimp: 8 cups, peeled, deveined
- Parmesan cheese: 2/3 cup(grated)
- Onion powder: 1 teaspoon
- Pepper: 1 teaspoon
- Four cloves of minced garlic
- Oregano: 1/2 teaspoon
- Basil: 1 teaspoon
- Lemon wedges

Instructions

Mix the Parmesan, onion powder, oregano, olive oil, garlic, basil and pepper in a bowl. Coat the shrimp in this mixture.

Spray oil on the basket of the air fryer, put the shrimp in it.

Bake for ten minutes, at 350 F, or until golden brown.

Season the shrimp with lemon before serving with a microgreen salad.

Nutritional value: per serving: Cal 198| Fat: 13 g| Carbs: 5.6 g| Protein: 12.7g

292. Fish Finger Sandwich

(Prep Time: 10 mints| Cook Time:20 mints| Servings: 3)

Ingredients

- Greek yogurt: 1 tbsp.
- Cod fillets: 4, without skin
- Flour: 2 tbsp.
- Whole-wheat breadcrumbs: 5 tbsp.
- Kosher salt and pepper, to taste
- Capers: 10–12
- Frozen peas: 3/4 cup
- Lemon juice

Instructions

Allow the air fryer to preheat.

Sprinkle the cod fillets with salt and kosher pepper and pass them in the flour, then in the breadcrumbs

Spray the fryer basket with oil. Put the cod fillets in the basket.

Cook for 15 minutes at 200 C.

Meanwhile, cook the peas in boiling water for a few minutes. Remove from the water and blend with Greek yogurt, lemon juice and capers until smooth.

On a sandwich, add the cooked fish with the pea puree. Add the lettuce and tomato.

Nutritional value : per serving: Cal 240| Fat: 12g| Net Carbs: 7g| Protein: 20g

293. Healthy Air Fryer Tuna Patties

(Prep Time: 15 mints| Cook Time:10 mints| Servings: 10)

Ingredients

- Whole wheat breadcrumbs: half cup
- Fresh tuna: 4 cups, diced
- Lemon zest
- Lemon juice: 1 Tablespoon

- 1 egg
- Grated parmesan cheese: 3 Tablespoons
- One chopped stalk celery
- Garlic powder: half teaspoon
- Dried herbs: half teaspoon
- Minced onion: 3 Tablespoons
- Salt , to taste
- Freshly ground black pepper

Instructions

In a bowl, add the lemon zest, breadcrumbs, salt, pepper, celery, eggs, dried herbs, lemon juice, garlic powder, parmesan and onion. Mix everything. Then gently add the tuna. Shape of the meatballs. If the mixture is too loose, chill in the refrigerator.

Add the air fryer parchment paper to the air fryer basket. Spray the baking paper with cooking spray.

Sprinkle the meatballs with oil.

Cook for ten minutes at 360 ° F. Turn the meatballs in half.

Serve with lemon slices and microgreens.

Nutritional value : per serving: Cal 214| Fat: 15g| Net Carbs: 6g| Protein: 22g

294.   Crab Cakes

(Prep Time: 10 mints| Cook Time:20 mints| Servings: 6)

Ingredients

- Crab meat: 4 cups
- Two eggs
- Whole wheat bread crumbs: ¼ cup
- Mayonnaise: 2 tablespoons
- Worcestershire sauce: 1 teaspoon
- Old Bay seasoning: 1 and ½ teaspoon
- Dijon mustard: 1 teaspoon
- Freshly ground black pepper to taste
- Green onion: ¼ cup, chopped

Instructions

In a bowl, add the Dijon mustard, Old Bay, eggs, Worcestershire and mayonnaise and mix well. Then add the chopped green onion and mix.

Incorporate the crab meat into the mayonnaise. Then add the breadcrumbs, so as not to mix too much.

Chill the mixture in the refrigerator for at least 60 minutes. Then shape into meatballs.

Allow the air fryer to preheat to 350F. Cook for 10 minutes. Flip the meatballs in half.

Serve with lemon wedges.

Nutritional value : per serving: Cal 218| Fat: 13 g| Net Carbs: 5.6 g| Protein: 16.7g

295.   Air Fryer Crispy Fish Sandwich

(Prep Time: 10 mints| Cook Time:10 mints| Servings: 2)

Ingredients

- Cod :2 fillets.
- All-purpose flour: 2 tablespoons
- Pepper: 1/4 teaspoon
- Lemon juice: 1 tablespoon
- Salt: 1/4 teaspoon
- Garlic powder : half teaspoon
- One egg

- Mayo : half tablespoon
- Whole wheat bread crumbs : half cup

Instructions

In a bowl, add salt, flour, pepper, and garlic powder.

In a separate bowl, add the lemon juice, mayonnaise and egg.

In another bowl, add the breadcrumbs.

Pass the fish in the flour, then in the egg, then in the breadcrumbs.

With cooking oil, spray the basket and place the fish in the basket. Also, sprinkle the fish with cooking oil.

Cook at 400 F for ten minutes. This fish is soft, be careful if you turn it.

Nutritional Value: per serving: Cal 218| Net Carbs:7g| Fat:12g| Protein: 22g

296.   Crispy Air Fryer Fish

(Prep Time: 10 mints| Cook Time:17 mints| Servings: 4)

Ingredients

- Old bay: 2 tsp
- 4-6, cut in half, Whiting Fish fillets
- Fi ne cornmeal: ¾ cup
- Flour: ¼ cup
- Paprika : 1 tsp
- Garlic powder : half tsp
- Salt: 1 and ½ tsp
- Freshly ground black pepper: half tsp

Instructions

In a zip lock bag, add all the ingredients and cover them with the fish fillets.

Spray oil on the basket of the air fryer and put the fish in it.

Cook for ten minutes at 400 F. Flip the fish if necessary and coat with oil spray and cook for another seven minutes.

Serve with green salad.

Nutritional value : per serving: 254 Kcal| fat 12.7g|carbohydrates8.2g |protein 17.5g.

297.   Air Fryer Fish and Chips

(Prep Time: 10 mints| Cook Time:35 mints| Servings: 4)

Ingredients

- 4 cups of any fish fillet
- flour: 1/4 cup
- Whole wheat breadcrumbs: one cup
- One egg
- Oil: 2 tbsp.
- Potatoes
- Salt : 1 tsp.

Instructions

Cut the potatoes into French fries. Then cover with oil and salt.

Cook in the air fryer for 20 minutes at 400 F, toss the fries in half.

Meanwhile pass the fish in the flour, then in the beaten egg and finally in the breadcrumbs.

Place the fish in the air fryer and let it cook at 330 ° C for 15 minutes.

Flip it halfway if necessary.

Serve with tartar sauce and green salad.

Nutritional value : per serving: Calories: 409kcal | Carbohydrates: 44g | Protein: 30g | Fat: 11g |

298.   Air-Fried Rosemary Garlic Grilled Prawns

(Prep Time: 5 mints| Cook Time:10 mints| Servings: 2)

Ingredients

- Melted butter: 1/2 tbsp.
- Green capsicum: slices
- Eight prawns
- Rosemary leaves
- Kosher salt& freshly ground black pepper
- 3-4 cloves of minced garlic

Instructions

In a bowl, mix all the ingredients and marinate the shrimp for at least 60 minutes or more

Add two prawns and two slices of pepper to each skewer.

Let the air fryer preheat to 360 F

Cook for 5-6 mints. Then change the temperature to 400F and cook for another minute.

Serve with lemon wedges.

Nutritional value : per serving: Cal 194 |Fat: 10g|Carbohydrates: 12g|protein: 26g

299.   Air Fryer Shrimp Tacos

(Prep Time: 20 mints| Cook Time:10 mints| Servings: 4)

Ingredients

- Flour tortillas: 12
- Avocado sliced: 1 cup
- Chipotle chili powder: 1 tsp
- Raw jumbo shrimp: 24 pieces, deveined, peeled, without tail
- Smoked paprika: 1/2 tsp
- Salt: 1/4 tsp
- Olive oil: 1 tbsp.
- Green salsa: ½ cup
- Light brown sugar: 1 and 1/2 tsp
- Garlic powder: 1/2 tsp
- Low-fat sour cream: 1/2 cup
- Red onion: 1/2 cup diced

Instructions

Allow the oven to preheat to 400 F and spray the air fryer basket with spray oil.

In a bowl, mix the chipotle pepper powder, salt, brown sugar, smoked paprika and garlic powder, mix well

Dry the shrimp, place them in a zip lock bag and add the toppings and mix well to coat

Place the shrimp in the basket of the air fryer in an even layer, cook for four minutes and turn too much for another four minutes

For the sauce, mix the sour cream and salsa verde.

Place the shrimp in a tortilla, garnish with salsa, shrimp, red onion, sliced avocado and serve with lime wedges.

Nutritional value : per serving: Cal 228| Fat: 18 |carbs: 16 g| Protein: 20 g

300.   Sriracha & Honey Tossed Calamari

(Prep Time: 10 mints| Cook Time:20 mints| Servings: 2)

Ingredients

- Club soda: 1 cup
- Sriracha: 1-2 Tbsp.
- Calamari tubes: 2 cups
- Flour: 1 cup
- Pinches of salt, freshly ground black pepper, red pepper flakes, and red pepper
- Honey: 1/2 cup

Instructions

Cut the squid tubes into rings. Soak them with club soda. Let it sit for ten minutes.

Meanwhile, in a bowl, add freshly ground black pepper, flour, chilli and kosher salt and mix well.

Drain the squid and pat them with absorbent paper. Coat the squid well in the flour mixture and set aside.

Spray the oil into the basket of the air fryer and place the squid in a single layer.

Cook at 375 for 11 minutes. Throw the rings twice during cooking. Meanwhile, make the honey sauce, chili flakes and sriracha in a bowl, fine.

Remove the squid from the basket, mix them with the sauce and cook for another two minutes. Serve with green salad.

Nutritional value: per serving: Cal 252 | Fat: 38g| Carbs: 3.1g|Protein: 41g

301.   Air Fryer Lemon Pepper Shrimp

(Prep Time: 5 mints| Cook Time:10 mints| Servings: 2)

Ingredients

- Raw shrimp: 1 and 1/2 cup peeled, deveined
- Olive oil: 1/2 tablespoon
- Garlic powder: ¼ tsp
- Lemon pepper: 1 tsp
- Paprika: ¼ tsp
- Juice of one lemon

Instructions

Allow the air fryer to preheat to 400 F.

In a bowl, mix the lemon pepper, olive oil, paprika, garlic powder and lemon juice. Mix well. Add the prawns and cover well

Add shrimps in the air fryer, cook for 6,8 minutes and top with lemon slices and serve

Nutritional value : per serving: Calories 237 |Fat 6g|Carbohydrates 11g|Protein 36g

302.   Air Fryer Sesame Seeds Fish Fillet

(Prep Time: 10 mints| Cook Time:20 mints| Servings: 2)

Ingredients

- Plain flour: 3 tablespoons
- One egg, beaten
- Five frozen fish fillets

For Coating

- Oil: 2 tablespoons
- Sesame seeds: 1/2 cup
- Rosemary herbs

- 5-6 biscuit's crumbs
- Kosher salt& pepper, to taste

Instructions

For two minutes, brown the sesame seeds in a pan, without oil. Brown them and set aside.

In a dish, mix all the ingredients of the coating

Place the aluminum foil on the basket of the air fryer and let it preheat to 200 C.

First, sprinkle the fish in the flour. Then in the egg, then in the coating mixture.

Place in the air fryer. If the fillets are frozen, cook for ten minutes, then turn the fillet and cook for another four minutes.

If not frozen, cook for eight minutes and two minutes.

Nutritional value : per serving: Cal 250| Fat: 8g| Net Carbs: 12.4g| Protein: 20g

303.   Easy Shrimp Egg Rolls
(Prep Time: 20 mints| Cook Time:20 mints| Servings: 6)
Ingredients
- 2-3 cloves of minced garlic
- 12-14   egg roll wrappers
- 2-3 cloves of minced garlic
- Raw shrimp (roughly chopped): 4 cups, peeled and deveined
- Coleslaw mix: 3 cups
- Sesame oil : 1 and 1/2 teaspoons
- Soy sauce : 1 tablespoon
- Fish sauce : 1 teaspoon
- Salt, pepper to taste
- Grated ginger : half tsp.
- Two green onions chopped
- Water: one cup

Instructions

In a skillet, add the shrimp with garlic, kosher salt and pepper, drizzle with cooking oil and sauté until shrimp turn pink. Turn off the heat and set it aside.

In a bowl, add the coleslaw mixture, cooked shrimp, green onions, fish sauce, soy sauce, sesame oil, and ginger. Mix well.

Add two tablespoons. Filling, in each wrapper, seal tightly with water.

With cooking oil, spray the basket of the air fryer. Place the egg rolls in a single layer in the basket. Spray with cooking oil.

Cook for 7 minutes at 400 degrees. Flip the rolls, then cook for another five minutes.

Serve with green micro salad.

Nutritional value: per serving: 228 calories|11g fat|11g carbs|20g protein

304.   Perfect Air Fryer Salmon Fillets
(Prep Time: 5 mints| Cook Time:15 mints| Servings: 2)
Ingredients
- Low-fat Greek yogurt: 1/4 cup
- Two salmon fillets
- Fresh dill: 1 tbsp. (chopped)
- One lemon and lemon juice
- Garlic powder : half tsp.
- Kosher salt and pepper

Instructions

Cut the lemon into slices and place it on the bottom of the air fryer basket.

Season the salmon with kosher salt and pepper. Place the salmon on top of the lemons.

Cook at 330 degrees for 15 minutes.

Meanwhile, mix the garlic powder, lemon juice, salt, pepper with the yogurt and dill.

Serve the fish with the sauce.

Nutritional value : per serving: Calories: 194kcal | Carbohydrates: 6g | Protein: 25g | Fat: 7g

305.   Air Fryer Salmon with Maple Soy Glaze
(Prep Time: 5 mints| Cook Time:8 mints| Servings: 4)
Ingredients
- Pure maple syrup: 3 tbsp.
- Gluten-free soy sauce: 3 tbsp.
- Sriracha hot sauce: 1 tbsp.
- One clove of minced garlic
- Salmon: 4 fillets, skinless

Instructions

In a zip lock bag, mix sriracha, maple syrup, garlic and soy sauce with the salmon.

Mix well and leave to marinate for at least half an hour.

Allow the air fryer to preheat to 400F. spray the basket with oil

Remove the fish from the marinade and dry it.

Place the salmon in the air fryer, cook for 7 - 8 minutes or longer.

Meanwhile, in a saucepan, add the marinade, let it simmer until reduced by half.

Add the glaze on the salmon and serve.

Nutritional value : per serving: Calories 292| Carbohydrates: 12g| Protein: 35g|Fat: 11g|

306.   Basil-Parmesan Crusted Salmon
(Prep Time: 5 mints| Cook Time:15 mints| Servings: 4)
Ingredients
- Grated Parmesan: 3 tablespoons
- Skinless four salmon fillets
- Salt: 1/4 teaspoon
- Freshly ground black pepper
- Low-fat mayonnaise: 3 tablespoons
- Basil leaves, chopped
- Half lemon

Instructions

Allow the air fryer to preheat to 400F. Spray the basket with olive oil.

Season the salmon with salt, pepper and lemon juice.

In a bowl, mix two tablespoons of Parmesan cheese with the mayonnaise and basil leaves.

Add this mixture and more Parmesan on top of the salmon and cook for seven minutes or until cooked through.

Serve hot.

Nutritional value : per serving: Calories: 289kcal|Carbohydrates: 1.5g|Protein: 30g|Fat: 18.5g

307. VBreaded Air Fried Shrimp with Bang Bang Sauce

(Prep Time: 10 mints| Cook Time:20 mints| Servings: 4)

Ingredients
- Whole wheat bread crumbs : 3/4 cup
- Raw shrimp: 4 cups, deveined, peeled
- Flour: half cup
- Paprika : one tsp
- Chicken Seasoning, to taste
- 2 tbsp. of one egg white
- Kosher salt and pepper to taste

Bang Bang Sauce
- Sweet chili sauce: 1/4 cup
- Plain Greek yogurt: 1/3 cup
- Sriracha : 2 tbsp.

Instructions

Let the air fryer preheat to 400 degrees.

Add the seasonings to the shrimp and coat well.

In three separate bowls, add the flour, breadcrumbs and egg whites.

First pass the prawns in the flour, dab them lightly in the egg whites, then in the breadcrumbs.

With cooking oil, sprinkle the shrimp.

Place the shrimp in an air fryer, cook for four minutes, flip the shrimp and cook for another four minutes. Serve with micro green sauce and bang bang.

Bang Bang Sauce

In a small bowl, mix all the ingredients. And serve.

Nutritional value: per serving: 229 calories| total fat 10g | carbohydrates 13g |protein 22g.

308. Grilled Salmon with Lemon, Soy Sauce

(Prep Time: 10 mints| Cook Time:20 mints| Servings: 4)

Ingredients
- Olive oil: 2 tablespoons
- Two Salmon fillets
- Lemon juice
- Water: 1/3 cup
- Gluten-free soy sauce: 1/3 cup
- Honey: 1/3 cup
- Scallion slices
- Cherry tomato
- Freshly ground black pepper, garlic powder, kosher salt to taste

Instructions

Season salmon with pepper and salt

In a bowl, mix honey, soy sauce, lemon juice, water, oil. Add salmon in this marinade and let it rest for least two hours.

Let the air fryer preheat at 360F

Place fish in the air fryer and cook for 8 minutes.

Move to a dish and top with scallion slices.

Nutritional value : per serving: Cal 211| fat 9g |protein 15g|

carbs 4.9g

309. Garlic Parmesan Crusted Salmon

(Prep Time: 5 mints| Cook Time:15 mints| Servings: 2)

Ingredients
- Whole wheat breadcrumbs: 1/4 cup
- 4 cups of salmon
- Butter melted: 2 tablespoons
- ¼ tsp of freshly ground black pepper
- Parmesan cheese: 1/4 cup(grated)
- Minced garlic: 2 teaspoons
- Half teaspoon of Italian seasoning

Instructions

Allow the air fryer to preheat to 400 F, spray the oil on the basket of the air fryer.

Dry the salmon. In a bowl, mix the Parmesan, Italian dressing, and breadcrumbs. In another pan, mix the melted butter with the garlic and add it to the breadcrumbs mixture. Mix well

Add kosher salt and freshly ground black pepper to the salmon. On top of each piece of salmon, add the crust mixture and press gently.

Let the air fryer preheat to 400 F and add the salmon. Cook until ready.

• Serve hot with vegetable side dishes.

Nutritional value : per serving: Calories 330 |Fat 19g|Carbohydrates 11g|Protein 31g

310. Air Fried Cajun Salmon

(Prep Time: 10 mints| Cook Time:20 mints| Servings: 1)

Ingredients
- Fresh salmon: 1 piece
- Cajun seasoning: 2 tbsp.
- Lemon juice.

Instructions

Allow the air fryer to preheat to 180 C.

Dry the salmon fillet. Rub the lemon juice and Cajun seasoning on the fish fillet.

Place in the air fryer, cook for 7 minutes. Serve with salad and lime wedges.

Nutritional value : per serving: 216 Cal| total fat 19g |carbohydrates 5.6g |protein 19.2g

311.   Air Fryer Lemon Cod

(Prep Time: 5 mints| Cook Time:10 mints| Servings: 1)

Ingredients

- One cod fillet
- Dried parsley
- Kosher salt and pepper, to taste
- Garlic salt
- One lemon

Instructions

In a bowl, mix all the ingredients and cover the fish fillet with the spices.

Slice the lemon and place it on the bottom of the air fryer basket.

Put the spiced fish on top. Cover the fish with lemon slices.

Cook for ten minutes at 375F, the internal temperature of the fish should be 145F.

Serve with green micro salad.

Nutritional value : per serving: Calories: 101kcal | Carbohydrates: 10g | Protein: 16g | Fat: 1g |

312.   Air-Fried Panko-Crusted Fish Nuggets

(Prep Time: 15 mints| Cook Time:10 mints| Servings: 4)

Ingredients

- Fish fillets in cubes: 2 cups(skinless)
- 1 egg, beaten
- Flour: 5 tablespoons
- Water: 5 tablespoons
- Kosher salt and pepper, to taste
- Breadcrumbs mix
- Smoked paprika: 1 tablespoon
- Whole wheat breadcrumbs: ¼ cup
- Garlic powder: 1 tablespoon

Instructions

Season the fish cubes with salt and kosher pepper.

In a bowl, add the flour and gradually add the water, stirring as you add.

Then incorporate the egg. And keep mixing but don't mix too much.

Sprinkle the cubes with the batter and then with the breadcrumbs. Coat well

Put the cubes in a pan and sprinkle with oil.

Allow the air fryer to preheat to 200 C.

Place the cubes in the air fryer and cook for 12 minutes or until they are well cooked and golden.

Serve with salad.

Nutritional value : per serving: Cal   184.2|Protei n : 1 9g| Total Fa t : 3.3 g| Net Carb: 10g

313.   Roasted Salmon with Fennel Salad

(Prep Time: 15 mints| Cook Time:10 mints| Servings: 4)

Ingredients

- Skinless and center-cut: 4 salmon fillets
- Lemon juice: 1 teaspoon(fresh)
- Parsley: 2 teaspoons(chopped)
- Salt: 1 teaspoon, divided
- Olive oil: 2 tablespoons
- Chopped thyme: 1 teaspoon
- Fennel heads: 4 cups (thinly sliced)
- One clove of minced garlic
- Fresh dill: 2 tablespoons, chopped
- Orange juice: 2 tablespoons(fresh)
- Greek yogurt: 2/3 cup(reduced-fat)

Instructions

In a bowl, add half a teaspoon of salt, parsley and thyme, mix well. Rub the oil on the salmon and sprinkle with the thyme mixture.

Place the salmon fillets in the basket of the air fryer, cook for ten minutes at 350 ° F.

Meanwhile, mix garlic, fennel, orange juice, yogurt, half a teaspoon. of salt, dill, lemon juice in a bowl.

Serve with fennel salad.

Nutritional value : per serving: Calories 364|Fat 30g|Protein 38g|Carbohydrate 9g

314.   Air-Fried Crumbed Fish

(Prep Time: 10 mints| Cook Time:12 mints| Servings: 2)

Ingredients

- Four fish fillets
- Olive oil: 4 tablespoons
- One egg beaten
- Whole wheat breadcrumbs: ¼ cup

Instructions

- Let the air fryer preheat to 360F
- In a bowl, mix breadcrumbs with oil. Mix well
- First, coat the fish in the egg mix (egg mixwith water) then in the breadcrumb mix. Coat well
- Place in the air fryer, let it cook for 10-12 minutes.
- Serve hot with salad green and lemon.

Nutritional value : per serving: 254 Cal| fat 12.7g|carbohydrates10.2g |protein 15.5g.

315.   Air-Grilled Honey-Glazed Salmon

(Prep Time: 10 mints| Cook Time:15 mints| Servings: 2)

Ingredients

- Gluten-free Soy Sauce: 6 tsp
- Salmon Fillets: 2 pcs
- Sweet rice wine: 3 tsp
- Water: 1 tsp
- Honey: 6 tbsp.

Instructions

In a bowl, mix the sweet rice wine, soy sauce, honey and water.

Set half aside.

In half marinate the fish and let it rest for two hours.

Allow the air fryer to preheat to 360 ° F

Cook the fish for 8 minutes, turn it in half and cook for another five minutes.

Baste the salmon with the marinade mixture after 3.4 minutes.

Half of the marinade, pour into a saucepan reduce in half, serve with a sauce.

Nutritional value : per serving: calories 254| carbs 9.9 g| fat 12 g| protein 20 g|

316. Herb & Garlic Fish Fingers

(Prep Time: 10 mints| Cook Time:20 mints| Servings: 4)

Ingredients

- Lemon juice: 2 tbsp.
- Fish: 1 cup
- Salt: half tsp
- Turmeric powder: 1/2 tsp
- Garlic Ginger paste: 1 tsp
- Red chili flakes: half tsp
- One large Egg
- Freshly ground black pepper: half tsp
- All-Purpose Flour: 2 tbsp.
- Whole wheat Bread crumbs: one cup
- Rice Flour: 1 tsp
- Baking soda: 1/4 tsp

Instructions

In a bowl, add the fish fingers, turmeric powder, freshly ground black pepper, red chilli flakes, garlic and ginger paste, kosher salt and lemon, mix well

Keep it aside for ten minutes.

In another bowl, mix the rice flour, all-purpose flour, baking soda, and egg

Coat the fish in this flour mixture, hold it for ten minutes and then sprinkle with breadcrumbs.

Preheat the air fryer to 360 ° F, cook for ten minutes until golden brown and crisp.

Serve with tartar sauce and microgreen.

Nutritional value : per serving: Calories 233 |Fat 4g|Carbohydrates 24g|Protein 26g

317. Air Fryer Crispy Fish Sticks

(Prep Time: 10 mints| Cook Time:15 mints | Serving 4)

Ingredients

- Whitefish such as cod 1 lb.
- Mayonnaise ¼ c
- Dijon mustard 2 tbsp.
- Water 2 tbsp.
- Pork rind 1&1/2 c
- Cajun seasoning ¾ tsp
- Kosher salt& pepper to taste

Instructions

Spray non-stick cooking spray on the air fryer grill.

Dry the fish and cut into sticks about 1 "by 2" wide

Mix the mayonnaise, mustard and water together in a small saucer. Mix the pork rinds and Cajun seasoning in another small container.

Add kosher salt and pepper to taste (both pork rinds and seasoning can contain a fair amount of kosher salt so you can dip a finger to see how salty it is).

Working one slice of fish at a time, dip to cover the mayonnaise and then tap to remove excess. Dip in the rind mixture, then flip to cover. Place on the grill of an air fryer.

Set to 400F on Air Fry and cook for 5 minutes, then turn the fish with the tongs and cook for another 5 minutes. To serve

Nutritional value : per serving: Cal: 263| Fat: 16g| Net Carbs: 1g| Protein: 26.4g

318. Air Fryer Lemon Garlic Shrimp

(Prep Time: 5 mints| Cook Time:10 mints| Servings: 2)

Ingredients

- Olive oil: 1 Tbsp.
- Small shrimp: 4 cups, peeled, tails removed
- One lemon juice and zest
- Parsley: 1/4 cup sliced
- Red pepper flakes(crushed): 1 pinch
- Four cloves of grated garlic
- Sea salt: 1/4 teaspoon

Instructions

Let the air fryer heat up to 400F

Mix the olive oil, lemon zest, red pepper flakes, shrimp, kosher salt and garlic in a bowl and coat the shrimp well.

Place the shrimp in the basket of the air fryer, coat them with spray oil.

Cook at 400 F for 8 minutes. Toss the shrimp in half

Serve with lemon slices and parsley.

Nutritional value : per serving: Cal 140| Fat: 18g |Net Carbs: 8g|Protein: 20g

319. Air Fryer Catfish with Cajun seasoning

(Prep Time: 5 mints| Cook Time:20 mints| Servings: 4)

Ingredients

- Cajun seasoning: 3 teaspoons
- Cornmeal: 3/4 cup
- Four catfish fillets

Instructions

In a zip lock bag, add the Cajun seasoning and cornmeal

Wash and dry the catfish fillets. Add them to the zip lock bag.

Sprinkle the fillets well with the sauce

Place the catfish fillets in the air fryer. And cook for 15 minutes at 390 ° F, turn the fillets in half. To get a golden color on the fillets, cook for another five minutes.

Serve with lemon wedges and spicy tartar sauce.

Nutritional value : per serving: Cal 324| Fat: 13.9g| |Carbohydrates: 15.6g|Protein: 26.3g

320. California Sushi Rolls Stuffed Avocados

(Prep Time: 10 mints| Cook Time:10 mints| Serving 4)

Ingredients

- Avocados 2
- Softened Cream cheese 2 oz.
- White crabmeat Can 1
- Dried chopped sushi nor, one-sheet
- Finely chopped Cucumber 2 c
- Green onion Chopped 2 tbsp.
- Pickled ginger Chopped 2-3 tbsp.
- Soy sauce Gluten-free ½ tsp
- Rice vinegar 1 tsp
- Sesame oil ¼ tsp
- Sea salt
- Minced Dried onion flakes, 2 tbsp.
- Olive oil, 2 tbsp.

- Optional Sriracha mayonnaise & sesame seeds, for serving

Instructions

Mash the cream cheese with the back of a fork in a medium bowl.

Add crabmeat, cucumber, green onion, soy sauce, vinegar, pickled ginger, kosher salt, and sesame oil.

Stir, until blended well, using a fork. Pour half of it into the avocado. Season the mayonnaise with the sriracha.

Nutritional value: per serving: Per serving: Cal: 313, Fat: 24g, Carbs: 12.5g, Protein: 14g

321. Air Fryer Cajun Shrimp Dinner

(Prep Time: 10 mints| Cook Time:20 mints| Servings: 4)

Ingredients

- Peeled, 24 extra-jumbo shrimp
- Olive oil: 2 tablespoons
- Cajun seasoning: 1 tablespoon
- one zucchini, thick slices (half-moons)
- Cooked Turkey: ¼ cup
- Yellow squash, sliced half-moons
- Kosher salt: 1/4 teaspoon

Instructions

In a bowl, mix the prawns with the Cajun seasoning.

In another bowl, add the zucchini, turkey, salt, pumpkin and grease with oil.

Allow the air fryer to preheat to 400F

Move the shrimp and vegetable mixture into the fryer basket and cook for three minutes.

Serve hot.

Nutritional value: per serving: Calories: 284kcal|Carbohydrates: 8g| Protein: 31|Fat: 14g

322. Red Lobsters Coconut Shrimp

(Prep Time: 10 mints| Cook Time:30 mints | Serving 4)

Ingredients

- Pork Rinds: ½ cup (Crushed)
- Jumbo Shrimp:4 cups. (deveined)
- Coconut Flakes preferably: ½ cup
- Eggs: two
- Flour of coconut: ½ cup
- Any oil of your choice for frying at least half-inch in pan
- Freshly ground black pepper & kosher salt to taste

Dipping sauce (Pina colada flavor):

- Powdered Sugar as Substitute : 2-3 tablespoon
- Mayonnaise : 3 tablespoons
- Sour Cream: ½ cup
- Coconut Extract or to taste: ¼ tsp
- Coconut Cream: 3 tablespoons
- Pineapple Flavoring as much to taste: ¼ tsp
- Coconut Flakes   preferably unsweetened this is optional: 3 tablespoons

Instructions

Pina Colada (Salsa)

Mix all the ingredients in a small bowl for the dipping sauce (Pina colada flavor). Combine well and refrigerate until ready to serve.

Preparation of the shrimp

Whip all the eggs in a deep bowl and in a small shallow bowl, add the crushed pork rinds, coconut flour, sea salt, coconut flakes and freshly ground black pepper.

Put the prawns one by one in the mixed eggs to be dipped, then in the coconut flour smoothie. Put them on a clean plate or put them in the basket of your deep fryer.

To make in an air oven:

Place the battered shrimp in a single layer on the basket of the air fryer. Sprinkle the shrimp with oil and cook for 8-10 minutes at 360 degrees, turning them in half.

Nutritional value: per serving: Calories 340 |Proteins 25g |Carbs 9g |Fat 16g |Fiber 7g

323. Air Fried Crispy Cod Steak

(Prep Time: 10 mints| Cook Time:10 mints| Servings: 2)

Ingredients

- Two big cod steaks
- Ginger powder: half tsp
- Plum sauce: 1 tbsp.
- Garlic powder: half tsp
- 1/4 cup Kentucky powder
- Turmeric powder: 1/4 tsp
- 1/4 cup corn flour
- Slices of ginger
- Salt, pepper

Instructions

In a bowl, mix the ginger powder, turmeric powder, pepper, garlic powder and salt. Cover the fish well with the spice. Then dip the fish in the cornmeal and Kentucky powder mixture.

Spray the oil on the fish fillets

Let the air fryer preheat to 360F

Place the fish in the air fryer and cook for 15 minutes, then at 400F for five minutes.

In a pan, sauté the ginger slices until golden brown. Turn off the heat and mix in the diluted plum sauce with the water.

Season on the fish and serve.

Nutritional value : per serving:219 Cal| total fat 11.8g |carbohydrates 11.1g |protein 22.2g

324. Air Fryer Salmon cakes

(Prep Time: 10 mints| Cook Time:10 mints| Serving 2)

Ingredients

- Fresh salmon fillet 8 oz.
- Egg 1
- Salt 1/8 tsp
- Garlic powder ¼ tsp
- Sliced lemon 1

Instructions

In the bowl, chop the salmon, add the egg and spices.

Form small cakes. Air fryers preheat to 390. At the bottom of the air fryer bowl, lay the sliced lemons and place the cakes on top.

Cook them for seven minutes. Based on your dietary preferences, eat with the sauce of your choice.Nutritional value : per serving: Kcal: 194, Fat: 9g, Carbs: 1g, Protein: 25g

325. South West Tortilla Crusted Tilapia Salad

(Prep Time: 15 mints| Cook Time:15 mints| Serving 2)

Ingredients

- Tilapia fillets (Tortilla Crusted)
- Mixed greens: six cups
- Chipotle Lime Dressing: half cup
- Diced red onion: 1/3 cup
- One avocado
- Cherry tomatoes: one cup

Instructions

On the frozen tilapia fillet, sprinkle the olive oil.

Place in the basket of the air fryer, cook at 390 ° for 15-18 minutes.

In a bowl, add the tomatoes, red onion and half of the vegetables. Top with the Chipotle lime dressing.

Serve the fish with the vegetables.

Nutritional value : per serving: 260cal| total fat 19g |carbohydrates 7.6g |protein 19.2g

Optavia Greens & VEGETABLES Air-fry Recipes

326. Japanese Tempura Bowl

Preparation time: 20 minutes Serves: 3

Ingredients

- tbps whey protein isolate 1 tsp. baking powder
- Kosher salt and ground black pepper, to taste 1/2 tsp. paprika
- tsp. dashi granules
- eggs
- 1 tablespoon mirin
- tbps soda water
- 1 cup parmesan cheese, grated 1 onion, cut into rings
- 1 bell pepper
- zucchini, cut into slices 3 asparagus spears
- tbps olive oil

Cooking Instructions

In a shallow bowl, mix the whey protein isolate, yeast, salt, black pepper, paprika, dashi grains, eggs, mirin and soda water.

In another shallow bowl, put the grated Parmesan cheese.

Dip the vegetables in the tempura batter; finally, roll over the Parmesan to coat evenly. Season each piece with olive oil.

Cook in the preheated air fryer at 400 ° F for 10 minutes, shaking the basket halfway through the cooking time. Work in batches until the vegetables are crisp and golden.

327. Balsamic Keto Vegetables

Preparation time: 15 minutes Serves: 3

Ingredients

- 1/2 pound cauliflower florets
- 1/2 pound button mushrooms, whole 1 cup pearl onions, whole
- Pink Himalayan salt and ground black pepper, to taste 1/4 tsp. smoked paprika
- tsp. garlic powder 1/2 tsp. dried thyme 1/2 tsp.
- dried marjoram 3 tbps olive oil
- tbps balsamic vinegar

Cooking Instructions

Throw all the ingredients into a large pan.

Roast in a preheated air fryer at 400 ° F for 5 minutes. Shake the basket and cook for another 7 minutes.

Serve with some extra fresh herbs if desired.

328. Winter Vegetables with Herbs

Preparation time: 25 minutes Serves: 2

Ingredients

- 1/2 pound broccoli florets
- celery root, peeled and cut into 1-inch pieces 1 onion, cut into wedges
- tbps unsalted margarine, melted 1/2 cup chicken broth
- 1/4 cup ketchup
- 1 tsp. parsley
- 1 tsp. rosemary
- 1 tsp. thyme

Cooking Instructions

Start by preheating the air fryer to 380 ° F. Place all ingredients in a lightly greased baking dish. Stir to mix well.

Cook in the preheated air fryer for 10 minutes. Gently mix the vegetables with a large spoon and cook for another 5 minutes.

Serve in individual bowls with a few drizzles of lemon juice.

329. Shrimp and Cauliflower Casserole

Preparation time: 25 minutes Serves: 4

Ingredients

- pound shrimp cleaned and deveined 2 cups cauliflower, cut into florets
- bell pepper, sliced 1 shallot, sliced
- tbps sesame oil
- cup tomato paste

Cooking Instructions

Start by preheating the air fryer to 360 ° F. Spray the pan with cooking spray.

Now, arrange the prawns and vegetables in the pan. Next, season the sesame oil on the vegetables. Pour the tomato paste over the vegetables.

Cook for 10 minutes in the preheated air fryer. Stir with a large spoon and cook for another 12 minutes. Serve hot.

330. Brussels Sprout Salad with Pancetta

Preparation time: 35 minutes + chilling time Serves: 4

Ingredients

- 2/3 pound Brussels sprouts 1 tablespoon olive oil
- Coarse sea salt and ground black pepper, to taste
- ounces baby arugula 1 shallot, thinly sliced
- ounces pancetta, chopped
- Lemon Vinaigrette:
- tbps extra virgin olive oil 2 tbps fresh lemon juice
- tablespoon honey

- 1 tsp. Dijon mustard

Cooking Instructions

Start by preheating the air fryer to 380 ° F.

Add the Brussels sprouts to the cooking basket. Brush with olive oil and cook for 15 minutes. Let it cool at room temperature for about 15 minutes.

Season the Brussels sprouts with salt, black pepper, rocket and shallot.

Mix all the ingredients for the dressing. Then dress your salad, garnish with the bacon and serve very cold.

331. Keto Buddha Bowl

Preparation time: 20 minutes Serves: 3

Ingredients

- (1-pound head cauliflower, food-processed into rice-like particles 2 bell pepper, spiralized
- Coarse sea salt and ground black pepper, to taste
- cups baby spinach
- tbps champagne vinegar 4 tbps mayonnaise
- 1 tsp. yellow mustard
- tbps olive oil, divided
- tbps cilantro leaves, chopped 2 tbps pine nuts

Cooking Instructions

Start by preheating the air fryer to 400 ° F.

Place the cauliflower florets and peppers in the basket of the lightly greased air fryer. Season with salt and black pepper; cook for 12 minutes, stirring halfway through cooking.

Season with baby spinach. Add the champagne vinegar, mayonnaise, mustard and olive oil. Garnish with fresh cilantro and pine nuts.

332. Italian-Style Eggplant with Mozzarella Cheese

Preparation time: 45 minutes Serves: 4

Ingredients

- pound eggplant, sliced 1 tablespoon sea salt
- 1/2 cup Romano cheese, preferably freshly grated
- Sea salt and cracked black pepper, to taste 1 egg, whisked
- ounces Pancetta rinds
- 1/2 cup mozzarella cheese, grated
- tbps fresh Italian parsley, roughly chopped

Cooking Instructions

Skip the aubergines with 1 tablespoon of salt and leave to rest for 30 minutes. Drain and rinse.

Mix the cheese, salt and black pepper in a bowl. Then add the beaten egg.

Dip the eggplant slices into the batter and press to coat on all sides. Roll them on the bacon rinds. Transfer to lightly greased air fryer basket.

Bake at 370 ° F for 7-9 minutes. Flip each slice over and garnish with mozzarella. Cook for another 2 minutes or until the cheese melts.

Serve garnished with fresh Italian parsley.

333. Authentic Peperonata Siciliana

Preparation time: 25 minutes Serves: 4

Ingredients

- tbps olive oil
- bell peppers, seeded and sliced
- serrano pepper, seeded and sliced 1/2 cup onion, peeled and sliced
- garlic cloves, crushed
- 1 large tomato, pureed Sea salt and black pepper
- 1 tsp. cayenne pepper
- fresh basil leaves
- Sicilian olives green, pitted and sliced

Cooking Instructions

Brush the sides and bottom of the cooking basket with 1 tablespoon of olive oil. Add the peppers, onions and garlic to the cooking basket. Cook for 5 minutes or until tender.

Add the tomatoes, salt, black pepper and cayenne pepper; add the remaining tablespoon of olive oil and cook in the preheated air fryer at 380 ° F for 15 minutes, stirring occasionally.

Divide between individual bowls and garnish with basil leaves and olives.

334. Asparagus Salad with Boiled Eggs

Preparation time: 10 minutes + chilling time Serves: 4

Ingredients

- 1/4 cup olive oil
- pound asparagus, trimmed 1 cup cherry tomatoes,halved 1/4 cup balsamic vinegar
- garlic cloves, minced
- scallion stalks, chopped 1/2 tsp. oregano
- Coarse sea salt and ground black pepper, to your liking
- hard-boiled eggs, sliced

Cooking Instructions

Start by preheating the air fryer to 400 ° F. Brush the cooking basket with 1 tablespoon of olive oil.

Add the asparagus and cherry tomatoes to the cooking basket. Drizzle 1 tablespoon of olive oil over all the vegetables.

Cook for 5 minutes, shaking the basket halfway through cooking. Let it cool slightly.

Season with the remaining olive oil, balsamic vinegar, garlic, shallot, oregano, salt and black pepper.

Next, add the hard-boiled eggs over the salad and serve.

335. Traditional Indian Kofta

Preparation time: 35 minutes Serves: 4

Ingredients

Veggie Balls:
- 3/4 pound zucchini, grated and well drained
  1/4 pound kohlrabi, grated and well drained
  2 cloves garlic, minced
- tablespoon Garam masala 1 cup paneer, crumbled
- 1/4 cup coconut flour
- 1/2 tsp. chili powder
- Himalayan pink salt and ground black pepper, to

taste Sauce:
- tablespoon sesame oil
- 1/2 tsp. cumin seeds
- cloves garlic, roughly chopped 1 onion, chopped
- 1 Kashmiri chili pepper, seeded and minced 1
  (1-inch piece ginger, chopped
- 1 tsp. paprika
- 1 tsp. turmeric powder 2 ripe tomatoes, pureed
- 1/2 cup vegetable broth
- 1/4 full fat coconut milk

Cooking Instructions

Start by preheating the air fryer to 360 ° F. Combine the courgettes, kohlrabi, garlic, garam masala, paneer, coconut flour, chili powder, salt and ground black pepper.

Shape the vegetable mixture into balls and place them in the lightly greased cooking basket.

Cook in the preheated air fryer at 360 ° F for 15 minutes or until completely cooked and crisp. Repeat the process until you run out of ingredients.

Heat the sesame oil in a saucepan over medium heat and add the cumin seeds. When the cumin seeds turn brown, add the garlic, onions, red pepper and ginger. Fry for 2-3 minutes.

•Add the paprika, turmeric powder, tomatoes and broth; let it simmer, covered, for 4-5 minutes, stirring occasionally.

Add the coconut milk. Heat up; add the vegetarian meatballs and mix gently to combine.

336.   Super-Crispy Asparagus Fries

Preparation time: 20 minutes Serves: 4

Ingredients

- Eggs
- tsp. Dijon mustard
- cup Parmesan cheese, grated
- Sea salt and ground black pepper, to taste 18 asparagus spears, trimmed
- 1/2 cup sour cream

Cooking Instructions

Start by preheating the air fryer to 400 ° F.

In a shallow bowl, beat the eggs and mustard. In another shallow bowl, combine the Parmesan, salt and black pepper.

Dip the asparagus spears in the egg mixture, then in the Parmesan mixture; press to join.

Cook for 5 minutes; work in three batches. Serve with sour cream on the side. To enjoy!

337.   Easy Shepherd's Pie

Preparation time: 30 minutes Serves: 5

Ingredients

- tbps olive oil
- bell peppers, seeded and sliced 1 celery, chopped
- onion, chopped
- garlic cloves, minced
- 1 cup cooked bacon, diced 1 ½ cups beef bone broth
- ounces green beans, drained
- Sea salt and freshly ground black pepper, to taste
- ounces cauliflower pulsed in a food processor to a

fine-crumb like consistency
- 1/2 cup milk
- tbps margarine, melted

Cooking Instructions

Heat the olive oil in a saucepan over medium-high heat. At this point, cook the peppers, celery, onion and garlic until softened, about 7 minutes add the bacon and broth. Bring to a boil and cook for another 2 minutes. Mix the green beans, salt and black pepper; continue cooking until everything has heated up.

Transfer the mixture to the lightly greased pan. Microwave cauliflower rice for 5 minutes.

In a small bowl, combine the cauliflower, milk and melted margarine. Stir until the mixture is homogeneous and pour the vegetable mixture evenly. Smooth it with a spatula and transfer it to the Air Fryer cooking basket.

Cook in the preheated air fryer at 400 ° F for 12 minutes. Place on a wire rack to cool slightly before slicing and serving.

338.   Cheesy Spinach Wontons

(Prep Time: 8 mints| Cook Time:20 mints| Servings: 6)

Ingredients

- Low-fat cream cheese: 1/4 cup, softened
- Wonton wrappers: 16-20
- Baby spinach: 1 and 1/2 cups chopped

Instructions

In a small bowl, mix the spinach and soften the cream cheese, mix well

Place the wonton wrappers on a flat surface, add a teaspoon of cream cheese in the center

With the help of water, fold the corners to join the edges. Give it a wonton shape.

Cook for six minutes at 400 degrees

Serve with lean proteins.

Nutritional value : per serving: calories 123|fat 10 g| protein 13 g| net Carb 10 g

339.   Bell Peppers with Spicy Mayo

Preparation time: 20 minutes Serves: 2

Ingredients

- bell peppers, seeded and sliced (1-inch pieces 1 onion, sliced (1-inch pieces
- 1 tablespoon olive oil
- 1/2 tsp. dried rosemary 1/2 tsp. dried basil Kosher salt, to taste
- 1/4 tsp. ground black pepper 1/3 cup mayonnaise
- 1/3 tsp. Sriracha

Cooking Instructions

Season the peppers and onions with the olive oil, rosemary, basil, salt and black pepper.

Arrange the peppers and onions on an even layer in the cooking basket. Bake at 400 ° F for 12-14 minutes.

Meanwhile, prepare the sauce by beating the mayonnaise and Sriracha. Serve quickly.

340. Easy Sesame Broccoli

Preparation time: 15 minutes Serves: 3

Ingredients

- pound broccoli florets 2 tbps sesame oil
- 1/2 tsp. shallot powder 1/2 tsp. porcini powder 1 tsp. garlic powder
- Sea salt and ground black pepper, to taste 1/2 tsp. cumin powder
- 1/4 tsp. paprika
- tbps sesame seeds

Cooking Instructions

Start by preheating the air fryer to 400 ° F.

Blanch the broccoli in boiling salted water until al dente, about 3 or 4 minutes. Drain well and transfer to lightly greased air fryer basket.

Add sesame oil, shallot powder, porcini mushrooms, garlic powder, salt, black pepper, cumin powder, paprika and sesame seeds.

Cook for 6 minutes, stirring halfway through cooking.

341. Fennel with Shirataki Noodles

Preparation time: 20 minutes + chilling time Serves: 3

Ingredients

- fennel bulb, quartered
- Salt and white pepper, to taste 1 clove garlic, finely chopped 1 green onion, thinly sliced
- 1 cup Chinese cabbage, shredded 2 tbps rice wine vinegar 2 tbps sesame oil
- 1 tsp. ginger, freshly grated 1 tablespoon soy sauce
- 1 1/3 cups Shirataki noodles, boiled

Cooking Instructions

Start by preheating the air fryer to 370 ° F.

At this point, cook the fennel in the lightly greased cooking basket for 15 minutes, shaking the basket once or twice.

Allow to cool completely and season with the remaining ingredients. Serve very cold.

342. Cauliflower Croquettes with Colby Cheese

Preparation time: 25 minutes Serves: 4

Ingredients

- pound cauliflower florets 2 eggs
- tablespoon olive oil
- tbps scallions, chopped 1 garlic clove, minced
- 1 cup Colby cheese, shredded 1/2 cup parmesan cheese, grated
- Sea salt and ground black pepper, to taste
- 1/4 tsp. dried dill weed 1 tsp. paprika

Cooking Instructions

Blanch the cauliflower in boiling salted water for about 3 or 4 minutes until al dente. Drain well and blend in a food processor.

Add the remaining ingredients; stir to mix well. Form the cauliflower mixture into small bites.

Spray the air fryer basket with cooking spray.

Bake in preheated air fryer at 375 ° F for 16 minutes, shaking halfway through cooking time. Serve with your fa-

vorite dipping sauce.

343. Mediterranean Tomatoes with Feta Cheese

Preparation time: 20 minutes Serves: 2

Ingredients

- medium-sized tomatoes, cut into four slices, pat dry 1 tsp. dried basil
- tsp. dried oregano
- 1/4 tsp. red pepper flakes, crushed 1/2 tsp. sea salt
- slices Feta cheese

Cooking Instructions

Spray the tomatoes with cooking oil and transfer them to the basket of the air fryer. Sprinkle with seasonings.

Cook at 350 ° F for about 8 minutes, turning them halfway through cooking.

Add the cheese and cook for another 4 minutes.

344. Zucchini Casserole with Cooked Ham

Preparation time: 30 minutes Serves: 4

Ingredients

- tbps margarine, melted 1 zucchini, diced
- bell pepper, seeded and sliced
- 1 red chili pepper, seeded and minced 1 medium-sized leek, sliced
- 3/4 pound ham, cooked and diced 5 eggs
- 1 tsp. cayenne pepper
- Sea salt, to taste
- 1/2 tsp. ground black pepper
- 1 tablespoon fresh cilantro, chopped

Cooking Instructions

Start by preheating the air fryer to 380 ° F. Grease the sides and bottom of a pan with the melted margarine.

Place the courgettes, peppers, leeks and ham in the pan. Cook in the preheated air fryer for 6 minutes.

Break the eggs over ham and vegetables; season with cayenne pepper, salt and black pepper. Cook for another 20 minutes or until the whites are completely solidified.

Garnish with fresh coriander and serve.

345. Cauliflower Fritters with Mustard and Cheese

Preparation time: 30 minutes Serves: 2

Ingredients

- 1/2 pound cauliflower florets 2 garlic cloves, minced
- 1/2 cup goat cheese, shredded
- Sea salt and ground black pepper, to taste 1/2 tsp. shallot powder
- 1/4 tsp. cumin powder 1/2 cup sour cream
- tsp. Dijon mustard

Cooking Instructions

Put the cauliflower florets in a saucepan of water; bring to the boil; reduce heat and cook for 10 minutes or until tender.

Mash the cauliflower using your blender; add the garlic,

cheese and spices; stir to mix well.
Form the cauliflower mixture into the shape of croquettes.
Bake in preheated air fryer at 375 ° F for 16 minutes, shaking halfway through cooking time. Serve with sour cream and mustard.

346.   Asian Cauliflower Rice with Eggs
Preparation time: 20 minutes Serves: 4
Ingredients
- cups cauliflower, food-processed into rice-like particles 2 tbps peanut oil
- 1/2 cup scallions, chopped 2 bell pepper, chopped
- eggs, beaten
- Sea salt and ground black pepper, to taste 1/2 tsp. powdered garlic

Cooking Instructions
Grease a baking sheet with non-stick cooking spray.
Add the cauliflower rice and other ingredients to the pan.
Bake at 400 ° F for 12 minutes, checking from time to time to ensure even cooking. To enjoy!

347.   Fried Yellow Beans with Blue Cheese and Pecans
Preparation time: 15 minutes Serves: 3
Ingredients
- 3/4 pound wax yellow beans, cleaned 2 tbps peanut oil
- tbps Romano cheese, grated
- Sea salt and ground black pepper, to taste 1/2 tsp. red pepper flakes, crushed
- tbps pecans, sliced
- 1/3 cup blue cheese, crumbled

Cooking Instructions
Mix the wax grains with the peanut oil, Roman cheese, salt, black pepper and chilli.
Place the wax grains in the lightly greased cooking basket.
Cook in the preheated air fryer at 400 ° F for 5 minutes. Shake the basket once or twice.
Add pecans and cook for another 3 minutes or until lightly toasted. Serve topped with blue cheese and enjoy your meal!

348.   Italian-Style Broccoli
Preparation time: 25 minutes Serves: 4
Ingredients
- 1/3 cup Asiago cheese
- 1 large-sized head broccoli, stemmed and cut small florets 2 1/2 tbps canola oil
- 1 tablespoon Italian seasoning blend Salt and ground black pepper, to taste

Cooking Instructions
Bring a medium skillet filled with lightly salted water to a boil. Then, boil the broccoli florets for about 3 minutes.
Then, drain the broccoli florets well; season with canola oil, rosemary, basil, salt and black pepper.
Set the air fryer to 390 ° F; place the seasoned broccoli in the cooking basket; set the timer for 17 minutes. Toss the

broccoli halfway through the cooking process.
Serve hot topped with grated cheese and enjoy your meal!

349.   Dilled Asparagus with Cheese
Preparation time: 15 minutes Serves: 3
Ingredients
- bunch of asparagus, trimmed 1 tablespoon olive oil
- 1/2 tsp. kosher salt
- 1/4 tsp. cracked black pepper, to taste 1/2 tsp. dried dill weed
- 1/2 cup goat cheese, crumbled

Cooking Instructions
Place the asparagus spears in the lightly greased cooking basket. Season the asparagus with the olive oil, salt, black pepper and dill.
Bake in preheated air fryer at 400 ° F for 9 minutes. Serve garnished with goat cheese.

350.   Air Fryer Onion Rings
(Prep Time: 105 mints| Cook Time:10 mints| Servings: 4)
Ingredients
- 1 egg whisked
- One large onion
- Whole-wheat breadcrumbs: 1 and 1/2 cup
- Smoked paprika: 1 teaspoon
- Flour: 1 cup
- Garlic powder: 1 teaspoon
- Buttermilk: 1 cup
- Kosher salt and pepper, to taste

Instructions
Cut the onion stalks. Then cut into half-inch thick rounds.
In a bowl, add the flour, pepper, garlic powder, smoked paprika and salt. Then add the egg and buttermilk. Stir to combine.
In another bowl, add the breadcrumbs.
Sprinkle the onions in the buttermilk mix and then in the breadcrumbs.
Freeze these breaded onions for 15 minutes. Spray the fryer basket with spray oil.
Place the onions in the basket of the air fryer in a single layer. Spray the onion with cooking oil
Cook at 370 degrees for 10-12 minutes. Flip only if necessary.
Serve with lean proteins.
Nutritional value : per serving: 205 Kcal |total fat 5.5g |carbohydrates 7.5g | protein 18g

351. Crispy Fried Okra

(Prep Time: 20 mints| Cook Time:10 mints| Servings: 4)

Ingredients
- Water: 1 cup
- Okra: 1.25 cups
- Rice flour: half cup
- Fennel Seeds: 1/2 tsp
- Red chili powder: 1/2 tsp
- Kosher salt:1 tsp
- Semolina: fine,1/4 cup
- Ground Turmeric: 1/2 tsp

Instructions

Wash and dry the okra completely. Cut in half.

In a bowl combine the semolina, fennel seeds, flour, turmeric, chilli, salt, mix the powder well and add the water to make the batter. It should be should.

Cover the okra with the batter.

Place the slices of okra in the basket of the air fryer in a single layer. Sprinkle with a little oil

Cook for ten minutes at 330 ° F.

Toss the okra, then cook for 2-5 mints, 350 ° F or until crisp.

Serve hot

Nutritional value : per serving: Calories: 151kcal|Carbohydrates: 30g|Protein: 4g|Fat: 1g|

352. Easy Vegetable Kabobs

Preparation time: 30 minutes Serves: 4

Ingredients
- medium-sized zucchini, cut into 1-inch pieces 2 red bell peppers, cut into 1-inch pieces
- green bell pepper, cut into 1-inch pieces 1 red onion, cut into 1-inch pieces
- tbps olive oil
- Sea salt, to taste
- 1/2 tsp. black pepper, preferably freshly cracked 1/2 tsp. red pepper flakes

Cooking Instructions

Soak the wooden skewers in water for 15 minutes.

Put the vegetables on the skewers; a drizzle of olive oil on the vegetable skewers; sprinkle with spices.

Cook in a preheated air fryer at 400 ° F for 13 minutes. Serve hot and enjoy your meal!

353. Air Fryer Buffalo Cauliflower

(Prep Time: 5 mints| Cook Time: 10 mints| Servings: 4)

Ingredients
- One egg
- Half head of cauliflower
- Whole wheat breadcrumbs: one cup
- Salt: 1/2 teaspoon
- Garlic powder: 1/2 teaspoon
- One cup of low-fat ranch dressing
- Freshly ground black pepper
- Hot sauce: 1/2 cup

Instructions

Cut the cauliflower into a flower. In a bowl, mix the egg with the garlic powder, salt, and pepper.

Pass the flower in the eggs then in the breadcrumbs.

Add them to the air fryer and cook for 8-10 minutes at 400 F.

Mix the hot sauce with the ranch and serve with fried cauliflower.

Nutritional value: per serving: Calories: 94kcal | Carbohydrates: 14g | Protein: 4g | Fat: 2g |

354. Salad Green

(Prep Time: 15 mints| Cook Time:0 mints| Serving 8)

Ingredients
- Cucumber: 2 cups, diced
- One Romaine heart
- Green olives: half cup, chopped
- Leafy lettuce: 5 cups
- Red pepper flakes: 1/4 teaspoon
- Cherry tomatoes: half cup

Instructions

Chop and dice all the vegetables. Mix them.

Add salt and kosher pepper along with the chilli flakes.

Season with any Italian seasoning if needed.

Serve with any lean protein.

Nutritional value : per serving: Total Fat 7g|Total Carbohydrate 2.2| Protein 1.5G

355. Air Fryer Falafel

(Prep Time: 10 mints| Cook Time:20 mints| Servings: 6)

Ingredients
- Paprika: 1 teaspoon
- Two cans of chickpeas drained and rinsed
- Cloves of garlic
- One chopped large onion
- Fresh parsley: 1/4 cup
- Gluten-free flour: 3 tablespoons
- Sesame seeds: 2 tablespoons
- Ground cumin: 2 teaspoons
- Cilantro: 1/4 cup
- Juice only: half lemon
- Salt: 1 teaspoon

Instructions

In a food processor, add the sesame seeds, lemon, chickpeas, cumin, garlic, coriander, shallot, parsley, paprika, salt and flour. Pulse up, so it all comes together, but it shouldn't be a smooth paste.

Make one inch in diameter, spoon full balls or make discs

Spray olive oil on the basket of the air fryer, then add the falafel to the basket in one layer and cook for 8 minutes at 350 F. Stir and then cook for six minutes.

Serve in warm pita bread, with slices of vegetables and your favorite sauce

Nutritional value : per serving: Cal 150| Fat: 8g| Net Carbs: 9g| Protein: 18g

356. Air Fryer Egg Rolls

(Prep Time: 10 mints| Cook Time:20 mints| Servings: 3)

Ingredients

*   Coleslaw mix: half bag
*   Half onion
*   Salt: 1/2 teaspoon
*   Half cups of mushrooms
*   Lean ground pork: 2 cups
*   One stalk of celery
*   Wrappers (egg roll)

Instructions

Place a skillet over medium heat, add the onion and lean ground pork and cook for 5-7 minutes

Add the coleslaw mixture, salt, mushrooms and celery to the pan and cook for almost five minutes

Flatten the egg wrap paper and add the filling (1/3 cup), roll it up, seal with water.

Spray the rollers with oil.

• Place in the air fryer for 6-8 minutes at 400 ° F, turning halfway once.

Serve hot

Nutritional value : per serving: Cal 245| Fat: 10g| Net Carbs: 9g|Protein: 11g

357. Air Fryer Sweet Potato Fries

(Prep Time: 5 mints| Cook Time: 8 mints| Servings: 2)

Ingredients

*   One sweet potato
*   Pinch of kosher salt and freshly ground black pepper
*   1 tsp olive oil

Instructions

Cut the peeled sweet potato into French fries. Sprinkle with salt, pepper and oil.

Cook in an air fryer for 8 minutes at 400 degrees. Cook the

potatoes in batches, in single layers.

Shake once or twice.

Serve with a leaner protein meal.

Nutritional value : per serving: Calories: 60 | Carbohydrates: 13g | Protein: 1g | fat 6 g

358. Air Fryer Avocado Fries

(Prep Time: 10 mints| Cook Time: 10 mints| Servings: 2)

Ingredients

*   One avocado
*   One egg
*   Whole wheat bread crumbs: 1/2 cup
*   Salt: 1/2 teaspoon

Instructions

The avocado must be firm and compact. Cut into wedges.

In a bowl, beat the egg with the salt. In another bowl, add the crumbs.

Coat the wedges in the egg then in the crumbs.

Air-fry them at 400 ° C for 8-10 minutes. Throw in half.

Serve with a lean protein meal.

Nutritional value : per serving: Calories: 251kcal | Carbohydrates: 19g | Protein: 6g | Fat: 17g |

359. Ranch Seasoned Air Fryer Chickpeas

(Prep Time: 5 mints| Cook Time:17 mints| Servings: 8)

Ingredients

*   Lemon juice: 1 tablespoon
*   One can chickpeas (not rinsed but drained) save the liquid from the can
*   Olive oil: 1 tablespoon
*   Garlic powder: 2 teaspoons
*   Onion powder: 2 teaspoons
*   Dried dill: 4 teaspoons
*   Sea salt: 3/4 teaspoon

Instructions

In a bowl, add the chickpeas, a spoon. of its liquid. Air fry for 12 minutes at 400 F.

Then in a bowl add the fried chickpeas with olive oil, lemon juice, onion powder, dill, salt, garlic powder, cover the chickpeas well

Return these chickpeas to the air fryer and cook for five minutes at 350 ° F minutes

Serve hot or cold.
Nutritional value : per serving: Cal 113.2 |Total Fat2.0 g | Total Carbohydrate 9.1| Protein 16 g

360.   Air Fryer Spanakopita Bites
(Prep Time: 10 mints| Cook Time:15 mints| Servings: 4)
Ingredients
- 4 sheets phyllo dough
- Baby spinach leaves: 2 cups
- Grated Parmesan cheese: 2 tablespoons
- Low-fat cottage cheese: 1/4 cup
- Dried oregano: 1 teaspoon
- Feta cheese: 6 tbsp. crumbled
- Water: 2 tablespoons
- One egg white only
- Lemon zest: 1 teaspoon
- Cayenne pepper: 1/8 teaspoon
- Olive oil: 1 tablespoon
- Kosher salt and freshly ground black pepper: 1/4 teaspoon, each

Instructions
In a pot over high heat, add the water and spinach, cook until wilted.

Drain it and let it cool for ten minutes. Squeeze out excess moisture.

In a bowl, mix the ricotta, Parmesan, oregano, salt, cayenne pepper, egg white, freshly ground black pepper, feta cheese, spinach, and zest. Stir well or in the food processor.

Place a sheet of phyllo on a flat surface. Spray with oil. Add the second sheet of phyllo dough on top, sprinkle oil. Add a total of 4 oiled sheets.

Form 16 strips from these four oiled sheets. Add a spoon. To fill a strip. Roll up the filling.

Spray oil into the basket of the air fryer. Put eight bites in the basket, spray with oil. Bake for 12 minutes at 375 ° F until crisp and golden. Flip in half.

Serve with leaner proteins.

Nutritional value : per serving: Calories 82|Fat 4g|Protein 4g|Carbohydrate 7g

361.   Air Fryer Frittata
(Prep Time: 3mints| Cook Time: 6 mints| Servings: 2)
Ingredients
- Three eggs
- Kosher salt and pepper to taste
- 1/4 chopped bell pepper
- 2 tbsp. milk
- 1/4 onion, diced
- Two mushrooms
- 1 tbsp. shredded cheese

Instructions
In a bowl, beat the milk with the eggs, pepper and kosher salt with the vegetables.

Let the air fryer preheat to 400 degrees.

Pour the eggs into the basket of the air fryer before spraying the basket with olive oil.

Cook for five minutes, cheese over and cook for one minute.

Serve with tomatoes, avocados and lean proteins.
Nutritional value : per serving: Calories: 162kcal | Carbohydrates: 4g | Protein: 12g | Fat: 10g |

362.   Air Fryer Delicata Squash
(Prep Time: 5 mints| Cook Time:10 mints| Servings: 2)
Ingredients
- Olive oil: 1/2 Tablespoon
- One delicata squash
- Salt: 1/2 teaspoon
- Rosemary: 1/2 teaspoon

Instructions
Chop the pumpkin into 1/4 thick slices. Sow the seeds.

In a bowl, add the olive oil, salt, rosemary with the pumpkin slices. Mix well.

Cook the squash for ten minutes at 400 F. Flip the squash in half.

Make sure it is completely cooked.

Serve hot with a plate of lean protein.

Nutritional value : per serving: Cal: 69|Fat: 4g| Carbs: 9g|Protein 1g

363.   Vegetable Spring Rolls
(Prep Time: 10 mints| Cook Time: 15 mints| Servings: 4)
Ingredients
- Toasted sesame seeds
- Large carrots – grated
- Spring roll wrappers
- One egg white
- Gluten-free soy sauce, a dash
- Half cabbage: sliced
- Olive oil: 2 tbsp.

Instructions
In a frying pan, heat 2 tablespoons over high heat. of oil and brown the chopped vegetables. Then add the soy sauce. Don't overcook the vegetables.

Turn off the heat and add the toasted sesame seeds.

Place the spring rolls on a surface and add the egg white with a brush on the sides.

Add some vegetable mix to the package and fold.

Spray the spring rolls with spray oil and air dry for 8 minutes at 400 F.

serve with dipping sauce.

Nutritional value : per serving: 129 calories| fat 16.3g |carbohydrates 8.2g |protein 12.1 g

364.   Air Fryer Roasted Corn
(Prep Time: 10 mints| Cook Time:10 mints| Servings: 4)
Ingredients
- 4 corn ears
- Olive oil: 2 to 3 teaspoons
- Kosher salt and pepper to taste

Instructions
Clean the corn, wash and pat dry.

Insert into the basket of the air fryer, cut it if necessary.

Top with olive oil, kosher salt and pepper.

Cook for ten minutes at 400 F

Nutritional value : per serving: Per serving: Kcal 28|Fat 2g|Net carbs 0 g |Protein 7 g

365. Baked Sweet Potato Cauliflower Patties

(Prep Time: 15 mints| Cook Time:20 mints| Servings: 7)

Ingredients

- Organic ranch seasoning mix: 2 tbsp.
- One sweet potato
- One diced green onion
- Chili powder: 1/2 tsp
- Minced garlic: 1 tsp
- Packed cilantro: 1 cup
- Cauliflower florets: 2 cup
- Cumin: 1/4 tsp
- Gluten-free flour
- Kosher salt and pepper
- Ground flaxseed: 1/4 cup

Instructions

Preheat the air fryer to 370 F.

Peel the sweet potato and cut it into small pieces. Blend in the food processor with the onion, garlic and cauliflower. Clean it again.

Then add the flax seeds, coriander, flour, remaining seasoning and blend again to form a thick batter. Make medium-density meatballs.

Place them on a baking tray and put them in the freezer for ten minutes.

Place them in the air fryer in one layer and cook for 18 or 20 minutes.

Serve with any dipping sauce.

Nutritional value : per serving: Calories: 85 | Fat: 2.9 g | Carbohydrates: 9 g| Protein: 2.7 g

366. Mac & Cheese Bites

(Prep Time: 20 mints| Cook Time:29 mints| Servings: 36 bites)

Ingredients

- Cheddar cheese: 3/4 cup, shredded
- Cooked mac and cheese cooked with broccoli: for four people
- Broccoli florets: 1 cup
- One egg
- Bacon: 4 slices

Instructions

Cook the mac and cheese with the broccoli, add the broccoli in the last few minutes.

Cook the bacon.

Then add the crumbled bacon and egg cooked in mac and cheese

In molds or muffin tins, spray with oil.

Add the mac and cheese to the molds, garnish with the cheddar cheese

Air fry, cook for 6-8 minutes, 400 F or until bites are light brown.

Serve hot.

Nutritional value : per serving: Cal 258| Fat: 13 g| Net Carbs: 5.6 g| Protein: 12.7g

367. Lemony Green Beans

(Prep Time: 10 mints| Cook Time:10 mints| Servings: 6)

Ingredients

- Salt, freshly ground black pepper to taste
- Green beans: 4 cups, trimmed
- One lemon
- 1/4 teaspoon oil

Instructions

Add the green beans to the basket of the air fryer, season with oil, salt, pepper and lemon juice.

Cook for 10-12 minutes at 400 F.

Serve with a lean protein meal.

Nutritional value : per serving: Cal 58|Fat 9g|Net carbs 5.3 g |Protein 9.0 g

368. Avocado Egg Rolls

(Prep Time: 15mints| Cook Time: 15 mints| Servings: 10)

Ingredients

- Ten egg roll wrappers
- Diced sundried tomatoes: ¼ cup oil drained
- Avocados, cut in cube
- Red onion: 2/3 cup chopped
- 1/3 cup chopped cilantro
- Kosher salt and freshly ground black pepper
- Two small limes: juice

Instructions

In a bowl, add the dried tomatoes, avocado, coriander, lime juice, pepper, onion and kosher salt and mix well and gently.

Place the egg roll wrap on a surface, add ¼ cup of filling to the bottom of the wrap.

Seal with water and turn it into a roll.

Spray the sandwiches with olive oil.

Cook at 400 F in the air fryer for six minutes. Turn halfway.

Serve with a leaner protein meal.

Nutritional value : per serving: 160 Cal| total fat 19g |carbohydrates 5.6g |protein 19.2g

369. Zucchini Parmesan Chips

(Prep Time: 10 mints| Cook Time:20 mints| Servings: 6)

Ingredients

- Seasoned, whole wheat Breadcrumbs: ½ cup
- Thinly slices of two zucchinis
- Parmesan Cheese: ½ cup (grated)
- 1 Egg whisked
- Kosher salt and pepper, to taste

Instructions

Dry the courgette slices, so that no moisture remains.

In a bowl, beat the egg with a few teaspoons. of water and salt, pepper. In another bowl, mix the grated cheese, smoked paprika (optional), and breadcrumbs.

Dip the courgette slices in the egg mix and then in the breadcrumbs. Put everything on a rack and sprinkle with olive oil.

In a single layer, add the air fryer and cook for 8 minutes at 350 F. Add kosher salt and pepper if needed, serve with lean protein.

Nutritional value : per serving: Cal 101|Fat: 8g|Net Carbs: 6g|Protein: 10g

370. Air Fryer Bacon-Wrapped Jalapeno Poppers

(Prep Time: 10 mints| Cook Time: 8 mints| Servings: 10)

Ingredients

- Cream cheese: 1/3 cup
- Ten jalapenos
- Thin bacon: 5 strips

Instructions

Wash and dry the jalapenos. Cut them in half and remove the seeds.

Add the cream cheese in the center, but not too much

Allow the air fryer to preheat to 370 F. Cut the bacon strips in half.

Wrap the cream cheese-filled jalapenos with slices of bacon.

Secure with a toothpick.

Place the wrapped jalapenos in an air fryer, cook at 370 F and cook for 6-8 minutes or until the bacon is crispy.

Serve hot.

Nutritional value: per serving: Calories: 76kcal | Carbohydrates: 1g | Protein: 2g | Fat: 7g |

371. Creamy Cauliflower and Broccoli

Preparation time: 20 minutes Serves: 6

Ingredients

- pound cauliflower florets 1 pound broccoli florets
- ½ tbps sesame oil
- 1/2 tsp. smoked cayenne pepper 3/4 tsp. sea salt flakes
- tablespoon lemon zest, grated
- 1/2 cup Colby cheese, shredded

Cooking Instructions

Prepare the cauliflower and broccoli using your preferred steaming method. Then drain them well; add the sesame oil, cayenne pepper and salt flakes.

Air fry at 390 ° F for about 16 minutes; be sure to check the vegetables halfway through cooking time.

Subsequently, incorporate the lemon zest and Colby cheese; mix well to cover and serve quickly!

372. Famous Fried Pickles

Preparation time: 20 minutes Serves: 6

Ingredients

- 1/3 cup milk
- 1 tsp. garlic powder 2 medium-sized eggs
- tsp. fine sea salt 1/3 tsp. chili powder 1/3 cup all-purpose flour
- 1/2 tsp. shallot powder
- jars sweet and sour pickle spears

Cooking Instructions

Tap the pickled spears with a kitchen towel. So, take two bowls.

Beat the egg and milk in a bowl. In another bowl, combine all the dry ingredients.

First, dip the pickled spears into the dry mixture; then coat each pickle with the egg / milk mixture; dip them back into the flour mixture for an additional coating.

Fry the battered pickles for 15 minutes at 385 degrees. To enjoy!

373. Fried Squash Croquettes

Preparation time: 22 minutes Serves: 4

Ingredients

- 1/3 cup all-purpose flour
- 1/3 tsp. freshly ground black pepper, or more to taste 1/3 tsp. dried sage
- cloves garlic, minced
- 1 ½ tbps olive oil
- 1/3 margarinenut squash, peeled and grated 2 eggs, well whisked
- 1 tsp. fine sea salt
- A pinch of ground allspice

Cooking Instructions

Thoroughly combine all the ingredients in a bowl.

Preheat the air fryer to 345 degrees and set the timer for 17 minutes; cook until the pancakes are golden; serve immediately.

374. Cheese Stuffed Mushrooms with Horseradish Sauce

Preparation time: 15 minutes Serves: 5

Ingredients

- 1/2 cup parmesan cheese, grated 2 cloves garlic, pressed
- 2 tbps fresh coriander, chopped
- 1/3 tsp. kosher salt
- 1/2 tsp. crushed red pepper flakes 1 ½ tbps olive oil
- 20 medium-sized mushrooms, cut off the stems 1/2 cup Gorgonzola cheese, grated
- 1/4 cup low-fat mayonnaise
- 1 tsp. prepared horseradish, well-drained 1 tablespoon fresh parsley, finely chopped

Cooking Instructions

Mix the Parmesan with the garlic, coriander, salt, chilli and olive oil; stir to mix well.

Stuff the mushroom caps with the cheese filling. Complete with grated Gorgonzola.

Place the mushrooms in the pan of the air fryer and put them in the machine. Grill at 380 ° F for 8-12 minutes or until the filling has heated up.

Meanwhile, prepare the horseradish sauce by mixing the mayonnaise, horseradish and parsley. Serve the horseradish sauce with the hot fried mushrooms. To enjoy!

375. Mozzarella Cheese Sticks

(Prep Time: 10 mints| Cook Time: 15 mints| Servings: 4)

Ingredients

- Half-block of mozzarella cheese
- Olive oil
- Powder garlic: 1 tsp
- One egg
- Whole wheat bread crumbs: 1 cup
- Salt: 1/2 tsp

Instructions

Slice the mozzarella into six strips.

In a bowl, mix the garlic with the egg and salt.

Sprinkle the strips with the egg mix and then with the crumbs.

Freeze for at least half an hour.

Spray olive oil on the strips.

Cook for five minutes at 400 ° F in the basket of the air fryer.

Turn every 1.5 minutes to cook completely.

Serve with a lean protein meal.

Nutritional value : per serving: 224 calories| total fat 15g |carbohydrates 10.3g |protein 9.2g

376. Tomato Bites with Creamy Parmesan Sauce

Preparation time: 20 minutes Serves: 4

Ingredients

For the Sauce:

- 1/2 cup Parmigiano-Reggiano cheese, grated 4 tbps pecans, chopped
- tsp. garlic puree 1/2 tsp. fine sea salt
- 1/3 cup extra-virgin olive oil

For the Tomato Bites:

- 2 large-sized Roma tomatoes, cut into thin slices and pat them dry 8 ounces Halloumi cheese, cut into thin slices
- 1/3 cup onions, sliced 1 tsp. dried basil
- 1/4 tsp. red pepper flakes, crushed
- 1/8 tsp. sea salt

Cooking Instructions

Start by preheating the air fryer to 385 ° F.

Prepare the sauce by mixing all the ingredients, except extra virgin olive oil, in your food processor.

While the machine is running, slowly and gradually pour in the olive oil; puree until everything is well blended.

Now, distribute 1 tsp. of the sauce on top of each tomato slice. Place a slice of Halloumi cheese on each tomato slice. Complete with onion slices.

Sprinkle with basil, chilli and sea salt.

Transfer the assembled morsels to the cooking basket of the air fryer. Drizzle with non-stick cooking spray and cook for about 13 minutes.

Arrange these morsels on a nice serving dish, garnish with the remaining sauce and serve at room temperature.

377. Simple Green Beans with Margarine

Preparation time: 12 minutes Serves: 4

Ingredients

- 3/4 pound green beans, cleaned 1 tablespoon balsamic vinegar 1/4 tsp. kosher salt
- 1/2 tsp. mixed peppercorns, freshly cracked 1 tablespoon margarine
- 2 tbps toasted sesame seeds, to serve

Cooking Instructions

Set your air fryer to cook at 390 ° F.

Mix the green beans with all the above ingredients, apart from the sesame seeds. Set the timer for 10 minutes.

Meanwhile, toast the sesame seeds in a small non-stick pan; be sure to stir continuously.

Serve the sautéed green beans on a nice serving dish sprinkled with toasted sesame seeds.

378. Spanish-Style Eggs with Manchego Cheese

Preparation time: 40 minutes Serves: 4

Ingredients

- 1/3 cup grated Manchego, cheese 5 eggs
- small onion, finely chopped
- green garlic stalks, peeled and finely minced 1 ½ cups white mushrooms, chopped

- 1 tsp. dried basil
- 1 ½ tbps olive oil 3/4 tsp. dried oregano
- 1/2 tsp. dried parsley flakes or 1 tablespoon fresh flat-leaf Italian parsley
- 1 tsp. porcini powder
- Table salt and freshly ground black pepper, to savor

Cooking Instructions

Start by preheating the air fryer to 350 ° F. Add the oil, mushrooms, onion and green garlic to the pan of the air fryer. Cook this mixture for 6 minutes or until tender.

Meanwhile, break the eggs into a bowl; beat the eggs until they are well whipped. Then add the seasonings and mix again. Pause your air fryer and take the pan out of the pan.

Pour the beaten egg mixture into the pan with the sautéed mixture. Top with the grated Manchego cheese.Bake for about 32 minutes at 320 °F or until your frittata is set. Serve warm.

379. Air Fryer Kale Chips

(Prep Time: 3 mints| Cook Time: 5 mints| Servings: 2)

Ingredients

- One bunch of kale
- Half tsp. of garlic powder
- One tsp. of olive oil
- Half tsp. of salt

Instructions

Let the air fryer preheat to 370 degrees.

Cut the black cabbage into small pieces without the stem.

In a bowl, add all the ingredients with the black cabbage pieces.

Add the kale to the air fryer.

Cook for three minutes. Stir and cook for another two minutes.

Serve with a lean protein meal.

Nutritional value: per serving: Calories: 37kcal | Carbohydrates: 6g | Protein: 3g | Fat: 1g |

380. Mediterranean-Style Eggs with Spinach

Preparation time: 15 minutes Serves: 2

Ingredients

- 2 tbps olive oil, melted 4 eggs, whisked
- ounces fresh spinach, chopped
- 1 medium-sized tomato, chopped 1 tsp. fresh lemon juice
- 1/2 tsp. coarse salt
- 1/2 tsp. ground black pepper
- 1/2 cup of fresh basil, roughly chopped

Cooking Instructions

Add the olive oil to an air fryer baking pan. Make sure you tilt the pan to distribute the oil evenly.

Simply combine the remaining ingredients, except the basil leaves; whisk well until everything is well incorporated.

Cook in a preheated air fryer for 8-12 minutes at 280 ° F. Garnish with fresh basil leaves. Serve hot with a dollop of sour cream if desired.

381. Pecan Crusted Eggplant Recipe

(Prep Time: 15 mints| Cook Time:8 mints| Servings: 4)

Ingredients

- One eggplant
- Egg replacer: 2 tablespoons
- Whole wheat breadcrumbs: 1 cup
- Marjoram: 1/4 teaspoon
- Kosher salt and pepper: 1/4 teaspoon, each
- Dry mustard: 1/4 teaspoon
- Water: 4 tablespoons
- Pecans: 1/2 cup
- Almond milk: 6 tablespoons

Instructions

In a bowl, add the water, almond milk and egg substitute, mix and set aside.

In a food processor, add 1/4 teaspoon of pepper and kosher salt, marjoram, crumbs, pecans and mustard. Blend until well blended and chopped. Do not over mix.

Allow the air fryer to preheat to 390 F.

Cut the aubergines into half-inch slices and season with kosher salt and pepper.

Coat the slices in the egg mix and then in the crumb mix.

Add the coated slices into the air fryer in an even layer - Bake for 6-8 minutes at 390 F.

Serve with a lean protein meal.

Nutritional value : per serving: Cal 78|Fat 9g|Net carbs 8 g |Protein 9.9 g

382. Spicy Zesty Broccoli with Ketchup

Preparation time: 20 minutes Serves: 6

Ingredients

For the Broccoli Bites:

- 1 medium-sized head broccoli, broken into florets 1/2 tsp. lemon zest, freshly grated
- 1/3 tsp. fine sea salt 1/2 tsp. hot paprika 1 tsp. shallot powder
- 1 tsp. porcini powder 1/2 tsp. powdered garlic 1/3 tsp. celery seeds
- 1 ½ tbps olive oil For the Hot Sauce:
- 1/2 cup ketchup
- tablespoon balsamic vinegar 1/2 tsp. ground allspice

Cooking Instructions

Mix all the ingredients for the broccoli morsels in a mixing bowl, covering the broccoli flowers on all sides.

Cook them in the preheated 360 ° air fryer for 13-15 minutes. Meanwhile, mix all the ingredients for the hot sauce.

Pause the air fryer, mix the broccoli with the prepared sauce and cook for another 3 minutes.

383. Broccoli with Herbs and Cheese

Preparation time: 25 minutes Serves: 4

Ingredients

- 1/3 cup grated yellow cheese
- large-sized head broccoli, stemmed and cut small florets 2 1/2 tbps canola oil
- tsp.s dried rosemary 2 tsp.s dried basil

- Salt and ground black pepper, to taste

Cooking Instructions

Bring a medium skillet filled with lightly salted water to a boil. Then, boil the broccoli florets for about 3 minutes.

Then, drain the broccoli florets well; season with canola oil, rosemary, basil, salt and black pepper.

Set the air fryer to 390 ° F; place the seasoned broccoli in the cooking basket; set the timer for 17 minutes. Toss the broccoli halfway through the cooking process.

Serve hot topped with grated cheese and enjoy your meal!

384. Family Favorite Stuffed Mushrooms

Preparation time: 16 minutes Serves: 2

Ingredients

- 2 tsp.s cumin powder
- garlic cloves, peeled and minced 1 small onion, peeled and chopped 18 medium-sized white mushrooms
- Fine sea salt and freshly ground black pepper, to your liking A pinch ground allspice
- 2 tbps olive oil

Cooking Instructions

First clean the mushrooms; remove the central stems from the mushrooms to prepare the "shells".

Take a mixing dish and carefully combine the remaining elements. Fill the mushrooms with the prepared mixture.

Cook the mushrooms at 350 ° C for 12 minutes. To enjoy!

385. Tamarind Glazed Sweet Potatoes

Preparation time: 24 minutes Serves: 4

Ingredients

- 1/3 tsp. white pepper 1 tablespoon margarine, melted
- 1/2 tsp. turmeric powder
- garnet sweet potatoes, peeled and diced A few drops liquid Stevia
- tsp.s tamarind paste
- 1 1/2 tbps fresh lime juice 1 1/2 tsp. ground allspice

Cooking Instructions

In a bowl, mix all the ingredients until the sweet potatoes are well coated. Air-fry them at 335 ° F for 12 minutes.

• Pause the air fryer and restart it. Raise the temperature to 390 ° F and cook for another 10 minutes. Eat hot.

386. Roasted Cauliflower with Pepper Jack Cheese

Preparation time: 25 minutes Serves: 2

Ingredients

- 1/3 tsp. shallot powder
- 1 tsp. ground black pepper
- ½ large-sized heads of cauliflower, broken into florets 1/4 tsp. cumin powder
- ½ tsp. garlic salt
- 1/4 cup Pepper Jack cheese, grated 1 ½ tbps vege

table oil
- 1/3 tsp. paprika

Cooking Instructions

Boil the cauliflower in a large pot of salted water for about 5 minutes. Subsequently, drain the cauliflower florets; now transfer them to a baking dish.

Mix the cauliflower florets with the rest of the above ingredients.

Cook at 395 ° F for 16 minutes, turn them halfway through cooking. To enjoy!

387. Mexican-Style Cauliflower Fritters

Preparation time: 48 minutes Serves: 6

Ingredients

- tsp.s chili powder 1 1/2 tsp. kosher salt
- tsp. dried marjoram, crushed
- 1/2 cups cauliflower, broken into florets 1 1/3 cups tortilla chip crumbs
- 1/2 tsp. crushed red pepper flakes
- eggs, whisked
- 1 ½ cups Queso cotija cheese, crumbled

Cooking Instructions

Whisk the cauliflower florets in your food processor until crumbled (it is about the size of rice. Then, combine the cauliflower "rice" with the other elements.

Now, roll the cauliflower mixture into small balls; refrigerate for 30 minutes.

Preheat the air fryer to 345 degrees and set the timer for 14 minutes; cook until the balls are golden and serve immediately.

388. Zucchini Gratin

(Prep Time: 10 mints| Cook Time: 15 mints| Servings: 4)

Ingredient

- Olive oil: 1 tablespoon
- Chopped fresh parsley: 1 tablespoon
- Whole wheat bread crumbs: 2 tablespoons
- Medium zucchini
- Freshly ground black pepper & kosher salt to taste
- Grated Parmesan cheese: 4 tablespoons

Instructions

Let the air fryer preheat to 360F.

Cut the courgettes in half and another cut into eight pieces.

Place the pieces in the air fryer, but do not start frying.

In a bowl, add the cheese, freshly ground black pepper, parsley, breadcrumbs and oil. Mix well.

Add the mixture over the courgettes. Then cook the pieces for 15 minutes.

Until light brown.

Nutritional value : per serving: 81.7 calories| protein 3.6g carbohydrates 6.1g |fat 5.2g

389. Crispy Air Fryer Brussels Sprouts

(Prep Time: 5 mints| Cook Time: 10 mints| Servings: 4)

Ingredients

- Almonds sliced: 1/4 cup
- Brussel sprouts: 2 cups
- Kosher salt
- Parmesan cheese: 1/4 cup grated
- Olive oil: 2 Tablespoons
- Everything bagel seasoning: 2 Tablespoons

Instructions

In a saucepan, add the Brussels sprouts with two cups of water and cook over medium heat for almost ten minutes.
Drain the sprouts and cut them in half.
In a mixing bowl, add the sliced Brussels sprout with the chopped almonds, oil, salt, Parmesan and all the bagel dressing.
Completely cover the shoots.
Cook in the air fryer for 12-15 minutes at 375 F or until light brown.
Serve with a leaner protein meal.
Nutritional value : per serving: Calories: 155kcal | Carbohydrates: 3g | Protein: 6g | Fat: 3g |

390. Cheesy Omelet with Mixed Greens

Preparation time: 17 minutes Serves: 2

Ingredients

- 1/3 cup Ricotta cheese 5 eggs, beaten
- 1/2 red bell pepper, seeded and sliced
- 1 cup mixed greens, roughly chopped 1/2 green bell pepper, seeded and sliced 1/2 tsp. dried basil
- 1/2 chipotle pepper, finely minced 1/2 tsp. dried oregano

Cooking Instructions

Lightly coat the inside of a pan with a pan spray.
Then, throw all the ingredients into the pan; give it a nice stir. Bake at 325 ° F for 15 minutes.

391. Crispy Jicama Fries in Air Fryer

(Prep Time: 15 mints| Cook Time: 15 mints| Servings: 4)

Ingredients

Jicama fries

- Jicama chopped 8 cups
- Olive oil 2 tbsp.
- Garlic powder half tsp
- Cumin 1 tsp
- Sea salt 1 tsp
- Freshly ground black pepper ¼ tsp

Chili topping

- Olive oil 1 tbsp.
- Ground beef ½ lb.
- Diced tomatoes 7.5 oz.
- Chili powder ½ tbsp.
- Cumin ½ tbsp.
- Dried oregano 1 tsp
- Garlic powder ½ tsp
- Sea kosher salt½ tsp

Toppings

- Shredded Cheddar cheese ½ c
- Green chopped onions ¼ c

Instructions

Jicama fries

Boil a large pot of water on the fire. Add the jicama chips and simmer for 12-15 mints, before it is no longer crunchy.
If the jicama is no longer crunchy, take it out and remove it.
Place the French fries and olive oil, garlic powder, cumin and sea salt in a large cup. Throw to cover.
For an oven with an air fryer:
Move fries in a single layer on 2 oven racks with air fryer. Place the two grids inside the air fryer.
Cook for 10 minutes. Move the top shelf to the bottom and the bottom to the top, then bake for another 10-15 minutes, until the fries are cooked in gold.
For a basket air fryer:
You may have 2 batches to do. Arrange the fries in the basket, in a single layer, then bake for 20-25 mints. Repeat the 2nd set as well.
Remove the racks or basket from the air fryer when the fries are finished and set the temperature again to 400.
Chilli dressing
When you do, make the beef chili. Heat the oil in a large saucepan or small saucepan over medium heat.
Incorporate the minced meat. Increase to medium heat. Cook, splitting with a spatula, for about 10 minutes until golden brown.
Put the remaining chili ingredients in the pan / pot and mix. Cook for 5 minutes and modify the chili powder to fit it (I applied 1/2 tablespoon more).
Cook, stirring regularly, for about 5-10 mints or until the flavors grow to your taste as long as you want.
Assembly
Move the fries to an 8x8 pan or an oven-safe plate or bowl that works inside the oven of the fryer.
Let the chilli roll over the chips. Sprinkle with grated cheese.
In the center of the oven of the air fryer (or just in the center of a standard air fryer), place the baking dish or plate on the rack for about 2 to 3 minutes before the cheese melts.
To serve, garnish with sliced green onions.
Nutritional value : per serving: Cal 216|Fat 3g| |Protein 22g|-

Carbohydrates 12g

392. Swiss Creamed Eggs
Preparation time: 25 minutes Serves: 2

Ingredients

- 1 tsp. garlic paste
- 1 ½ tbps olive oil 1/2 cup crème fraîche
- 1/3 tsp. ground black pepper, to your liking 1/3 cup Swiss cheese, crumbled
- 1 tsp. cayenne pepper
- 1/3 cup Swiss chard, torn into pieces 5 eggs
- 1/4 cup yellow onions, chopped
- 1 tsp. fine sea salt

Cooking Instructions

Break the eggs in a baking dish; then add the fresh cream, salt, ground black pepper and cayenne pepper.

Next, cover the inside of a baking dish with olive oil and tilt it to distribute it evenly. Scrape the egg and cream mixture into the pan. Add the other ingredients; stir to mix well.

Bake for 18 minutes at 292 ° F. Serve quickly.

393. Air Fryer Tofu
(Prep Time: 10 mints| Cook Time: 10 mints| Servings: 4)

Ingredients

- Avocado oil: 1 tablespoon
- Extra firm tofu of 12 oz.
- Cornstarch: 2 teaspoon
- Salt: 1/2 teaspoon
- Onion powder: 1 teaspoon
- Freshly ground black pepper: 1/2 teaspoon
- Garlic powder: 1 teaspoon
- Paprika: 1 teaspoon

Instructions

Take the block of tofu and press between two plates with absorbent paper in the middle.

Add a heavy object on top of it and press for half an hour.

Allow the air fryer to preheat to 390 F.

Carefully cut the tofu into half-inch or ¾-inch cubes

Pour the tofu cubes into the avocado oil and the corn starch

Cover all the tofu pieces. Then add the air fryer and cook for five minutes at 390 F.

Or cook according to your preferences.

Serve hot with lean proteins.

Nutritional value : Per Serving : 109 calories| total fat 10g | carbohydrates 3g |protein 14g.

394. Air-Fried Spinach Frittata
(Prep Time: 5 mints| Cook Time:10 mints| Servings: 4)

Ingredients

- 1/3 cup of packed spinach
- One small chopped red onion
- Shredded mozzarella cheese
- Three eggs
- Salt, pepper

Instructions

Allow the air fryer to preheat to 360 F

In a pan over medium heat, add the oil, the onion, cook until translucent, add the spinach and sauté until half cooked.

Beat the eggs and season with kosher salt and pepper - mix the spinach mixture.

Cook in the air fryer for 8 minutes or until cooked.

Slice and serve hot.

Nutritional Value : per serving: Cal 124| Fat: 10.9g|Net Carbs: 14.1g| Protein: 16.9 g

395. Decadent Omelet with Oyster Mushrooms
Preparation time: 42 minutes Serves: 2

Ingredients

- king oyster mushrooms, thinly sliced 1 lemongrass, chopped
- 1/2 tsp. dried marjoram
- eggs
- 1/3 cup Swiss cheese, grated 2 tbps sour cream
- 1/2 tsp. dried rosemary
- tsp.s red pepper flakes, crushed 2 tbps margarine, melted
- 1/2 red onion, peeled and sliced into thin rounds
- ½ tsp. garlic powder 1 tsp. dried dill weed
- Fine sea salt and ground black pepper, to your liking

Cooking Instructions

Melt the margarine in a pan over medium heat. Then, sauté the onion, mushrooms, and lemongrass until softened; Reserve.

Next, preheat the air fryer to 325 ° F. Next, break the eggs into a mixing bowl and beat them well. Then, stir in the sour cream and mix well.

Now, stir in the salt, black pepper, chilli, rosemary, garlic powder, marjoram and dill.

Next step, grease the inside of an air fryer pan with a thin layer of cooking spray. Pour the egg / seasoning mixture into the pan; discard the reserved mixture. Top with the Swiss cheese.

Set the timer for 35 minutes; cook until a knife inserted in the center comes out clean and dry.

396. Italian Tomatoes with Goat Cheese

Preparation time: 20 minutes Serves: 4

Ingredients

- ounces goat cheese, sliced 2 shallots, thinly sliced
- Pantano Romanesco tomatoes, cut into 1/2-inch slices 1 ½ tbps extra-virgin olive oil
- 3/4 tsp. sea salt
- Fresh parsley, for garnish Fresh basil, chopped

Cooking Instructions

Preheat your Air Fryer to 380 °F.

Now, pat each tomato slice dry using a paper towel. Sprinkle each slice with salt and chopped basil. Top with a slice of goat cheese.

Top with the shallot slices; drizzle with olive oil. Add the prepared tomato and feta "bites" to the air fryer food basket.

Cook in the Air Fryer for about 14 minutes. Lastly, adjust seasonings to taste and serve garnished with fresh parsley leaves. Enjoy!

397. Veggies with Middle-Eastern Tahini Sauce

Preparation time: 20 minutes Serves: 4

Ingredients

- pound cauliflower florets 1 pound button mushrooms 2 tbps olive oil
- 1/2 tsp. white pepper 1/2 tsp. dried dill weed 1/2 tsp. cayenne pepper 1/2 tsp. celery seeds 1/2 tsp. mustard seeds Salt, to taste

Yogurt Tahini Sauce:

- cup plain yogurt
- heaping tbps tahini paste 1 tablespoon lemon juice
- 1 tablespoon extra-virgin olive oil 1/2 tsp. Aleppo pepper, minced

Cooking Instructions

Season the cauliflower and mushrooms with olive oil and spices. Preheat your air fryer to 380 ° F.

Add the cauliflower to the cooking basket and cook for 10 minutes.

Add the mushrooms, bring the temperature to 390 degrees and cook for another 6 minutes.

While the vegetables are cooking, prepare the sauce by beating all the ingredients. Serve the vegetables warm with the sauce on the side.

398. Summer Vegetable Fritters

Preparation time: 20 minutes Serves: 2

Ingredients

- zucchini, grated and squeezed 1 cup cauliflower florets, boiled
- tbps Romano cheese, grated
- tbps fresh shallots, minced 1 tsp. fresh garlic, minced
- 1 tablespoon peanut oil
- Sea salt and ground black pepper, to taste 1 tsp. cayenne pepper

Cooking Instructions

In a bowl, carefully combine all the ingredients until everything is well incorporated.

Shape the mixture into meatballs. Spray the air fryer basket with cooking spray.

Cook in the preheated air fryer at 365 ° F for 6 minutes. Turn them over and cook for another 6 minutes

Serve quickly and enjoy!

399. Greek-Style Roasted Vegetable Salad

Preparation time: 20 minutes Serves: 4

Ingredients

- red onion, sliced
- 1 pound cherry tomatoes 1/2 pound asparagus
- cucumber, sliced 2 cups baby spinach
- tbps white vinegar 1/4 cup extra-virgin olive oil 2 tbps fresh parsley Sea salt and pepper to taste
- 1/2 cup Kalamata olives, pitted and sliced

Cooking Instructions

Start by preheating the air fryer to 400 ° F.

Place the onion, cherry tomatoes and asparagus in the basket of the lightly greased air fryer. Cook for 5 to 6 minutes, turning the basket from time to time.

Transfer to a salad bowl. Add the cucumber and baby spinach.

Next, whisk the vinegar, olive oil, parsley, salt and black pepper in a small bowl. Dress your salad; add the Kalamata olives.

Launch to mix well and serve.

400. Zucchini Parmesan Crisps

Preparation time: 20 minutes Serves: 4

Ingredients

- pound zucchini, peeled and sliced 1 egg, lightly beaten
- 1 cup parmesan cheese, preferably freshly grated

Cooking Instructions

Dry the courgettes with a kitchen towel.

In a baking dish, carefully combine the egg and cheese. Then, cover the courgette slices with the breadcrumbs mixture.

Cook in the preheated air fryer at 400 ° F for 9 minutes, shaking the basket halfway through the cooking time.

Work in batches until the fries are golden.

401. Vegetable and Egg Salad

Preparation time: 35 minutes Serves: 4

Ingredients

- 1/3 pound Brussels sprouts 1/2 cup radishes, sliced
- 1/2 cup mozzarella cheese, crumbled 1 red onion, chopped
- eggs, hardboiled and sliced
- Dressing:
- 1/4 cup olive oil
- tbps champagne vinegar 1 tsp. Dijon mustard
- Sea salt and ground black pepper, to taste

Cooking Instructions

Start by preheating the air fryer to 380 ° F.
Add the Brussels sprouts and radishes to the cooking basket. Spray with cooking spray and cook for 15 minutes. Let it cool at room temperature for about 15 minutes.
Season the vegetables with cheese and red onion.
Mix all the ingredients for the dressing and mix to mix well. Serve topped with hard-boiled eggs.

402.   Simple Stuffed Bell Peppers

Preparation time: 20 minutes Serves: 2

Ingredients

- bell peppers, tops and seeds removed Salt and pepper, to taste
- 2/3 cup cream cheese
- tbps mayonnaise
- tablespoon fresh celery stalks, chopped

Cooking Instructions

Place the peppers in the lightly greased cooking basket. Cook in the preheated air fryer at 400 ° C for 15 minutes, turning them halfway through the cooking time.
Season with salt and pepper.
Then, in a bowl, combine the cream cheese with the mayonnaise and the chopped celery. Stuff the pepper with the cream cheese and serve.

403.   Italian-Style Sausage Casserole

Preparation time: 20 minutes Serves: 4

Ingredients

- pound Italian sausage
- Italian peppers, seeded and sliced 1 cup mushrooms, sliced
- 1 shallot, sliced
- cloves garlic
- 1 tsp. dried basil
- tsp. dried oregano 1/4 tsp. black pepper 1/4 tsp. cayenne pepper Sea salt, to taste
- tbps Dijon mustard 1 cup chicken broth

Cooking Instructions

Toss all the ingredients into a lightly greased baking sheet. Make sure the sausages and vegetables are coated in oil and seasonings.
Cook in a preheated 380 ° F air fryer for 15 minutes. Divide between individual bowls and serve hot.

404.   Rustic Roasted Green Beans

Preparation time: 10 minutes + chilling time Serves: 4

Ingredients

- 3/4 pound trimmed green beans, cut into bite-sized pieces Salt and freshly cracked mixed pepper, to taste
- shallot, thinly sliced
- 1 tablespoon lime juice
- 1 tablespoon champagne vinegar 1/4 cup extra-virgin olive oil
- 1/2 tsp. mustard seeds 1/2 tsp. celery seeds
- 1 tablespoon fresh basil leaves, chopped

- 1 tablespoon fresh parsley leaves 1 cup goat cheese, crumbled

Cooking Instructions

Pour the green beans with salt and pepper into a lightly greased air fryer basket.
Cook in preheated air fryer at 400 ° F for 5 minutes or until tender.
Add the shallots and mix gently to combine.
In a bowl, beat the lime juice, vinegar, olive oil and spices. Dress the salad and garnish with the goat cheese. Serve at room temperature or cool. To enjoy!

405.   Garlic Fried Mushrooms

Preparation time: 15 minutes Serves: 4

Ingredients

- pound button mushrooms 1 ½ cups Pancetta rinds
- cup parmesan cheese, grated
- eggs, whisked ½ tsp. salt
- tbps fresh parsley leaves, roughly chopped

Cooking Instructions

Dry the mushrooms with absorbent paper.
To get started, set up your "breading" station. Mix the bacon rinds and Parmesan in a shallow pan. In a separate dish, beat the eggs.
Start by dipping the mushrooms in the eggs. Squeeze the mushrooms into the parm / pancetta mixture, coating evenly.
Spray the basket of the air fryer with cooking oil. Add the mushrooms and cook at 400 °F for 6 minutes, turning them halfway through cooking.
Sprinkle with salt. Serve garnished with fresh parsley leaves.

406.   Air Fryer Spicy Dill Pickle Fries

(Prep Time: 15 mints| Cook Time: 15 mints| Servings: 12)

Ingredient

- All-purpose flour: 1 cup
- One and a half jars(spears) of spicy dill pickle
- ¼ cup of milk
- Cooking spray
- One egg lightly beaten
- Half teaspoon of paprika
- Whole wheat bread crumbs: 1 cup

Instructions

Drain the pickles well and dry them with absorbent paper.
In a bowl, mix the paprika and flour. In another bowl, mix the beaten egg and milk.
Put the wholemeal breadcrumbs in another bowl.
Allow the air fryer to preheat to 400 F.
Coat the dill pickle first in the flour mixture, then in the egg mix, then in the breadcrumb mix.
Coat all the dill pickles.
Add dill-coated pickles in an even layer into the basket of the air fryer.
Cook for 14 minutes at 400 F
Flip the dill pickles in half, until cooked through
Nutritional value : Per Serving: 79.8 calories| protein 3.1g |carbohydrates 16.8g| fat 1g

407. Classic Cauliflower Hash Browns

Preparation time: 30 minutes Serves: 2

Ingredients

- 2/3 pound cauliflower, peeled and grated 2 eggs, whisked
- 1/4 cup scallions, chopped
- tsp. fresh garlic, minced
- Sea salt and ground black pepper, to taste 1/4 tsp. ground allspice
- 1/2 tsp. cinnamon 1 tablespoon peanut oil

Cooking Instructions

Boil the cauliflower over medium-low heat until the fork is tender, 5 to 7 minutes Drain the water; dab the cauliflower with a cloth.

Now add the remaining ingredients; stir to mix well.

Cook in a preheated air fryer at 400F for 20 minutes. Shake the basket once or twice. Serve with low carb ketchup.

408. Rainbow Cheese and Vegetable Bake

Preparation time: 50 minutes Serves: 4

Ingredients

- pound cauliflower, chopped into small florets 2 tbps olive oil
- 1/2 tsp. red pepper flakes, crushed
- 1/2 tsp. freshly ground black pepper Salt, to taste
- bell peppers, thinly sliced
- serrano pepper, thinly sliced
- medium-sized tomatoes, sliced 1 leek, thinly sliced
- garlic cloves, minced
- 1 cup Monterey cheese, shredded

Cooking Instructions

Start by preheating the air fryer to 350 ° F. Spray a saucepan with cooking oil.

Put the cauliflower in the saucepan in an even layer; drizzle 1 tablespoon of olive oil on top. Then add the red pepper, black pepper and salt.

Add 2 peppers and 1/2 of the leeks. Add the tomatoes and the remaining spoonful of olive oil.

Add the remaining chopped peppers, leeks and garlic. Top with the cheese.

Cover the saucepan with aluminum foil and cook for 32 minutes. Remove the film and raise the temperature to 400 ° F; cook for another 16 minutes.

409. Smoky Sweet Crunchy Chickpeas

(Prep Time: 10 mints| Cook Time: 10 mints| Servings: 4)

Ingredients

- Water from chickpeas: 2 tablespoons
- Chickpeas: 1 can
- Smoked paprika: 2 teaspoons
- Maple syrup: 1 tablespoon
- Garlic powder: 1 and 1/2 teaspoons
- Half tsp. of sea salt

Instructions

Do not wash the chickpeas, but rinse them and set aside the water from the can of chickpeas.

Place the chickpeas in the basket of the air fryer. Air-fry them for eight minutes at 390 F.

Meanwhile, in a bowl, add the maple syrup, kosher salt, garlic powder, two tablespoons. of water reserved from the cans, smoked paprika. Mix well.

Remove the chickpeas from the air fryer, cover them with the spice mixture. Then add the coated chickpeas back into the air fryer.

Cook for another five minutes, at 390 F.

Turn the basket, then return it to the deep fryer for another five minutes, until the chickpeas are golden and crisp.

Serve hot and cold with lean proteins.Nutritional value: Per Serving: 147 Kcal| total fat 19.3g |carbohydrates 15.6g | protein 24.7g

410. Easy Air Fryer Zucchini Chips

(Prep Time: 10 mints| Cook Time: 12 mints| Servings: 2)

Ingredients

- Parmesan Cheese: 3 Tbsp.
- Garlic Powder: 1/4 tsp
- Zucchini: 1 Cup (thin slices)
- Corn Starch: 1/4 Cup
- Onion Powder: 1/4 tsp
- Salt: 1/4 tsp
- Whole wheat Bread Crumbs: 1/2 Cup

Instructions

Allow the air fryer to preheat to 390 F. Cut the zucchini into thin slices, like chips.

In a food processor bowl, mix together the garlic powder, kosher salt, wholemeal breadcrumbs, parmesan and onion powder.

Blend into finer pieces.

Zucchini chips for air fryer

In three separate bowls, add the cornstarch in one, the egg mixture in another bowl and the wholemeal breadcrumb mixture in the other bowl.

Pour the zucchini flakes into the cornstarch mixture, into the egg mixture, then cover with wholemeal breadcrumbs.

Spray the basket of the air fryer with olive oil. Add the breaded courgette flakes in a single layer to the deep fryer and drizzle with olive oil.

Air fry for six minutes at preheated temperature. Cook for another four minutes after turning or until the zucchini flakes are golden brown.

Serve with a cooked lean protein meal.

Nutritional value: Per Serving: 219 calories| total fat 26.9g |carbohydrates 11.2g |protein 14.1g

411. Breakfast Veggie Mix

(Prep time: 10 min| Cook time: 25 min| Servings: 6)

Ingredients

- 1 yellow onion, sliced
- 1 red bell pepper, chopped
- 1 Tablespoon olive oil
- ¼ cup brie, trimmed and cubed
- One and a half cup sourdough bread, cubed
- 8 tbsp. of parmesan, grated
- 8 eggs (white only and 2 yellows)

- 1 Tablespoons mustard
- 2 cups of milk
- Salt and black pepper to the taste

Instructions

At 350 degrees F, turn on the air fryer, add fat, onion, potatoes, and bell pepper and cook for 5 minutes.

Mix the eggs with the sugar, salt, pepper and mustard in a cup, then blend well.

Add the bread and brie to the air fryer, add half of the egg mixture and add half of the Parmesan.

Add the remaining bread and Parmesan, mix just a little and cook for 20 minutes.

Serve at breakfast and divide between dishes.

To enjoy

Nutritional value: calories 231| fat 5g| fiber 10g|carbs 20g| protein 12g

412. Easy Spring Rolls (Air Fried)

(Prep Time: 20 mints| Cook Time: 24 mints| Servings: 20)

Ingredients

- Asian noodles: ¼ cup
- Sesame oil: 1 tablespoon
- Mince lean pork: one cup
- One chopped onion
- Cloves of minced garlic
- Mixed vegetables: 1 cup
- Gluten-free soy sauce: 1 teaspoon
- One packet of spring rolls
- Cold water: 2 tablespoons

Instructions

In hot water, soak the Asian noodles until tender, then drain the hot water and cut into smaller pieces, according to your preference.

In a wok, heat the oil until it smokes lightly, then add the mixed vegetables, minced meat, garlic and onion with soy sauce, cook until the meat is completely cooked.

Turn off the heat and then add the chopped tagliatelle, until all the sauce is absorbed.

Place the spring roll on a flat surface, one at a time, then add 1/4 cup of the filling and fold, seal with water.

Roll them up tightly.

Allow the air fryer to preheat to 360 ° F

Spray each spring roll with olive oil.

Arrange the rolls in a single layer and bake for eight minutes at 180 ° C or until golden brown. Repeat the process until all are cooked.

Nutritional value : Per serving: Cal 153 |Fat: 18g| Net Carbs: 10g| Protein: 20g|

413. Asparagus Frittata

(Prep Time: 10 mints| Cook Time: 5 mints| Servings: 2)

Ingredients

- 4 eggs, whisked
- 3 Tablespoons parmesan, grated
- 2 Tablespoons milk
- Salt and black pepper to the taste
- Ten asparagus tips, steamed
- Cooking spray

Instructions

Mix the eggs with the Parmesan, butter, salt, pepper and whisk well in a saucepan.

Heat the air fryer to 400 degrees F and spray with fat.

Add the asparagus, mix the eggs, mix a little and cook for 5 minutes.

Divide the omelette into plates and serve breakfast.

Enjoy!

Nutritional value: per serving: calories 312, fat 5g, fiber 8g, carbs 14g, Protein 2g

OPTAVIA LEAN & GREEN DESSERT AIR-FRY RECIPES

414. Tasty Banana Cake

Preparation time: 10 minutes Cooking duration: 30 minutes Serves: 4

Ingredients:

- 1 tablespoon margarine, soft
- 1 egg
- 1/3 cup brown sugar
- 2 tbps honey
- 1 banana, peeled and mashed
- 1 cup white flour
- 1 tsp. baking powder
- ½ tsp. cinnamon powder
- Cooking spray

Cooking Instructions:

Spray a cake pan with cooking spray and set aside.

In a bowl, mix the margarine with the sugar, banana, honey, egg, cinnamon, baking powder and flour and whisk

Pour it into a pan greased with cooking spray, pop into your air fryer and cook at 350 ° F for 30 minutes.

4. Allow the cake to cool, slice and serve.

415. Simple Cheesecake

Preparation time: 10 minutes Cooking duration: 15 minutes Serves: 15

Ingredients:

- 1 pound cream cheese
- ½ tsp. vanilla extract
- 2 eggs
- 4 tbps sugar
- 1 cup graham crackers, crumbled
- 2 tbps margarine

Cooking Instructions:

In a bowl, mix the crackers with the margarine.

Press the crackers mix to the bottom of a lined cake pan, introduce into the air fryer and bake at 350 ° F for 4 minutes.

Meanwhile, in a bowl, mix the sugar with the cream cheese, eggs and vanilla and beat well.

Spread the filling over the cracker crust and cook the cheesecake in the air fryer at 310 ° F for 15 minutes.

Leave the cake in the fridge for 3 hours, slice and serve.

416. Bread Pudding

Preparation time: 10 minutes Cooking duration: 1 hour Serves: 4

Ingredients

- 6 glazed doughnuts, crumbled
- 1 cup cherries
- 4 egg yolks
- 1 and ½ cups whipping cream
- ½ cup raisins
- ¼ cup sugar
- ½ cup chocolate chips.

Cooking Instructions:

In a bowl, mix the cherries with the egg yolks and whipped cream and mix well.

In another bowl, mix the raisins with the sugar, chocolate chips and donuts and mix.

Combine the 2 blends, transfer everything to a greased pan suitable for your air fryer and cook at 310 ° F for 1 hour.

Chill the pudding before cutting and serving.

417. Bread Dough and Amaretto Dessert

Preparation time: 10 minutes Cooking duration: 12 minutes Serves: 12

Ingredients:

- 1 pound bread dough
- 1 cup sugar
- ½ cup margarine, melted
- 1 cup heavy cream
- 12 ounces chocolate chips
- 2 tbps amaretto liqueur

Cooking Instructions:

Roll out the dough, cut it into 20 slices and then cut each slice in half.

Brush the pieces of dough with margarine, sprinkle with sugar, place them in the fryer basket after brushing some margarine, cook them at 350 ° F for 5 minutes, turn them, cook for another 3 minutes and transfer to a plate from scope.

Heat a pan with the cream over medium heat, add the chocolate chips and stir until they melt.

Add the liqueur, mix again, transfer to a bowl and serve ladles of bread with this sauce.

418. Cinnamon Rolls and Cream Cheese Dip

Preparation time: 2 hours Cooking duration: 15 minutes Serves: 8

Ingredients:

- 1 pound bread dough
- ¾ cup brown sugar
- 1 and ½ tbps cinnamon, ground
- ¼ cup margarine, melted

For the cream cheese dip:

- 2 tbps margarine
- 4 ounces cream cheese
- 1 and ¼ cups sugar
- ½ tsp. vanilla

Cooking Instructions:

Roll out the dough onto a floured work surface, shape into a rectangle and brush with ¼ cup margarine.

In a bowl, mix the cinnamon with the sugar, mix, sprinkle the dough, roll the dough into a log, seal tightly and cut into 8 pieces.

Let the rolls rise for 2 hours, place them in the basket of the air fryer, bake at 350 ° F for 5 minutes, flip, cook for another 4 minutes and transfer to a serving dish.

In a bowl, mix the cream cheese with the margarine, sugar and vanilla and whisk very well.

Serve your cinnamon rolls with this cream cheese sauce.

419. Pumpkin Pie

Preparation time: 10 minutes Cooking duration: 15 minutes Serves: 9

Ingredients:

- 1 tablespoon sugar
- 2 tbps flour
- 1 tablespoon margarine
- 2 tbps water
- For the pumpkin pie filling:
- 3.5 ounces pumpkin flesh, chopped
- 1 tsp. mixed spice
- 1 tsp. nutmeg
- 3 ounces water
- 1 egg, whisked
- 1 tablespoon sugar

Cooking Instructions:

Put 3 ounces of water in a pot, bring to a boil over medium high heat, add pumpkin, egg, 1 tablespoon of sugar, spice and nutmeg, stir, boil for 20 minutes, remove from heat and blend with an immersion blender.

In a bowl, mix the flour with the margarine, 1 tablespoon of sugar and 2 tablespoons of water and knead the dough well.

Grease a pan suitable for the air fryer with margarine, press the dough into the pan, fill with the pumpkin pie filling, place in the air fryer basket and cook at 360 ° F for 15 minutes.

Slice and serve hot.

420. Wrapped Pears

Preparation time: 10 minutes Cooking duration: 15 minutes Serves: 4

Ingredients:

- 4 puff pastry sheets
- 14 ounces vanilla custard
- 2 pears, halved
- 1 egg, whisked
- ½ tsp. cinnamon powder
- 2 tbps sugar

Cooking Instructions:

Arrange the slices of puff pastry on a work surface, add a tablespoon of vanilla cream in the center of each, garnish with half of pears and wrap.

Brush the pears with the egg, sprinkle with sugar and cinnamon, place them in the basket of the air fryer and cook at 320 ° C for 15 minutes.
Divide the packages on plates and serve.

421. Flourless Almond and Ginger Cookies

Preparation time: 50 minutes Serves: 8

Ingredients

- 1/4 cup slivered almonds
- 1 stick margarine, room temperature 4 ounces monk fruit
- 3/3 cup blanched almond flour 1/4 cup coconut flour
- 1/4 tsp. ground cloves
- 1 tablespoon ginger powder
- 3/4 tsp. pure vanilla extract

Cooking Instructions:

In a baking dish, whisk the monk fruit, margarine, vanilla extract, ground cloves and ginger until the mixture is light and fluffy. Then, add the coconut flour, almond flour, and flaked almonds.

Continue to mix until a soft dough is formed. Cover and refrigerate for 35 minutes. Meanwhile, preheat the air fryer to 315 ° F.

Roll the dough into small biscuits and place them on the Air Fryer cake pan; gently press each cookie using the back of a spoon.

Bake these margarine cookies for 13 minutes.

422. Strawberry Donuts

Preparation time: 10 minutes Cooking duration: 15 minutes Serves: 4

Ingredients:

- 8 ounces flour
- 1 tablespoon brown sugar
- 1 tablespoon white sugar
- 1 egg
- 2 and ½ tbps margarine
- 4 ounces whole milk
- 1 tsp. baking powder
- For the strawberry icing:
- 2 tbps margarine
- 3.5 ounces icing sugar
- ½ tsp. pink coloring
- ¼ cup strawberries, chopped
- 1 tablespoon whipped cream

Cooking Instructions:

In a bowl, mix the margarine, 1 tablespoon of brown sugar, 1 tablespoon of white sugar and the flour and mix.

In a second bowl, mix the egg with 1 1/2 tablespoons of margarine and the milk and mix well.

Combine the 2 mixes, mix, form donuts from this mix and place them in the basket of the air fryer and cook at 360 ° F for 15 minutes.

Add 1 tablespoon of margarine, powdered sugar, food coloring, whipped cream and strawberry puree and blend well.

Arrange the donuts on a serving plate and serve with strawberry glaze.

423. Air Fried Bananas

Preparation time: 10 minutes Cooking duration: 15 minutes Serves: 4

Ingredients:

- 3 tbps margarine
- 2 eggs
- 8 bananas, peeled and halved
- ½ cup corn flour
- 3 tbps cinnamon sugar
- 1 cup panko

Cooking Instructions:

1. Heat a pan with the margarine over medium-high heat, add the panko, stir and cook for 4 minutes, then transfer to a bowl.
2. Roll each in flour, eggs and panko, place in air fryer basket, sprinkle with cinnamon sugar and bake at 280 ° F for 10 minutes.

Serve immediately.

424. Easy Fruitcake with Cranberries

Preparation time: 30 minutesServes: 8

Ingredients

- 1 cup almond flour
- 1/4 tsp. baking soda 1/4 tsp. baking powder 3/4 cup
- erythritol
- 1/4 tsp. ground cloves 1/4 tsp. ground cinnamon 1/4 tsp. cardamom
- stick margarine
- 1/4 tsp. vanilla paste
- eggs plus 1 egg yolk, beaten
- 1/4 cup cranberries, fresh or thawed 1 tablespoon browned margarine

For Ricotta Frosting:

- 1/4 stick margarine
- 1/4 cup firm Ricotta cheese 1 cup powdered
- erythritol 1/4 tsp. salt
- Zest of 1/4 lemon

Cooking Instructions:

1 Start by preheating the air fryer to 355 ° F.

In a mixing bowl, combine the flour with the baking soda, baking powder, erythritol, ground cloves, cinnamon and cardamom.

In a separate bowl, whisk 1 stick of margarine with the vanilla paste; mix the eggs until light and fluffy. Add the flour / sugar mixture to the margarine / egg mixture. Incorporate the cranberries and browned margarine. 4 Scrape the mixture into the greased pan. Then cook in the preheated air fryer for about 35 minutes. 5 Meanwhile, in a food processor, whip 1/4 stick of margarine and ricotta until there are no lumps.

Slowly add the powdered erythritol and salt until a thick consistency is obtained. Incorporate the lemon zest; stir to combine and cool completely before use.

Glaze the cake and enjoy your meal!

425. Classic White Chocolate Cookies

Preparation time: 40 minutes Serves: 10

Ingredients

- 3/4 cup margarine
- 3/3 cups almond flour 1/4 cup coconut flour
- tbps coconut oil 3/4 cup powdered swerve
- 1/4 tsp. ground anise star 1/4 tsp. ground allspice 1/4 tsp. grated nutmeg 1/4 tsp. fine sea salt
- ounces white chocolate, unsweetened 3 eggs, well beaten

Cooking Instructions:

Place all the above ingredients, minus 1 egg, in a baking dish. Then, knead with your hand until it forms a soft dough. Refrigerate for 35 minutes.

Roll the cold dough into small balls; flatten the balls and preheat the air

350 ° F fryer r.

Prepare a washed egg using the remaining egg. Then, glaze the biscuits with the beaten egg; bake about 11 minutes.

426. Birthday Chocolate Raspberry Cake

Preparation time: 30 minutes Serves: 4

Ingredients

- 1/4 cup monk fruit
- 1/4 cup unsalted margarine, room temperature 1 egg plus 1 egg white, lightly whisked
- ounces almond flour
- 3 tbps Dutch-process cocoa powder 1/4 tsp. ground cinnamon
- tablespoon candied ginger 1/8 tsp. table salt
- For the Filling:
- ounces fresh raspberries 1/4 cup monk fruit
- 1 tsp. fresh lime juice

Cooking Instructions:

First, set the air fryer to cook at 315 ° F. Then, spray the inside of two cake pans with the margarine-flavored cooking spray.

In a mixing bowl, beat the monk fruit and margarine until smooth and creamy. Then, incorporate the beaten eggs. Stir in the almond flour, cocoa powder, cinnamon, ginger and salt.

Press the batter into the pans; use a wide spatula to level the surface of the batter. Bake for 35 minutes or until a wooden stick inserted in the center of the cake is completely dry.

While the cake is cooking, mix all the ingredients for the filling together in a medium saucepan. Cook over high heat, stirring often and mashing with the back of a spoon; bring to a boil and lower the temperature.

Continue to cook, stirring until the mixture thickens, for another 7 minutes. Let the filling cool to room temperature.

Spread 1/4 of the raspberry filling on the first crust. Top with another crust; distribute the remaining filling on top. Spread the frosting on top and sides of the cake.

427. Picnic Blackberry Muffins

Preparation time: 35 minutes Serves: 8

Ingredients

- 1/2 cups almond flour 1/4 tsp. baking soda 1 tsp. baking powder 1/4 tsp. kosher salt 1/4 cup swerve
- eggs, whisked 1/4 cup milk
- 1/4 cup coconut oil, melted 1/4 tsp. vanilla paste
- 1/4 cup fresh blackberries

Cooking Instructions:

In a bowl, combine the almond flour, baking soda, baking powder, sandwich and salt. Whisk to mix well.

In another bowl, combine the eggs, milk, coconut oil and vanilla.

Now, add the wet egg mixture to dry the flour mixture. Then, carefully incorporate the fresh blackberries; mix gently to combine.

Scrape the batter mixture into the muffin molds. Bake the muffins at 350 ° F for 13 minutes or until the tops are golden brown.

Sprinkle some extra icing sugar on top of each muffin if desired.

428. Sunday Tart with Walnuts

Preparation time: 35 minutes Serves: 6

Ingredients

- 1 cup coconut milk 3 eggs
- 1/4 stick margarine, at room temperature 1 tsp. vanilla essence
- 1/4 tsp. ground cardamom
- 1/4 tsp. ground cloves 1/4 cup walnuts, ground 1/4 cup swerve
- 1/4 cup almond flour

Cooking Instructions:

Start by preheating the air fryer to 360 ° F. Spray the sides and bottom of a pan with non-stick cooking spray.

Mix all ingredients until they are well combined. Scrape the batter into the prepared pan.

Cook for about 13 minutes; use a toothpick to check cooking.

429. Perfectly Puffy Coconut Cookies

Preparation time: 35 minutes Serves: 13

Ingredients

- 1 cup margarine, melted
- ¾ cups powdered swerve 3 eggs
- tbps coconut milk 1 tsp. coconut extract 1 tsp. vanilla extract 1 cup coconut flour
- 1 ¼ cups almond flour
- 1/4 tsp. baking powder 1/4 tsp. baking soda 1/4 tsp. fine table salt
- 1/4 cups coconut chips, unsweetened

Cooking Instructions:

Start by preheating the air fryer to 350 ° F.

In the bowl of an electric hand mixer, whisk the margarine and swirl until well blended. Now add the eggs one at a time and mix well; add coconut milk, coconut extract and vanilla; beat until the mixture is creamy and uniform.

Mix the flour with the baking powder, baking soda and salt. Next, mix the flour mixture into the margarine mixture and stir until everything is well incorporated.

Finally, combine the coconut flakes and mix again. Collect 1 scoop-sized balls of batter on a baking sheet, leaving 3 inches between each cookie.

Cook for 10 minutes or until golden brown, turning the pan once or twice during the cooking time. Let your cookies cool on racks.

430.   Ultimate Chocolate and Coconut Pudding

Preparation time: 35 minutes Serves: 10

Ingredients

- 1 stick margarine
- ¼ cups bakers' chocolate, unsweetened 1 tsp. liquid stevia
- tbps full fat coconut milk
- eggs, beaten
- 1/4 cup coconut, shredded

Cooking Instructions:

Begin by preheating the air fryer to 330 ° F.

In a microwave-safe bowl, melt the margarine, chocolate, and stevia. Let it cool to room temperature.

Add the remaining ingredients to the chocolate mixture; stir to mix well. Scrape the batter into a lightly greased pan.

Cook in the preheated air fryer for 15 minutes or until a toothpick comes out dry and clean. To enjoy!

431.   Chocolate Paradise Cake

Preparation time: 35 minutes + chilling time Serves: 6

Ingredients

- eggs, beaten
- 3/3 cup sour cream 1 cup almond flour 3/3 cup swerve
- 1/4 cup coconut oil, softened 1/4 cup cocoa powder
- tbps chocolate chips, unsweetened 1 1/2 tsp.s baking powder
- 1 tsp. vanilla extract
- 1/4 tsp. pure rum extract Chocolate Frosting:
- 1/4 cup margarine, softened
- 1/4 cup cocoa powder 1 cup powdered swerve 3 tbps milk

Cooking Instructions:

Mix all the ingredients for the chocolate cake with a hand mixer on low speed. Scrape the batter into a cake pan.

Bake at 330 ° F for 35-30 minutes. Transfer the cake to a wire rack

Meanwhile, whip the margarine and cocoa until smooth. Stir in the steering powder. Slowly and gradually, pour in the milk until the glaze reaches the desired consistency.

Whip until smooth and fluffy; then, glaze the cooled cake. Refrigerate for a couple of hours. Serve very cold.

432.   Puffy Coconut and Pecan Cookies

Preparation time: 30 minutes Serves: 10

Ingredients

- 3/4 cup coconut oil, room temperature 1 1/2 cups coconut flour
- 1 cup pecan nuts, unsalted and roughly chopped
- eggs plus an egg yolk, whisked 1 1/2 cups extra-fine almond flour 3/4 cup monk fruit
- 1/4 tsp. freshly grated nutmeg 1/4 tsp. ground cloves
- 1/4 tsp. baking powder
- 1/4 tsp. baking soda
- 1/4 tsp. pure vanilla extract 1/4 tsp. pure coconut extract 1/8 tsp. fine sea salt

Cooking Instructions:

In a bowl, combine both types of flour, baking soda and baking powder. In a separate bowl, beat the eggs with the coconut oil. Combine the egg mixture with the flour mixture.

Add the other ingredients, mixing well. Form the mixture into cookies. Bake at 370 ° F for about 35 minutes.

433.   Double Chocolate Whiskey Brownies

Preparation time: 55 minutesServes: 10

Ingredients

- tbps whiskey
- ounces white chocolate 3/4 cup almond flour
- 1/4 cup coconut flakes 1/4 cup coconut oil
- eggs plus an egg yolk, whisked 3/4 cup monk fruit
- tbps cocoa powder, unsweetened
- 1/4 tsp. ground cardamom 1 tsp. pure rum extract

Cooking Instructions:

Microwave white chocolate and coconut oil until everything is melted; let the mixture cool to room temperature.

Next, beat the eggs, monk fruit, rum extract, cocoa powder and cardamom thoroughly.

Next step, add the rum / egg mixture to the chocolate mixture. Incorporate the flour and coconut flakes; mix to combine.

Mix the cranberries with the whiskey and leave them to soak for 15 minutes. Fold them into the batter. Press the batter into a lightly margarine pan.

Air fry for 35 minutes at 340 ° F. Allow them to cool slightly on a wire rack before slicing and serving.

434.   Old-Fashioned Walnut and Rum Cookies

Preparation time: 40 minutesServes: 8

Ingredients

- 1/4 cup walnuts, ground 1/4 cup coconut flour
- 1 cup almond flour 3/4 cup swerve
- stick margarine, room temperature
- tbps rum
- 1/4 tsp. pure vanilla extract 1/4 tsp. pure almond extract

Cooking Instructions:

In a baking dish, beat the margarine with the swerve, vanilla and almond extract until light and fluffy. Then, throw in the flour and chopped nuts; add the rum.

Continue to mix until a soft dough is formed. Cover and refrigerate for 35 minutes. Meanwhile, preheat the air fryer to 330 ° F.

Roll the dough into small biscuits and place them on the Air Fryer cake pan; gently press each cookie using a spoon.

Bake the margarine cookies for 15 minutes in the preheated air fryer.

435.   Chocolate and Blueberry Cupcakes

Preparation time: 35 minutes Serves: 6

Ingredients

- 3 tsp.s cocoa powder, unsweetened 1/4 cup blueberries
- 1 ¼ cups almond flour 1/4 cup milk
- 1 stick margarine, room temperature
- 3 eggs
- 3/4 cup powdered erythritol 1 tsp. pure rum extract 1/4 tsp. baking soda
- 1 tsp. baking powder 1/4 tsp. grated nutmeg
- 1/4 tsp. ground cinnamon 1/8 tsp. salt

Cooking Instructions:

1 Take two bowls. In the first bowl, carefully combine the erythritol, almond flour, baking soda, baking powder, salt, nutmeg, cinnamon and cocoa powder.

Take the second bowl and cream the margarine, egg, rum extract and milk; whisk to mix well. Now add the wet mixture to the dry mixture. Incorporate the blueberries.

Press the prepared batter mixture into a lightly greased muffin mold. Bake at 345 ° for 15 minutes. Use a toothpick to check if your cupcakes are cooked.

436.   Peanut Margarine and Chocolate Chip Cookies

Preparation time: 35 minutes Serves: 8

Ingredients

- 1 stick of margarine, at room temperature 1 ¼ cup steer
- 1/4 cup coarse peanut margarine 1 tsp. vanilla paste
- Fine almond flour
- 3/3 cup of coconut flour
- 1/4 cup of cocoa powder, unsweetened 1 1/2 teaspoon of baking powder
- 1/4 tsp. ground cinnamon 1/4 tsp. crystallized ginger
- 1/4 cup of unsweetened chocolate chips

Cooking Instructions:

In a mixing dish, beat the margarine and swerve until creamy and uniform. Stir in the peanut margarine and vanilla.

In another mixing dish, thoroughly combine the flour, cocoa powder, baking powder, cinnamon, and crystallized ginger.

Add the flour mixture to the peanut margarine mixture; mix to combine well. Afterwards, fold in the chocolate chips.

Drop by large spoonfuls onto a parchment-lined Air Fryer basket. Bake at 365 °F for 11 minutes or until golden brown on the top.

437.   Cocoa Cake

Preparation time: 10 minutes Cooking duration: 17 minutes Serves: 6

Ingredients:

- 3.5 ounces margarine, melted
- 3 eggs
- 3 ounces sugar
- 1 tsp. cocoa powder
- 3 ounces flour
- ½ tsp. lemon juice

Cooking Instructions:

In a bowl, mix 1 tablespoon of margarine with the cocoa powder and blend.

In another bowl, mix the rest of the margarine with the sugar, eggs, flour and lemon juice, beat well and pour half into a pan suitable for your air fryer.

Add half of the cocoa mixture, spread, add the rest of the margarine layer and garnish with the rest of the cocoa.

Place in the air fryer and cook at 360 ° F for 17 minutes.

Allow the cake to cool before slicing and serving.

438.   Old-Fashioned Muffins

Preparation time: 35 minutes Serves: 6

Ingredients

- 1/4 cup raspberries 3/4 cup swerve
- 1/4 cup coconut oil
- 1 cup sour cream
- ¼ tsp.s baking powder 3 cups almond flour
- eggs
- 1/4 tsp. ground allspice 1/4 tsp. ground anise star 1/4 tsp. grated lemon zest 1/4 tsp. salt

Cooking Instructions:

Get two bowls. In the first bowl, carefully combine the almond flour, baking powder, swerve, salt, anise, all the spices and lemon zest.

Take the second bowl; whisk the coconut oil, sour cream and eggs; whisk to mix well. Now add the wet mixture to the dry mixture. Incorporate the raspberries.

Press the batter mixture into a lightly greased muffin mold. Bake at 345 ° for 15 minutes. Use a toothpick to check if your muffins are cooked.

439.   Chocolate Coffee Cake

Preparation time: 40 minutes Serves: 8

Ingredients

- 1 1/2 cups almond flour 1/4 cup coconut meal 3/3 cup swerve
- 1 tsp. baking powder 1/4 tsp. salt
- 1 stick margarine, melted
- 1/4 cup hot strongly brewed coffee 1/4 tsp. vanilla
- 1 egg
- Topping:
- 1/4 cup coconut flour
- 1/4 cup confectioner's swerve 1/4 tsp. ground cardamom 1 tsp. ground cinnamon
- tbps coconut oil

Cooking Instructions:

Mix all the dry ingredients for your cake; then, mix the wet ingredients. Mix until everything is well incorporated.

Spray a baking sheet with cooking spray. Scrape the batter into the pan. Next, make the garnish by mixing all the ingredients. Place the cake on top.

Smooth the top with a putty knife.

Bake at 330 ° F for 30 minutes or until the top of the cake comes back when gently pressed with your fingers. Serve with your favorite hot drink.

440. Peanut Margarine Fudge Cake

(Preparation time: 30 minutes Serves: 10)

Ingredients

- 1 cup peanut margarine 1 ¼ cups monk fruit 3 eggs
- 1 cup almond flour
- 1 tsp. baking powder 1/4 tsp. kosher salt
- 1 cup unsweetened bakers' chocolate, broken into chunks

Cooking Instructions:

Start by preheating the air fryer to 350 degrees F. Now, spritz the sides and bottom of a pan with cooking spray.

In a mixing dish, carefully combine the peanut margarine with the monk fruit until creamy. Then, incorporate the egg and beat until soft.

Next, add the almond flour, baking powder, salt and baking chocolate. Stir until everything is well blended.

Cook in the preheated air fryer for 30-33 minutes. Transfer to a wire rack to cool before slicing and serving.

441. Keto Mixed Berry Crumble Pots

Preparation time: 40 minutes Serves: 6

Ingredients

- ounces unsweetened mixed berries 1/4 cup powdered swerve
- tbps golden flaxseed meal
- 1/4 tsp. ground star anise 1/4 tsp. ground cinnamon 1 tsp. xanthan gum
- 3/3 cup almond flour
- 1 cup powdered swerve
- 1/4 tsp. baking powder
- 1/4 cup unsweetened coconut, finely shredded 1/4 stick margarine, cut into small pieces

Cooking Instructions:

Mix the berries with the golden flaxseed meal, star anise, cinnamon and xanthan gum. Divide between six cups of custard coated with cooking spray.

In a baking dish, carefully combine the remaining ingredients. Sprinkle the berry mixture.

Cook in the preheated air fryer at 330 ° F for 35 minutes. If necessary, work in batches.

442. Chocolate Cake

Preparation time: 10 minutes Cooking duration: 30 minutes Serves: 12

Ingredients:

- ¾ cup white flour

- ¾ cup whole wheat flour
- 1 tsp. baking soda
- ¾ tsp. pumpkin pie spice
- ¾ cup sugar
- 1 banana, mashed
- ½ tsp. baking powder
- 2 tbps canola oil
- ½ cup Greek yogurt
- 8 ounces canned pumpkin puree
- Cooking spray
- 1 egg
- ½ tsp. vanilla extract
- 2/3 cup chocolate chips

Cooking Instructions:

In a bowl, mix the white flour with the wholemeal flour, salt, baking soda, and pumpkin powder and spices and mix.

In another bowl, mix the sugar with the oil, banana, yogurt, pumpkin puree, vanilla and egg and mix with a mixer.

Combine the 2 mixes, add the chocolate chips, mix and pour into a greased Bundt pan suitable for your air fryer.

Place in the air fryer and cook at 330 ° F for 30 minutes.

Allow the cake to cool before cutting and serving.

443. Apple Bread

Preparation time: 10 minutes Cooking duration: 40 minutes Serves: 6

Ingredients:

- 3 cups apples, cored and cubed
- 1 cup sugar
- 1 tablespoon vanilla
- 2 eggs
- 1 tablespoon apple pie spice
- 2 cups white flour
- 1 tablespoon baking powder
- 1 stick margarine
- 1 cup water

Cooking Instructions:

In a bowl, mix the egg with 1 stick of margarine, the spices for the apple pie and the sugar and mix using the mixer.

Add the apples and mix well again.

In another bowl, mix the yeast with the flour and mix.

Combine the 2 mixtures, mix and pour into a springform pan.

Place the spring-shaped pan in your air fryer and cook at 320 ° F for 40 minutes

Slice and serve.

444. Banana Bread

Preparation time: 10 minutes Cooking duration: 40 minutes Serves: 6

Ingredients:

- ¾ cup sugar
- 1/3 cup margarine
- 1 tsp. vanilla extract
- 1 egg
- 2 bananas, mashed
- 1 tsp. baking powder

- 1 and ½ cups flour
- ½ tsp.s baking soda
- 1/3 cup milk
- 1 and ½ tsp.s cream of tartar
- Cooking spray

Cooking Instructions:

In a bowl, mix milk with cream of tartar, sugar, margarine, egg, vanilla and bananas and stir everything.

In another bowl, mix flour with baking powder and baking soda.

Combine the 2 mixtures, stir well, pour this into a cake pan greased with some cooking spray, introduce in your air fryer and cook at 320 °F for 40 minutes.

Take bread out, leave aside to cool down, slice and serve it.

445. Mini Lava Cakes

Preparation time: 10 minutes Cooking duration: 20 minutes Serves: 3

Ingredients:

- 1 egg
- 4 tbps sugar
- 2 tbps olive oil
- 4 tbps milk
- 4 tbps flour
- 1 tablespoon cocoa powder
- ½ tsp. baking powder
- ½ tsp. orange zest

Cooking Instructions:

In a bowl, mix the egg with the sugar, oil, milk, flour, salt, cocoa powder, baking powder and orange zest, mix well and pour into greased molds.

Add the molds to the air fryer and cook at 320 ° F for 20 minutes.

Serve the hot lava cakes.

446. Crispy Apple

Preparation time: 10 minutes Cooking duration: 10 minutes Serves: 4

Ingredients:

- 2 tsp.s cinnamon powder
- 5 apples, cored and cut into chunks
- ½ tsp. nutmeg powder
- 1 tablespoon maple syrup
- ½ cup water
- 4 tbps margarine
- ¼ cup flour
- ¾ cup old fashioned rolled oats
- ¼ cup brown sugar

Cooking Instructions:

Place the apples in a pan suitable for your air fryer, add the cinnamon, nutmeg, maple syrup and water.

In a bowl, mix the margarine with the oats, sugar, salt and flour, mix, pour a tablespoon of this mixture over the apples, place in the deep fryer and cook at 350 ° F for 10 minutes.

Serve hot.

447. Carrot Cake

Preparation time: 10 minutes Cooking duration: 45 minutes Serves: 6

Ingredients:

- 5 ounces flour
- ¾ tsp. baking powder
- ½ tsp. baking soda
- ½ tsp. cinnamon powder
- ¼ tsp. nutmeg, ground
- ½ tsp. allspice
- 1 egg
- 3 tbps yogurt
- ½ cup sugar
- ¼ cup pineapple juice
- 4 tbps sunflower oil
- 1/3 cup carrots, grated
- 1/3 cup pecans, toasted and chopped
- 1/3 cup coconut flakes, shredded
- Cooking spray

Cooking Instructions:

In a bowl, mix the flour with baking soda and powder, salt, allspice, cinnamon, and nutmeg and mix.

In another bowl, mix the egg with the yogurt, sugar, pineapple juice, oil, carrots, pecans and coconut flakes and mix well.

Combine the two blends and mix well, pour into a spring pan suitable for your air fryer that you greased with cooking spray, transfer to air fryer and cook at 320 ° F for 45 minutes.

Allow the cake to cool, then cut and serve.

448. Ginger Cheesecake

Preparation time: 2 hours and 10 m. Cooking: 20 minutes Serves: 6

Ingredients:

- 2 tsp.s margarine, melted
- ½ cup ginger cookies, crumbled
- 16 ounces cream cheese, soft
- 2 eggs
- ½ cup sugar
- 1 tsp. rum
- ½ tsp. vanilla extract
- ½ tsp. nutmeg, ground

Cooking Instructions:

Grease a pan with margarine and spread the biscuit crumbs on the bottom.

In a bowl, beat the cream cheese with nutmeg, vanilla, rum and eggs, beat well and spread over the biscuit crumbs.

Place in the air fryer and cook at 340 ° F for 20 minutes.

Allow the cheesecake to cool and keep it in the fridge for 2 hours before slicing and serving.

449. Coffee Cheesecakes

Preparation time: 10 minutes Cooking duration: 20 minutes Serves: 6

Ingredients:

For the cheesecakes:

- 2 tbps margarine
- 8 ounces cream cheese
- 3 tbps coffee
- 3 eggs
- 1/3 cup sugar
- 1 tablespoon caramel syrup

For the frosting:
- 3 tbps caramel syrup
- 3 tbps margarine
- 8 ounces mascarpone cheese, soft
- 2 tbps sugar

Cooking Instructions:

In your blender, mix the cream cheese with the eggs, 2 tablespoons of margarine, coffee, 1 tablespoon of caramel syrup and 1/3 cup of sugar and blend very well, pour one tablespoon into a pan for cupcakes that suitable for your air fryer, pop into the fryer and cook at 320 ° F and bake for 20 minutes.

Leave to cool and then keep in the freezer for 3 hours. Meanwhile, in a bowl, mix 3 tablespoons of margarine with 3 tablespoons of caramel syrup, 2 tablespoons of sugar and mascarpone, mix well, pour this spoon over the cheesecakes and serve.

450.   Cocoa Cookies

Preparation time: 10 minutes Cooking duration: 14 minutes Serves: 12

Ingredients:
- 6 ounces coconut oil, melted
- 6 eggs
- 3 ounces cocoa powder
- 2 tsp.s vanilla
- ½ tsp. baking powder
- 4 ounces cream cheese
- 5 tbps sugar

Cooking Instructions:

In a blender, mix the eggs with the coconut oil, cocoa powder, baking powder, vanilla, cream cheese and mix and mix with a mixer.

Pour it into a lined pan that fits your air fryer, place in the 320 ° F fryer and bake for 14 minutes.

Slice the pan into rectangles and serve.

451.   Tasty Orange Cake

Preparation time: 10 minutes Cooking duration: 32 minutes Serves: 12

Ingredients:
- 6 eggs
- 1 orange, peeled and cut into quarters
- 1 tsp. vanilla extract
- 1 tsp. baking powder
- 9 ounces flour
- 2 ounces sugar+ 2 tbps
- 2 tbps orange zest
- 4 ounces cream cheese
- 4 ounces yogurt

Cooking Instructions:

In your food processor, the orange pulsates very well.

Add the flour, 2 tablespoons of sugar, eggs, baking powder, vanilla extract and blend well again.

Transfer to 2 spring-loaded pans, place each in the deep fryer and cook at 330 ° F for 16 minutes.

Meanwhile, in a bowl, mix the cream cheese with the orange zest, the yogurt and the rest of the sugar and mix well.

Place one layer of cake on a plate, add half of the cream cheese, add the other layer of cake and top with the rest of the cream cheese.

Roll it out well, slice and serve.

452.   Macaroons

Preparation time: 10 minutes Cooking duration: 8 minutes Serves: 20

Ingredients:
- 2 tbps sugar
- 4 egg whites
- 2 cup coconut, shredded
- 1 tsp. vanilla extract

Cooking Instructions:

In a bowl, mix the egg whites with the stevia and beat with the mixer.

Add the coconut and vanilla extract, mix again, form balls with this mixture, place them in the air fryer and cook at 340 ° F for 8 minutes.

Serve the macaroons cold.

453.   Lime Cheesecake

Preparation time: 4 hours and 10 minutes Cooking: 4 minutes Serves: 10

Ingredients:
- 2 tbps margarine, melted
- 2 tsp.s sugar
- 4 ounces flour
- ¼ cup coconut, shredded

For the filling:
- 1 pound cream cheese
- Zest from 1 lime, grated
- Juice form 1 lime
- 2 cups hot water
- 2 sachets lime jelly

Cooking Instructions:

In a bowl, mix the coconut with the flour, margarine and sugar, mix well and press it into the bottom of a pan suitable for your air fryer.

In the meantime, put the hot water in a bowl, add the gelatin sachets and stir until dissolved.

Put the cream cheese in a bowl, add the gelatin, lime juice and zest and blend very well.

Add this to the crust, spread, put in the air fryer and cook at 300 ° F for 4 minutes.

Refrigerate for 4 hours before serving.

454. Easy Granola

Preparation time: 10 minutes Cooking duration: 35 minutes Serves: 4

Ingredients:
- 1 cup coconut, shredded
- ½ cup almonds
- ½ cup pecans, chopped
- 2 tbps sugar
- ½ cup pumpkin seeds
- ½ cup sunflower seeds
- 2 tbps sunflower oil
- 1 tsp. nutmeg, ground
- 1 tsp. apple pie spice mix

Cooking Instructions:

In a bowl, mix almonds and pecans with pumpkin seeds, sunflower seeds, coconut, nutmeg and apple pie spice mix and mix well.

Heat a pan with oil over medium heat, add sugar and mix well.

Pour this over nuts and coconut and mix well.Spread it on a lined baking sheet that fits your air fryer, pop into the air fryer and cook at 300 ° F and bake for 25 minutes.

Let the muesli cool, cut and serve.

455. Blueberry Scones

Preparation time: 10 minutes Cooking duration: 10 minutes Serves: 10

Ingredients:
- 1 cup white flour
- 1 cup blueberries
- 2 eggs
- ½ cup heavy cream
- ½ cup margarine
- 5 tbps sugar
- 2 tsp.s vanilla extract
- 2 tsp.s baking powder

Cooking Instructions:

In a bowl, mix flour, salt, baking powder and blueberries and mix.

In another bowl, mix the cream with the margarine, vanilla extract, sugar and eggs and mix well.

Combine the 2 mixes, knead until you have your dough, form 10 triangles from this mixture, arrange them on a lined pan that fits your air fryer and cook at 320 ° F for 10 minutes.

Serve them cold.

456. Special Brownies

Preparation time: 10 minutes Cooking duration: 17 minutes Serves: 4

Ingredients:
- 1 egg
- 1/3 cup cocoa powder
- 1/3 cup sugar
- 7 tbps margarine
- ½ tsp. vanilla extract
- ¼ cup white flour
- ¼ cup walnuts, chopped
- ½ tsp. baking powder
- 1 tablespoon peanut margarine

Cooking Instructions:

Heat a pan with 6 tablespoons of margarine and sugar over medium heat, mix, cook for 5 minutes, transfer to a bowl, add salt, vanilla extract, cocoa powder, egg, baking powder, nuts and flour, mix everything really good thing and pour into a pan that fits your air fryer.

In a bowl, mix 1 tablespoon of margarine with the peanut margarine, heat in the microwave for a few seconds, mix well and season with the brownie mixture.

Place in the air fryer and bake at 320 ° F and bake for 17 minutes.

Allow brownies to cool, cut and serve.

457. Black Tea Cake

Preparation time: 10 minutes Cooking duration: 35 minutes Serves: 12

Ingredients:
- 6 tbps black tea powder
- 2 cups milk
- ½ cup margarine
- 2 cups sugar
- 4 eggs
- 2 tsp.s vanilla extract
- ½ cup olive oil
- 3 and ½ cups flour
- 1 tsp. baking soda
- 3 tsp.s baking powder

For the cream:
- 6 tbps honey
- 4 cups sugar
- 1 cup margarine, soft

Cooking Instructions:

Put the milk in a saucepan, heat over medium heat, add the tea, mix well, remove from heat and allow to cool.

In a bowl, mix ½ cup of margarine with 2 cups of sugar, eggs, vegetable oil, vanilla extract, baking powder, baking soda and 3 ½ cups of flour and mix well.

Pour this into 2 greased round pans, place each in the 330 ° F fryer and bake for 25 minutes.

In a bowl, mix 1 cup of margarine with honey and 4 cups of sugar and mix very well.

Arrange a cake on a tray, spread the cream all over, garnish with the other cake and refrigerate until needed.

458. Plum Cake

Preparation time: 1 hour and 20 minutes Cooking duration: 36 minutes Serves: 8

Ingredients:
- 7 ounces flour
- 1 package dried yeast
- 1 ounce margarine, soft
- 1 egg, whisked
- 5 tbps sugar
- 3 ounces warm milk

- 1 and ¾ pounds plums, pitted and cut into quarters Zest from 1 lemon, grated
- 1 ounce almond flakes

Cooking Instructions:

In a bowl, mix the yeast with the margarine, flour and 3 tablespoons of sugar and mix well.

Add the milk and the egg and blend for 4 minutes until you get a paste.

Place the dough in a spring-shaped pan suitable for your air fryer and greased with a little margarine, cover and set aside for 1 hour.

Arrange the lumps on top of the margarine, sprinkle the rest of the sugar, place in the 350 ° F air fryer, bake for 36 minutes, cool, sprinkle with almond flakes and lemon zest, slice and serve.

459. Chocolate Cookies

Preparation time: 10 minutes Cooking duration: 25 minutes Serves: 12

Ingredients:

- 1 tsp. vanilla extract
- ½ cup margarine
- 1 egg
- 4 tbps sugar
- 2 cups flour
- ½ cup unsweetened chocolate chips

Cooking Instructions:

Heat a pan with the margarine over medium heat, stir and cook for 1 minute.

In a bowl, mix the egg with the vanilla extract and sugar and mix well.

Add the melted margarine, flour and half of the chocolate chips and mix everything together.

Transfer to a pan suitable for your air fryer, spread the rest of the chocolate chips, place in the deep fryer at 330 ° F and bake for 25 minutes.

460. Lentils Cookies

Preparation time: 10 minutes Cooking duration: 25 minutes Serves: 36

Ingredients:

- 1 cup water
- 1 cup canned lentils, drained and mashed
- 1 cup white flour
- 1 tsp. cinnamon powder
- 1 cup whole wheat flour
- 1 tsp. baking powder
- ½ tsp. nutmeg, ground
- 1 cup margarine, soft
- ½ cup brown sugar
- ½ cup white sugar
- 1 egg
- 2 tsp.s almond extract
- 1 cup raisins
- 1 cup rolled oats
- 1 cup coconut, unsweetened and shredded

Cooking Instructions:

In a bowl, mix the white and wholemeal flour with the salt,

cinnamon, baking powder and nutmeg and mix.

In a bowl, mix the margarine with the white and brown sugar and mix with the kitchen mixer for 2 minutes.

Add the egg, almond extract, lentil mix, flour mix, oats, raisins and coconut and mix well.

Pour tablespoons of pasta onto a lined pan that fits the air fryer, place them in the deep fryer and cook at 350 ° F for 15 minutes.

Arrange the biscuits on a serving plate and serve

461. Lentils and Dates Brownies

Preparation time: 10 minutes Cooking duration: 15 minutes Serves: 8

Ingredients:

- 28 ounces canned lentils, rinsed and drained
- 12 dates
- 1 tablespoon honey
- 1 banana, peeled and chopped
- ½ tsp. baking soda
- 4 tbps almond margarine
- 2 tbps cocoa powder

Cooking Instructions:

In your food processor, mix the lentils with the margarine, banana, cocoa, baking soda and honey and mix very well.

Add the dates, blend a few more times, pour into a greased pan suitable for the air fryer, distribute evenly, place in the 360 ° F fryer and cook for 15 minutes.

Remove the brownies from the oven, cut them, arrange them on a serving dish and serve.

462. Strawberry Cobbler

Preparation time: 10 minutes Cooking duration: 25 minutes Serves: 6

Ingredients:

- ¾ cup sugar
- 6 cups strawberries, halved
- 1/8 tsp. baking powder
- 1 tablespoon lemon juice
- ½ cup flour
- A pinch of baking soda
- ½ cup water
- 3 and ½ tablespoon olive oil
- Cooking spray

Cooking Instructions:

In a bowl, mix the strawberries with half the sugar, sprinkle some flour, add the lemon juice, blend and pour into the pan that fits your air fryer and greased with cooking spray

In another bowl, mix the flour with the rest of the sugar, baking powder and soda and mix well.

• Add the olive oil and mix until all with your hands.

• Add ½ cup of water and spread over the strawberries.

• Place in the fryer at 355 ° F and bake for 25 minutes.

• Let the cobbler cool, slice and serve.

463. Maple Cupcakes

Preparation time: 10 minutes Cooking duration: 20 minutes Serves: 4

Ingredients:

- 4 tbps margarine
- 4 eggs
- ½ cup pure applesauce
- 2 tsp.s cinnamon powder
- 1 tsp. vanilla extract
- ½ apple, cored and chopped
- 4 tsp.s maple syrup
- ¾ cup white flour
- ½ tsp. baking powder

Cooking Instructions:

Heat a pan with the margarine over medium heat, add the applesauce, vanilla, eggs and maple syrup, stir and remove from the heat and allow to cool.

Add the flour, cinnamon, baking powder and apples, blend, pour into a baking dish, place in the 350 ° F air fryer and bake for 20 minutes.

Allow the cupcakes to cool, transfer them to a serving dish and serve.

464. Strawberry Pie

Preparation time: 10 minutes Cooking duration: 20 minutes Serves: 12

Ingredients:

For the crust:

- 1 cup coconut, shredded
- 1 cup sunflower seeds
- ¼ cup margarine

For the filling:

- 1 tsp. gelatin
- 8 ounces cream cheese
- 4 ounces strawberries
- 2 tbps water
- ½ tablespoon lemon juice
- ¼ tsp. stevia
- ½ cup heavy cream
- 8 ounces strawberries, chopped for serving

Cooking Instructions:

In your food processor, mix the sunflower seeds with the coconut, a pinch of salt and the margarine, fry and press this into the bottom of a pan suitable for your air fryer.

Heat a skillet with water over medium heat, add gelatin, stir until dissolved, allow to cool, add to food processor, mix with 4 oz of strawberries, cream cheese, lemon juice and stevia and blend well .

Add the cream, mix well and spread it over the crust.

Top with 8 ounces of strawberries, place in the air fryer and cook at 330 ° F for 15 minutes.

Keep in the fridge until you serve it.

465. Famous New York Cheesecake

Preparation time: 1 hour + chilling time Serves: 8

Ingredients

- 1 1/2 cups almond flour 3 ounces swerve
- 1/4 stick margarine, melted
- 30 ounces full-fat cream cheese 1/4 cup heavy cream
- 1 ¼ cups powdered swerve 3 eggs, at room temperature 1 tablespoon vanilla essence 1 tsp. grated lemon zest

Cooking Instructions:

Coat the sides and bottom of a pan with a little flour.

In a bowl, combine the almond flour and steer. Add the melted margarine and mix until you have a breadcrumb mixture.

Press the mixture into the bottom of the prepared pan to form an even layer. Bake at 330 ° F for 7 minutes until golden brown. Leave to cool completely on a wire rack.

In the meantime, in a planetary mixer fitted with a spatula, prepare the filling by mixing the soft cheese, cream and powdered swerve; beat until the mixture is creamy and fluffy.

Break the eggs into the bowl, one at a time; add the vanilla and lemon zest and keep stirring until they are completely blended.

Pour the prepared cover over the cooled crust and distribute evenly.

Bake in preheated air fryer at 330 ° F for 35-30 minutes; leave it in the air fryer to keep warm for another 30 minutes.

Cover your cheesecake with cling film. Refrigerate and let cool for at least 6 hours or overnight. Serve very cold.

466. Mixed Berries with Pecan Streusel

Preparation time: 35 minutes Serves: 3

Ingredients

- tbps pecans, chopped 3 tbps almonds, slivered 3 tbps walnuts, chopped 3 tbps powdered swerve 1/4 tsp. ground cinnamon 1 egg
- tbps cold salted margarine, cut into pieces 1/4 cup mixed berries

Cooking Instructions:

Blend the dried fruit, corn, cinnamon, egg, and margarine until smooth.

Place the berries on the bottom of a lightly greased air dish. Complete with the prepared garnish.

Bake at 340 ° F for 17 minutes. Serve at room temperature.

467. Easy Fluffy Pancakes

Preparation time: 35 minutes Serves: 3

Ingredients

- 1/4 cup coconut flour
- tsp. baking powder 1/4 tsp. salt
- tbps erythritol 1/4 tsp. cinnamon
- 1 tsp. red paste food color
- 1 egg
- 1/4 cup milk

- tsp. vanilla Topping:
- ounces cream cheese, softened 3 tbps margarine, softened 3/4 cup powdered swerve

Cooking Instructions:
Mix the coconut flour, baking powder, salt, erythritol, cinnamon and red paste food coloring in a large bowl.

Gradually add the egg and milk, whisking constantly, until they are well blended. Let it sit for 35 minutes.

Spray the pan of the air fryer with cooking spray. Pour the batter into the pan using a measuring cup.

Bake at 330 ° F for 4-5 minutes or until golden brown. Repeat with the remaining batter.

Meanwhile, prepare the dressing by mixing the ingredients until you get a creamy and fluffy mixture. Decorate your pancakes with topping.

468. Easy Spanish Churros
Preparation time: 35 minutes Serves: 4

Ingredients
- 3/4 cup water
- 1 tablespoon swerve 1/4 tsp. sea salt
- 1/4 tsp. grated nutmeg 1/4 tsp. ground cloves 6 tbps margarine
- 3/4 cup almond flour 3 eggs

Cooking Instructions:
To make the dough, boil the water in a pan over medium-high heat; now add the swerve, salt, nutmeg and cloves; cook until melted.

Add the margarine and reduce the heat. Gradually incorporate the almond flour, stirring constantly, until the mixture forms a ball.

Remove from the heat; add the eggs one at a time, stirring to mix well.

Pour the mixture into a pastry bag with a large star tip. Squeeze 4-inch strips of dough into the greased pan of the air fryer.

Bake at 410 ° F for 6 minutes, working in batches.

469. Rhubarb Pie
Preparation time: 30 minutes Cooking duration: 45 minutes Serves: 6

Ingredients:
- 1 and ¼ cups almond flour
- 8 tbps margarine
- 5 tbps cold water
- 1 tsp. sugar
For the filling:
- 3 cups rhubarb, chopped
- 3 tbps flour
- 1 and ½ cups sugar
- 2 eggs
- ½ tsp. nutmeg, ground
- 1 tablespoon margarine
- 2 tbps low fat milk

Cooking Instructions:
In a bowl, mix 1 ¼ cups of flour with 1 tsp. sugar, 8 tablespoons of margarine and cold water, mix and knead until you get a dough.

Transfer the dough to a floured work surface, form a disk, flatten it, wrap it in plastic, store in the fridge for about 30 minutes, roll up and press on the bottom of a pan suitable for your air fryer.

In a bowl, mix the rhubarb with 1 ½ cups of sugar, nutmeg, 3 tablespoons of flour and blend.

In another bowl, beat the eggs with the milk, mix them with the rhubarb mixture, pour the entire mixture into the pie crust, place in your air fryer and cook at 390 ° C for 45 minutes.

Cut it and serve it cold.

470. Mixed Berry Compote with Coconut Chips
Preparation time: 35 minutes Serves: 6

Ingredients
- 1 tablespoon margarine
- 13 ounces mixed berries 1/4 cup powdered swerve 1/4 tsp. grated nutmeg 1/4 tsp. ground cloves
- 1/4 tsp. ground cinnamon 1 tsp. pure vanilla extract 1/4 cup coconut chips

Cooking Instructions:
Begin by preheating the air fryer to 330 ° F. Grease a baking sheet with margarine.

Place all ingredients, except the coconut flakes, in a baking dish. Cook in the preheated air fryer for 35 minutes.

Serve in individual bowls, garnished with coconut flakes.

471. Vanilla Coconut Cupcakes
Preparation time: 30 minutes Serves: 4

Ingredients
- 1/4 cup coconut flour 1/4 cup coconut milk 3 eggs
- 1 tablespoon coconut oil, melted 1 tsp. vanilla
- A pinch of ground cardamom
- 1/4 cup coconut chips

Cooking Instructions:
Mix the flour, coconut milk, eggs, coconut oil, vanilla and cardamom in a large bowl.

Leave to rest for 35 minutes. Pour the batter into a greased muffin pan.

Bake at 330 ° F for 4-5 minutes or until golden brown. Repeat with the remaining batter.

Decorate your cupcakes with coconut flakes.

472. Autumn Walnut Crisp
Preparation time: 40 minutes Serves: 8

Ingredients
- 1 cup walnuts 1/4 cup swerve Topping:
- 1 1/2 cups almond flour 1/4 cup coconut flour 1/3 cup swerve
- 1 tsp. crystallized ginger 1/3 tsp. ground cardamom A pinch of salt
- 1 stick margarine, cut into pieces

Cooking Instructions:
Place the walnuts and 1/4 cup sauce in a lightly greased baking dish with nonstick cooking spray.

In a baking dish, carefully combine all ingredients for garnish. Sprinkle the topping ingredients on the walnut layer. Cook in the preheated air fryer at 330 ° F for 35 minutes.

473. Fudge Cake with Pecans

Preparation time: 30 minutes Serves: 6

Ingredients

- 1/4 cup margarine, melted 1/4 cup swerve
- 1 tsp. vanilla essence
- 1 egg
- 1/4 cup almond flour
- 1/4 tsp. baking powder 1/4 cup cocoa powder
- 1/4 tsp. ground cinnamon 1/4 tsp. fine sea salt
- 1 ounce bakers' chocolate, unsweetened 1/4 cup pecans, finely chopped

Cooking Instructions:

Start by preheating the air fryer to 350 ° F. Now lightly grease six silicone molds.

In a baking dish, whisk the melted margarine with the steering wheel until frothy. Then, stir in the vanilla and egg and beat again.

Next, add the almond flour, baking powder, cocoa powder, cinnamon and salt. Stir until everything is well blended.

Incorporate the chocolate and pecans; mix to combine. Cook in the preheated air fryer for 30-33 minutes.

474. French Blueberry Flan

Preparation time: 30 minutes Serves: 6

Ingredients

- 3/4 cup extra-fine almond flour 1 cup fresh blueberries
- 1/4 cup coconut cream
- 3/4 cup coconut milk 3 eggs, whisked
- 1/4 cup swerve
- 1/4 cup confectioner's swerve 1/4 tsp. baking soda
- 1/4 tsp. baking powder
- 1/4 tsp. ground cinnamon 1/4 tsp. crystalized ginger 1/4 tsp. grated nutmeg

Cooking Instructions:

Lightly grease 3 cake tins using non-stick cooking spray.
Put the blueberries in the bottom of the pots.
In a preheated saucepan over medium heat, heat the cream together with the coconut milk until completely heated.
Remove the pan from the heat; add the flour together with the baking soda and baking powder.
In a medium-sized bowl, beat the eggs, whisk and spices; whip until creamy.
Add the creamy milk mixture. Carefully distribute this mixture on the fruits.
Bake at 330 ° for about 35 minutes. To serve, sprinkle with the swerve of the pastry chef.

475. Stuffed Apple Bake

Preparation time: 5 minutes Cooking time: 10 minutes Serves: 4

Ingredients

- 4 medium sized apples, cored 6 tsp.s of sugar 4 tbps of breadcrumbs 2 tbps of margarine 1 tsp. of mixed spice 1½ ounce of mixed seeds Zest of 1 lemon

Cooking Instructions

Cut the skin of the apples with a knife around the circumference to prevent them from dividing during cooking.
Mix the sugar, breadcrumbs, margarine, zest, spices and mixed seeds in a bowl and stuff the apples with the mixture.
Heat the Airfryer to 356 ° F and cook the stuffed apples for 10 minutes.

476. Sweet Cinnamon Bananas Sticks

Preparation time: 15 minutes Cooking time: 10 minutes Serves: 6-8

Ingredients

- 8 ounces of breadcrumbs 8 ripe bananas, peeled and halved 7 tsp.s of sugar 4 ounces of corn flour 3 tbps of coconut oil 2 large eggs, whisked 2 tsp.s of cinnamon

Cooking Instructions

Put the coconut oil in a skillet over medium heat. Put the breadcrumbs and mix for 4 minutes until it is lightly golden. Remove from the heat and transfer to a deep plate.
Roll the bananas first in the cornmeal, then pass them in the eggs and finally in the breadcrumbs to cover.
Put the coated bananas in the cooking basket. Mix the cinnamon and sugar well in a bowl and sprinkle the mixture over the bananas to cover them.
Slide the basket into the airfryer and cook for 10 minutes at 280 ° F. When finished, shake off the excess crumbs, if any.

477. Berry And Apricot Crumble

Preparation time: 10 minutes Cooking time: 20 minutes Serves: 6

Ingredients

- 2½ ounces of margarine 2¼ cups of apricot ½ pound of flour 8 tbps of sugar 6 tsp.s of lemon juice 5½ ounces fresh blackberries Salt to taste

Cooking Instructions

Cut the apricots in 2 and remove the stones, then cut them into cubes.
Put them in a bowl and add 2 tablespoons of sugar, blackberries and lemon juice and mix. Pour and distribute the mixture evenly in a baking dish.
Put the flour in a bowl and add 6 tablespoons of sugar, margarine, salt and a little water and mix well. Rub the mixture with your fingertips until crumbly.
Heat your Airfryer to 390 ° F.
Spread the mixture over the fruits and press lightly.
Place in the Airfryer basket and cook for 20 minutes until the crumble is golden.

478. Coconut Pineapples & Yoghurt Dip

Preparation time: 15 minutes Cooking time: 10 minutes Serves: 4

Ingredients

- 2 ounces of dried coconut flakes 1 sprig of mint, finely chopped ½ medium size pineapple 8 ounces of vanilla yogurt

Cooking Instructions

Heat the Airfryer to 390 ° F.

Cut the pineapple into chips (sticks) and dip them in the diced coconut to allow the coconut to stick.

Place the sticks in the fryer basket and cook for about 10 minutes.

Mix the mint leaves in the vanilla yogurt. Serve with pineapple sticks.

479. Air Fried Marble Cake

Preparation time: 10 minutes Cooking time: 17 minutes Serves: 6

Ingredients

* 7 tbps of caster sugar ½ cup of flour, sieved 4 eggs, whisked
* 1 tsp. of baking powder 5 tsp.s of cocoa powder 2/3 cup of margarine, melted ½ tsp. of lime juice

Cooking Instructions

Heat your deep fryer to 356 ° F.

Mix 3 tablespoons of melted margarine with cocoa powder to form a paste. Add the sugar to the remaining margarine and mix well. Incorporate the eggs, flour and baking powder and mix well until smooth. Pour in the lime and mix.

Place a greased baking sheet in the airfryer and let it heat for one minute.

Pour some batter into the hot oven, then add a layer of chocolate mix, then the batter, then the chocolate and finally top with the batter. Use a skewer to create a swirl.

Place in the air fryer and cook for 17 minutes. The cake must be cooled while it is in the pan before removing it.

480. Extra Crunchy Breakfast Casserole

Preparation time: 2 minutes Cooking time: 30 minutes Serves: 3-4

Ingredients

* 4 eggs
* 6 ounces of raw sweet sausage, remove from the casings ½ cup bread crumbs 1 cup shredded cheddar cheese Pinch salt and pepper

Cooking Instructions

Preheat the Airfryer to 350 ° F. Cook the raw sausage for 10 minutes over medium-high heat, breaking it with a wooden spoon to prevent it from clumping. Remove and set aside.

Beat the eggs in a bowl, until they are foamy. Incorporate half of the breadcrumbs, half of the cheese, the cooked sausage, salt and pepper. Pour into a baking dish and sprinkle the remaining breadcrumbs and grated cheese on top.

Place the tray in the Airfryer basket, set the timer for 20 minutes. Remove, serve and enjoy!

481. Vanilla Rum Cookies with Walnuts

Preparation time: 35 minutes Serves: 6

Ingredients

* 1/4 cup almond flour 1/4 cup coconut flour
* 1/4 tsp. baking powder
* 1/4 tsp. fine sea salt

* 1 stick margarine, unsalted and softened 1/4 cup swerve
* 1 egg
* 1/4 tsp. vanilla
* 1 tsp. margarine rum flavoring 3 ounces walnuts, finely chopped

Cooking Instructions:

Begin by preheating the air fryer to 360 ° F.

In a baking dish, carefully combine the flour with the baking powder and salt.

Beat the margarine and swerve with a hand mixer until it is light and fluffy; add the beaten egg, vanilla and rum margarine flavor; mix again to mix well. Now, add the dry ingredients.

Incorporate the chopped walnuts and toss to combine. Divide the mixture into balls; flatten each ball with a fork and transfer them to a tin lined with aluminum foil.

Cook in the preheated air fryer for 14 minutes. Work in a few batches and transfer to racks to cool completely.

482. Parmesan & Pesto Twists

Preparation time: 10 minutes Cooking time: 25 minutes Serves: 4

Ingredients

* 12 ounces of packed margarine puff pastry
* 1.8 ounces of cream cheese 3 tsp.s of flour ¼ cup of basil pesto 1 egg, whisked 1.8 ounces of grated Parmesan cheese

Cooking Instructions

Preheat your Airfryer to 460 ° F.

Lightly spread the flour on a surface and roll the margarine puff pastry into a rectangular shape.

Divide the half into 2 and spread the pesto and cream cheese on one half and place the other half on top.

Cut the sandwich in 2 from the center, then cut each rectangular piece into 0.4 "thick strips.

Twist the strips, pull slightly to stretch them. Using a pastry brush, sprinkle the tortelle with egg and sprinkle with Parmesan cheese.

Place in the Airfryer until leavened and golden for about 25 minutes.

483. Air Fried French Toast

Preparation time: 4 minutes Cooking time: 6 minutes Serves: 4

Ingredients

* 2 slices of sourdough bread 3 eggs
* 1 tablespoon of margarine 1 tsp. of liquid vanilla 3 tsp.s of honey 2 tbps of Greek yogurt Berries

Cooking Instructions

Preheat the air fryer to 356 ° F.

Pour the vanilla into the eggs and whisk to mix. Spread the margarine on all sides of the bread and dip the eggs into absorb.

Place the bread in the Airfryer basket and bake for 3 minutes. Turn the bread over and bake for another 3 minutes.

Transfer to a place, garnish with yogurt and berries with a sprinkle of honey.

484. Strawberry And Cream Chocolate Cupcake

Preparation time: 30 minutes Cooking time: 12 minutes Serves: 4

Ingredients

- 1 pound of refined flour 3 eggs
- 4 tbps of strawberry sauce 6 ounces of icing sugar 1 large strawberry, cut into 4
- ½ pound of cream cheese 6 ounces of peanut margarine 1 tsp. of vanilla extract 1 tsp. of cocoa powder ½ pound of hard margarine for frosting 2 tsp.s of beet powder A few crushed colorful chocolate, crushed

Cooking Instructions

Prepare a batter by mixing together flour, cocoa, peanut margarine, powdered sugar, beet powder and eggs using an electric mixer. Pour the batter into the cupcake molds.

Heat your deep fryer for 5 minutes at 360 ° F. Place the cupcakes in the airfryer and turn the heat down to 340 ° F. Bake for 12 minutes.

Remove the cakes from the fryer; cool for 10 minutes.

Combine the icing sugar, hard margarine and vanilla in an electric hand mixer and blend until smooth.

Add the icing to the cupcakes and sprinkle with strawberry sauce, crushed chocolates and garnish with a piece of strawberry.

485. Sesame And Poppy Cheese Cookies

Preparation time: 18 minutes Cooking time: 12 minutes Serves: 10

Ingredients

- 7 tbps of cream ¾ cup of grated Gruyere cheese 3 tsp.s of milk 2 egg yolks, beaten 1 tsp. of paprika powder 5.2 ounces of margarine 2/3 cup of flour ½ tsp. of baking powder ½ tsp. salt Poppy seeds and sesame seeds for garnishing

Cooking Instructions

Mix the cheese, margarine, salt, cream and paprika in a bowl until smooth.

Mix the baking powder and flour together and sift on a flat surface. Put the margarine and cheese mixture on the flour and knead until it forms a soft dough. Roll out the dough until it is thin and then cut it into a biscuit shape.

Mix the milk and eggs and use to coat the cookies with a brush. Sprinkle the poppy and sesame seeds on top of the cookies.

Place in the Airfryer basket and bake at 340 ° F for 12 minutes.

486. Chocolate Cake Airfry

Preparation time: 10 minutes Cooking time: 10 minutes Serves: 4

Ingredients

- ½ cup of chopped dark chocolate, melted 8 tbps of margarine, melted 5 tbps of sugar ½ tsp. of coffee 1 tsp. of baking powder 2 eggs
- small lemon, juiced 1/3 cup of flour ¼ tsp. of salt

Cooking Instructions

Add the melted chocolate, margarine and lemon and mix.

Put the egg, coffee and sugar in a bowl and blend until creamy. Add the chocolate margarine mixture and mix. Add and mix the yeast, flour and salt. Gently mix the batter.

Heat your deep fryer to 356 ° F.

Place the batter in a greased baking dish and place it in the fryer basket. Air fry for 10 minutes or until firm.

487. Wheat & Seed Bread

Preparation time: 70 minutes Cooking time: 18 minutes Serves: 4

Ingredients

- 3½ ounces of flour 1 tsp. of yeast 1 tsp. of salt 3½ ounces of wheat flour ¼ cup of pumpkin seeds

Cooking Instructions

Mix the wheat flour, baking powder, salt, seeds and 00 flour in a large bowl. Stir ¾ cup of warm water and keep stirring until the dough becomes soft.

Knead for another 5 minutes until the dough becomes elastic and smooth. Shape into a ball and cover with a plastic bag. Leave to rise for 30 minutes.

Heat your Airfryer to 392 ° F.

Transfer the dough to a pizza pan and place it in the airfryer. Cook for 18 minutes until golden brown. Remove and place on a wire rack to cool.

488. Quick N Easy Air Fried Scrambled Egg

Preparation time: 2 minutes Cooking time: 20 minutes Serves: 2

Ingredients

- 2 eggs
- ¾ tablespoon unsalted margarine Pepper and salt to taste Tomatoes, mushroom or cheese (optional)

Cooking Instructions

Beat the eggs in a bowl. Preheat the Airfryer to 140 ° F for about 5 minutes.

Melt the margarine in the preheated airfryer by tilting the pan to distribute it evenly.

Now, pour the egg into the airfryer at 140 ° F for 10 minutes. Add the other ingredients like tomatoes, mushrooms, and cheese if you use them.

Whisk continuously every few minutes until soft and yellow.

Serve the egg, seasoned on toast and enjoyed with milk.

489. Easy Chocolate Muffins

Preparation time: 10 minutes Cooking time: 15 minutes Serves: 12

Ingredients

- 1cup caster sugar 2 cups self raising flour ¾ cups milk chocolate ¼ cups cocoa powder 2 medium eggs ½ cup margarine 5tbps of milk ½ tsp. vanilla essence Water

Cooking Instructions

Preheat the Airfryer to 350F. Combine the flour, cocoa and

sugar in a large bowl. Add the margarine and rub until you get the consistency of breadcrumbs.

In a small bowl, break the eggs and add the milk, then add them to the large bowl, mixing well.

Add the vanilla essence, mix well and then add some water if too thick. Use a rolling pin to beat the milk chocolate in a sandwich bag until the sizes are all different. Add to bowl and mix again.

Pour into small sandwich containers, place in the airfryer, bake for 9 minutes at 350 ° F, then 6 minutes at 325 ° F. Serve!

490. Strawberry Ring Cake

Preparation time: 15 minutes Cooking time: 30 minutes
Serves: 4

Ingredients

- 1 egg
- 3½ tbps of margarine 3 strawberries, mashed ½ tsp. of cinnamon 2.6 ounces of sugar 8 ounces of flour 2 tbps of maple syrup A pinch of salt

Cooking Instructions

Heat the air fryer to 320 ° F. Spray a small ring cake pan with spray oil.

Put the sugar and margarine in a bowl and mix until creamy. Add the mashed strawberries, eggs and maple syrup and beat the mixture until smooth.

Sift the flour, cinnamon and salt and mix until a batter is formed. Pour the batter into the ring pan and level with a spoon. Insert the cake pan into the basket of the air fryer.

Bake for 30 minutes until a knife inserted in the heart of the cake comes out clean.

491. Anise and Orange Cake

Preparation time: 30 minutes Serves: 6

Ingredients

- 1/4 cup hazelnuts, roughly chopped
- tbps sugar free orange marmalade 1 stick margarine
- eggs plus 1 egg yolk, beaten 5 tbps liquid monk fruit
- ounces unbleached almond flour 1 tsp. baking soda
- 1/4 tsp. baking powder
- 1/4 ground anise seed
- 1/4 tsp. ground cinnamon 1/4 tsp. ground allspice Pan oil

Cooking Instructions:

Lightly grease a pan using a pan oil.

Now, whip the liquid monk fruit and margarine in a bowl; whisk until clear and smooth. Incorporate the eggs, hazelnuts and jam; beat again until everything is well mixed.

Add the almond flour, baking soda, baking powder, allspice, star anise and ground cinnamon. Cook in the preheated air fryer at 310 ° F for about 35 minutes.

Next, use a tester to check cooking. To finish, add the icing.

492. Croissant With Ham, Mushroom And Egg

Preparation time: 5 minutes Cooking time: 8 minutes
Serves: 1

Ingredients

- 1 store-bought Croissant 3 slices honey shaved ham 4 honey cherry tomato, halved 4 small button mushroom, quartered 1 Egg
- 1.8 oz shredded cheddar cheese Handful salad greens 1/2 Rosemary Sprig, roughly chopped (optional)

Cooking Instructions

Lightly grease a baking dish with margarine.

Arrange the ingredients in two layers, placing the cheese in the middle and top layer. Create a space in the center of the ham mixture, break the egg.

Sprinkle the mixture with black pepper, salt and rosemary and place it in the Airfryer basket together with the croissant.

In the oven at a temperature of 325 ° F preheated for 8 minutes. (Remove the croissant from the Airfryer basket after 4 minutes).

Serve croissants and cheese baked eggs on the plate along with some salads.

493. Oatmeal Muffins

Preparation time: 5 minutes Cooking time: 15 minutes
Serves: 2-4

Ingredients

- 2 Eggs
- 3½ ounce oats
- 3 ounce margarine, melted 1/2 cup flour
- 1/4 tsp. vanilla essence e 1/2 cup icing sugar Pinch baking powder 1 tablespoon raisins Cooking spray

Cooking Instructions

Combine the sugar and margarine until soft. Whisk together the eggs and vanilla essence. Add it to the sugar / margarine mixture until soft peaks form.

Combine flour, raisins, baking powder and oats in a separate bowl. Add it to the mixed ingredients.

Lightly grease the muffin tins with cooking spray and fill them with batter. Preheat AirFryer to 350 ° F.

Place the muffin tins in the Airfryer tray. Cook for 12 minutes. Chill, serve and enjoy!

494. Banana And Chocolate Muffins

Preparation time: 10 minutes Cooking time: 25 minutes
Serves: 6-8

Ingredients

- 3 medium sized bananas, mashed 4 tbps of cocoa ¾ cup of wheat flour ¾ cup of chocolate chips ¾ cup of plain flour ½ cup of sugar ¼ tsp. of baking powder 1 egg, whisked 1 tsp. of baking soda 1/3 cup of vegetable oil

Cooking Instructions

Mix the bananas, egg and oil in a bowl. Mix both flours, cocoa, baking soda, leavening flour and sugar using a wooden spatula until well blended.

Add the chocolate chips and mix lightly.

Grease the muffin pan with oil and pour the batter into the holes.

Heat the air fryer to 347 ° F and bake the muffins for 25 minutes. Leave to cool for about 15 minutes, then place on a wire rack.

495.   Snickerdoodle Cinnamon Cookies
Preparation time: 1 hour Serves: 10

Ingredients
- tbps liquid monk fruit 1/4 cup hazelnuts, ground
- 1 stick margarine, room temperature 3 cups almond flour
- cup coconut flour
- ounces powdered swerve
- tsp.s ground cinnamon

Cooking Instructions:
First, cream the liquid monk fruit with margarine until the mixture is fluffy. Sift both types of flour.

Now, incorporate the hazelnuts. Now, knead the mixture to form a dough; put in the refrigerator for about 35 minutes.

Finally, shape the prepared dough into small balls; arrange them on a baking dish; flatten the balls using the back of a spoon.

Mix the powdered swerve with the ground cinnamon. Press the cookies into the cinnamon mixture until they are completely covered.

Bake the cookies for 35 minutes at 310 ° F.

Let them cool for about 10 minutes before placing them on a wire rack.

496.   Boozy Baileys Fudge Brownies
Preparation time: 35 minutes Serves: 8

Ingredients
- cup powdered swerve
- tbps unsweetened cocoa powder, sifted 1/4 cup almond flour
- 1/4 cup coconut flour 1/4 tsp. salt
- 1/4 tsp. baking powder
- 1/4 cup margarine, melted then cooled 3 eggs room temperature
- tsp. vanilla
- tbps Baileys
- ounces unsweetened chocolate chips 1/4 cup sour cream
- 1/4 cup powdered erythritol
- ounces Ricotta cheese, room temperature

Cooking Instructions:
In a bowl, carefully combine the butter powder, cocoa powder, flour, salt and baking powder.

Mix the margarine, eggs and vanilla. Add the batter to a lightly greased pan.

Air fry for 35 minutes at 355 ° F. Let them cool slightly on a wire rack.

Heat the chocolate chips in the microwave until everything has melted; let the mixture cool to room temperature.

Next, add the ricotta, baileys, sour cream and powdered erythritol; mix until everything is blended.

Spread this mixture on top of the brownie. Serve very cold.

497.   Orange Swiss Roll
Preparation time: 1 hour 35 minutes Serves: 6

Ingredients
- 1/4 cup milk 1/4 cup swerve
- 1 tablespoon yeast
- 1/4 stick margarine, at room temperature 1 egg, at room temperature
- 1/4 tsp. salt
- cup almond flour 1 cup coconut flour
- tbps fresh orange juice Filling:
- tbps margarine
- tbps swerve
- tsp. ground star anise 1/4 tsp. ground cinnamon 1 tsp. vanilla paste
- 1/4 cup confectioners' swerve

Cooking Instructions:
Heat the milk in a microwave-safe bowl and transfer the hot milk to the bowl of a planetary mixer. Add 1/4 cup of swerve and yeast and mix to combine well. Cover and let stand until the yeast is frothy.

Then, whisk the margarine on low speed. Incorporate the egg and mix again. Add salt and flour. Add the orange juice and mix on medium speed until a smooth dough forms.

Knead the dough on a lightly floured surface. Cover it loosely and let it rest in a warm place for about 1 hour or until doubled in size. Next, spray the bottom and sides of a baking sheet with cooking oil (margarine flavored).

Roll out the dough into a rectangle.

Spread 3 tablespoons of margarine over the entire dough. In a baking dish, combine 4 tablespoons of swerve, ground star anise, cinnamon and vanilla; sprinkle evenly over the dough.

Then, roll up the dough to form a register. Cut them into 6 equal rolls and place them in the parchment-lined air fryer basket.

Bake at 350 ° for 13 minutes, turning them halfway through cooking. Dust off the swerve of the pastry chefs and enjoy!

498.   Classic Mini Cheesecakes
Preparation time: 30 minutes Serves: 8

Ingredients
For the Crust:
- 1/4 tsp. grated nutmeg 1 1/2 tbps erythritol 1 1/2 cups almond meal
- tbps melted margarine 1 tsp. ground cinnamon A pinch of kosher salt
- For the Cheesecake:
- eggs
- 1/4 cups unsweetened chocolate chips 1 1/2 tbps sour cream
- ounces soft cheese 1/4 cup swerve
- 1/4 tsp. vanilla essence

Cooking Instructions:
First, line eight mini muffin mold cups with paper liners.

To make the crust, mix the almond flour with erythritol,

cinnamon, nutmeg and kosher salt.

Now, add the melted margarine and mix well to moisten the crumb mixture.

Divide the crust mixture between muffin cups and press gently to create even layers.

In another bowl, whip together the soft cheese, sour cream and swirl until the mixture is homogeneous and smooth. Incorporate the eggs and vanilla essence.

Then divide the chocolate chips into the prepared muffin cups. Then, add the cheese mix to each muffin cup.

Bake for about 18 minutes at 345 ° F. Bake in batches if necessary. Finally, transfer the mini cheesecakes to a cooling rack; keep in the fridge.

499. Delicious Spiced Apples

Preparation time: 10 minutesCooking Time: 10 minutes
Serves: 6

Ingredients :

- small apples, sliced 1 tsp apple pie spice 1/4 cup erythritol
- tbsp coconut oil, melted

Cooking Instructions:

Add the apple slices to a mixing bowl and sprinkle sweetener, apple pie spice and coconut oil over the apple and mix to coat.

Transfer the apple slices to the baking dish. Place the dish in the basket of the air fryer and cook at 350 F for 10 minutes.

Serve and enjoy.

Nutritional value (Amount per serving):

Calories 73

Fat 4.6 g

Carbohydrates 8.3 g

Sugar 5.4 g

Protein 0 g

Cholesterol 0 mg

500. Air Fried Crab Sticks

Preparation time: 5 minutes Cooking time: 12 minutes
Serves: 1-2

Ingredients

- packet crabsticks, break length-wise &cut into small even pieces 2 tsp. oil, to toss Cajun or curry seasoning powder (Optional)

Cooking Instructions

Preheat the Airfryer to 325 ° F for 5 minutes. Place the cut, uniform crab sticks in a bowl and sprinkle with oil, stirring well to combine.

Airfry until golden brown for 12 minutes. Every few minutes, check to make sure they cook evenly.

Sprinkle with seasoning if desired.

501. Bread Rolls With Crisp Potato Stuffing

Preparation time: 20 minutes Cooking time: 15 minutes
Serves: 8

Ingredients

- 8 slice bread, white part only 5 large potatoes
- 2green chilies, seeded &finely chopped 1 small coriander bunch, finely chopped 1/2 tsp. turmeric 2 small onions, finely chopped 1/2 tsp. mustard seeds 2 tbps oil
- 2 sprigs curry leaf Salt to taste

Cooking Instructions

Add the potatoes, a spoonful of salt and water to a saucepan. Boil, peel and mash the potatoes well.

Heat a teaspoon. of oil and mustard seeds in a pan. Once they crackle, add the onions and fry until translucent and the curry leaves and add the turmeric. Fry and then add the mashed potatoes and salt. Mix well and let cool.

With the palms of your hands, shape the mixture into 8 oval shapes and set aside.

Now, cut the sides of the bread and wet it completely with water. Remove excess water by pressing with the palm of your hand.

Holding the wet bread in the palm of your hand, place the potato and roll the bread into a spindle shape. Next, seal the edges and make sure the potato filling is completely inside the bread.

Make all the rolls and brush them with oil. Keep aside. Preheat Airfryer to 400 ° F for 8 minutes and brush the basket with a little oil before placing the ready rolls.

Bake 12-13 minutes until crisp. Enjoy ketchup along with masala chai!

502. Crispy French Fries

Preparation time: 30 minutes Cooking time: 30 minutes
Serves: 4

Ingredients

- 6 tsp.s of vegetable oil
- 6 medium sized Irish potatoes

Cooking Instructions

Peel the potatoes and cut them into 3 "long strips. Soak them in water for 30 minutes, drain and then dry them with absorbent paper.

Heat your Airfryer to about 360 ° F.

Pour the oil into the potato strips and mix until a homogeneous mixture is obtained.

Place the potatoes in the fryer basket and cook until golden brown for 30 minutes, shaking at 10 minute intervals.

503. Chocolate Rum Lava Cake

Preparation time: 35 minutes Serves: 4

Ingredients

- 1/2 ounces margarine, at room temperature
  3 ounces chocolate, unsweetened
- eggs, beaten
- 1/4 cup confectioners' swerve 1/4 cup almond flour
- 1 tsp. rum extract
- 1 tsp. vanilla extract

Cooking Instructions:

Start by preheating the air fryer to 370 ° F. Spray the sides and bottoms of four molds with cooking spray.

Melt the margarine and chocolate in a microwave-safe bowl. Mix the eggs and confectioners until frothy.

Pour the margarine / chocolate mixture into the egg mixture. Incorporate the almond flour, rum extract and vanilla extract. Mix until everything is well incorporated.

Scrape the batter into the prepared molds. Cook in the pre-heated air fryer for 9-11 minutes.

Leave to rest for 3 to 3 minutes. Invert on a hot plate and serve.

504. Ketchupd Meatballs

Preparation time: 10 minutes Cooking time: 13minutes Serves: 3-4

Ingredients

- ¾ pounds (12oz) ground beef 1 small onion, finely chopped 1 tablespoon fresh parsley, chopped ½ tablespoon fresh thyme leaves, chopped 1 egg
- 3 tbps breadcrumbs Pepper & salt to taste 10oz ketchup of choice, extra

Cooking Instructions

Combine all the ingredients in the bowl, mixing well. Make 10 to 12 balls with this mixture.

Now preheat the Airfryer to 390 ° F. Place the meatballs in the Airfryer basket and in the Airfryer. Cook for 8 minutes.

Remove the meatballs in an ovenproof dish, add the ketchup and place the dish in the Airfryer basket. Put the basket back in the airfryer.

Heat everything to a temperature of 330 ° F and for 5 minutes.

505. Ultimate Lemon Coconut Tart

Preparation time: 15 minutes + chilling time Serves: 8

Ingredients

- eggs plus 6 egg yolks 1/4 cup lemon juice
- tbps unsalted margarine
- 1/4 cup powdered swerve 4 tbps heavy cream Crust:
- 1 cup blanched almond meal 3/4 cup shredded coconut
- 1 ¼ cups cream cheese, room temperature
- 1 tsp. apple pie spice blend 1 tsp. pure vanilla extract 1/8 tsp. salt
- 1/4 tsp. ground anise star

Cooking Instructions:

In a bowl, beat the eggs. Add the lemon juice, zest, margarine and powder. Place in a double boiler or place a stainless steel bowl over boiling water.

Keep stirring until the temperature reaches 170 degrees. Remove from heat and stir in the cream.

Put the plastic wrap on top and let it cool in the refrigerator.

Next, mix all the ingredients of the crust.

Transfer them to the Air Fryer dish and bake at 350 ° F for only 5 minutes. When the edges turn golden, they're ready.

Finally, spread the prepared cream on the crust. Keep them in the refrigerator until ready to serve.

506. Apple Chips with Dip

Preparation time: 10 minutesCooking Time: 13 minutes Serves: 4

Ingredients :

- 1 apple, thinly slice using a mandolin slicer 1 tbsp almond margarine
- 1/4 cup plain yogurt 3 tsp olive oil
- 1 tsp ground cinnamon 4 drops liquid stevia

Cooking Instructions:

Add the apple slices, oil and cinnamon to a large bowl and mix well.

Spray the basket of the air fryer with cooking spray.

Place the apple slices in the basket of the air fryer and cook at 375 F for 13 minutes. Turn every 4 minutes.

Meanwhile, in a small bowl, mix the almond margarine, yogurt, and sweetener.

Serve apple chips with gravy and enjoy.

Nutritional value (Amount per serving):

Calories 86

Fat 4.9 g

Carbohydrates 10 g

Sugar 7.1 g

Protein 1.9 g

Cholesterol 1 mg

507. Tasty Cheese Bites

Preparation time: 10 minutes Cooking Time: 3 minutes Serves: 16

Ingredients :

- oz cream cheese, softened 3 tbsp erythritol
- 1/4 cup almond flour 1/4 tsp vanilla
- tbsp heavy cream 1/4 cup erythritol

Cooking Instructions:

Add the cream cheese, vanilla, 1/4 cup of erythritol and 3 tablespoons of cream to a mixer and mix until smooth.

Pour the cream cheese mixture onto the parchment-lined plate and refrigerate for 1 hour.

In a small bowl, mix the almond flour and 3 tablespoons of erythritol.

Dip the cheesecake bites into the remaining cream and top with the almond flour mixture.

Place the prepared cheesecake morsels in the air fryer basket and fry for 3 minutes at 350 F.

Make sure the cheesecake bites are frozen before air frying, otherwise they will melt.

Drizzle with chocolate syrup and serve.

Nutritional value (Amount per serving):

1.   Calories 80
2.   Fat 7 g
3.   Carbohydrates 3 g
4.   Sugar 1 g
5.   Protein 3 g
6.   Cholesterol 16 mg

508. Classic Pound Cake

Preparation time: 35 minutes Serves: 8

Ingredients

- 1stick margarine, at room temperature 1 cup swerve
- eggs
- 1 1/2 cups coconut flour
- 1/4 tsp. baking powder 1/4 tsp. baking soda 1/4 tsp. salt
- A pinch of freshly grated nutmeg
- A pinch of ground star anise
- 1/4 cup margarinemilk
- tsp. vanilla essence

Cooking Instructions:

Start by preheating the air fryer to 330 ° F. Spray the bottom and sides of a pan with cooking spray.

Whisk the margarine and swerve with a hand mixer until creamy. Then, combine the eggs, one at a time, and mix well until frothy.

Incorporate the flour together with the remaining ingredients. Stir to mix well. Scrape the batter into the prepared pan.

Bake for 15 minutes; rotate the pan and bake for another 15 minutes, until the top of the cake comes back when gently pressed with your fingers.

509. Easy Cheesecake

Preparation time: 10 minutes Cooking Time: 10 minutes Serves: 6

Ingredients :

- eggs
- 16 oz cream cheese, softened 3 tbsp sour cream
- 1/4 tsp fresh lemon juice 1 tsp vanilla
- 3/4 cup erythritol

Cooking Instructions: :

Preheat the air fryer to 350 F.

Add the eggs, lemon juice, vanilla and sweetener to a large bowl and beat with a hand mixer until smooth.

Add the cream cheese and sour cream and beat until frothy.

Pour the batter into the 3-inch spring-shaped pan and place it in the air fryer basket and cook for 8-10 minutes at 350 F.

Remove from the air fryer and allow it to cool completely.

Refrigerate for the night.

Serve and enjoy.

Nutritional value (Amount per serving):

- Calories 396
- Fat 38 g
- Carbohydrates 3.4 g
- Sugar 0.4 g
- Protein 7.7 g
- Cholesterol 139 mg

510. Blackberry and Cocoa Margarine Cake

Preparation time: 30 minutes Serves: 8

Ingredients

- 1/4 cup fresh blackberries

- 1/4 cup margarine, room temperature 1/4 tsp. baking powder
- ounces swerve
- 1/4 cup cocoa powder, melted 1 tsp. baking soda
- whole eggs
- 1 cup almond flour
- 1 tsp. orange zest

Cooking Instructions:

In a bowl, beat the margarine, the steering and the orange zest with an electric mixer. Carefully incorporate the eggs, one at a time; beat well with your electric whisk after each addition.

Then, add the almond flour, baking soda, baking powder, cocoa powder and orange juice.

Pour the prepared batter into a pan. Complete with fresh blackberries. Cook in the preheated air fryer for 33 minutes at 335 ° F.

Check the baking of the cake; let it cool on a wire rack.

511. Spicy Coconut Coated Shrimp

Preparation time: 10 minutes Cooking time: 14 minutes Serves: 4

Ingredients

- 4 ounces of grated coconut 16 ounces of large sized shrimps, peeled, deveined 4 ounces of flour 2 egg whites, whisked 8 tbps of breadcrumbs ½ tsp. of salt Zest of 1 small lemon Sweet chili sauce ½ tsp. ground black pepper Oil spray

Cooking Instructions

Mix the breadcrumbs with the zest, pepper, coconut and salt on a plate and set aside. Season the flour with pepper and salt in a separate dish. Put the eggs in another dish.

Heat your deep fryer to 400 ° F.

Put each shrimp in the flour, pass it in the beaten eggs and finally cover evenly with the breadcrumb mixture.

Place the dredged shrimp on a plate and grease them with spray oil.

Divide the shrimp into two batches and place the first one in the airfryer. Cook for 6 minutes until they are firm. Do the same with the second batch. Lower the temperature to 340 ° F and add the first batch to the second in the airfryer. Air fry for another 2 minutes.

To be served with sweet chilli sauce.

512. Coconut Pie

Preparation time: 10 minutes Cooking Time: 13 minutes Serves: 6

Ingredients :

- eggs
- 1/4 cup coconut flour 1/4 cup erythritol
- 1 cup shredded coconut 1 1/4 tsp vanilla
- 1/4 cup margarine
- 1 1/4 cups coconut milk

Cooking Instructions:

Add all ingredients to the large bowl and mix until smooth.

Spray a 6-inch pan with cooking spray.

Pour the batter into the prepared dish and place it in the

basket of the air fryer.

Cook at 350 F for 10-13 minutes.

Slice and serve.

Nutritional value (Amount per serving):

- Calories 383
- Fat 38.9 g
- Carbohydrates 6.3 g
- Sugar 3.3 g
- Protein 4 g
- Cholesterol 75 mg

513. Easy Lava Cake

Preparation time: 10 minutesCooking Time: 9 minutes Serves: 3

Ingredients :

- 1 egg
- 1/4 tsp baking powder
- tbsp coconut oil, melted 1 tbsp flax meal
- tbsp erythritol
- tbsp water
- tbsp unsweetened cocoa powder Pinch of salt

Cooking Instructions:

Beat all the ingredients in the bowl and transfer them to two molds.

Preheat the air fryer to 350 F.

Place the molds in the fryer basket and cook for 8-9 minutes.

Carefully remove the molds from the air fryer and allow it to cool for 10 minutes.

Serve and enjoy.

Nutritional value (Amount per serving):

- Calories 119
- Fat 11 g
- Carbohydrates 4 g
- Sugar 0.3 g
- Protein 5 g
- Cholesterol 83 mg

514. Cranberry Almond Cake

Preparation time: 10 minutes Cooking Time: 16 minutes Serves: 6

Ingredients :

- Eggs
- tsp orange zest 3 tsp mixed spice 3 tsp cinnamon 1/4 cup swerve
- cup margarine, softened 3/3 cup dried cranberries
- 1 1/4 cups almond flour 1 tsp vanilla

Cooking Instructions: :

Preheat the air fryer to 335 F.

In a bowl, add the sweetener and the melted margarine and beat until frothy.

Add cinnamon, vanilla and mixed spices and mix well.

Add the eggs mixed until well combined.

Add the almond flour, orange zest and cranberries and mix to combine.

Pour the batter into a greased deep fryer pan and place in the deep fryer.

Bake the cake for 16 minutes.

Slice and serve.

Nutritional value (Amount per serving):

- Calories 485
- Fat 48 g
- Carbohydrates 8 g
- Sugar 3 g
- Protein 11 g
- Cholesterol 35 mg

515. Cheese Margarine Cookies

Preparation time: 10 minutes Cooking Time: 13 minutes Serves: 8

Ingredients :

- eggs
- tbsp margarine, melted 1/4 cup sour cream
- 1/4 cup mozzarella cheese, shredded 1 1/4 cup almond flour
- 1/4 tsp baking powder 1/4 tsp salt

Cooking Instructions:

Preheat the air fryer to 370 F.

Add all the ingredients to a large bowl and mix using a hand mixer.

Pour the batter into the silicone muffin molds and place it in the air fryer and cook for 13 minutes.

Serve and enjoy.

Nutritional value (Amount per serving):

4. Calories 305
5. Fat 30 g
6. Carbohydrates 4 g
7. Sugar 1 g
8. Protein 6 g
9. Cholesterol 35 mg

516. Favorite Cupcakes with Peanuts

Preparation time: 15 minutes Serves: 8

Ingredients

- egg whites
- whole egg
- 1/4 tsp. pure vanilla extract 1/4 cup swerve
- 1/4 cup confectioners' swerve 1/4 tsp. cream of tartar 1/4 stick margarine, softened
- 1/4 tsp. almond extract 1 cup almond flour
- 1/4 cup coconut flour
- tbps unsalted peanuts, ground

Cooking Instructions:

First, whisk the softened margarine and swerve until it becomes fluffy.

Subsequently, incorporate the egg and mix again; carefully throw the flour along with the chopped peanuts; add the almond extract and vanilla extract.

Divide the batter between muffin molds lined with muffin paper; Air fry at 335 ° F for 10 minutes.

In the meantime, prepare the filling; simply whip the egg and cream of tartar until you get an airy consistency.

Now, gradually add the deviation of the pastry chefs; continue to mix until stiff and shiny peaks form. Finally, decorate the cupcakes and serve them on a nice serving dish.

517.   Asian Barbecue Satay

Preparation time: 15 minutes Cooking time: 15 minutes Serves: 3

Ingredients

- 4 garlic cloves, chopped ¾ pound (12 oz) boneless skinless chicken tenders ½ cup pineapple juice ½ cup low sodium soy sauce ¼ cup sesame oil 4 scallions, chopped 2 tsp.s sesame seeds, toasted 1 tablespoon fresh ginger, grated 1 pinch black pepper

Cooking Instructions

Skewer the tender chicken, removing excess fat or meat.

Combine all the other ingredients in a large bowl. Add the skewered chicken to the bowl, combine, cover and refrigerate for 2 to 24 hours.

Preheat Airfryer to 390 ° F. Pat dry chicken. Add the skewers to the basket and cook for 5-7 minutes.

518.   25-Minute Orange Galettes

Preparation time: 25 minutes Serves: 6

Ingredients

- cup almond meal 1/4 cup coconut flour 3 eggs
- 1⁄3 cup milk
- tbps monk fruit
- tsp.s grated lemon peel
- 1⁄3 tsp. ground nutmeg, preferably freshly ground 1 1/2 tsp.s baking powder
- tbps orange juice A pinch of turmeric

Cooking Instructions:

Get two bowls. Combine the dry ingredients in the first bowl.

In the second bowl, combine all the wet ingredients. Add the wet mixture to the dry mixture and mix until smooth and uniform.

Air fry for 4-5 minutes at 345 ° F. Works in batches. If you wish, dust with the swerve of the pastry chefs.

519.   Garlic And Cheese Bread Rolls

Preparation time: 10 minutes Cooking time: 5 minutes Serves: 2

Ingredients

- 8 tbps of grated cheese 6 tsp.s of melted margarine Garlic bread spice mix 2 bread rolls

Cooking Instructions

Slice the sandwiches from the top crosswise but do not cut them at the bottom.

Place all the cheese in the slots and brush the tops of the sandwiches with the melted margarine. Sprinkle the garlic mix on the rolls.

Heat the air fryer to 350 ° F. Place the rolls in the basket and cook until the cheese has melted for about 5 minutes.

520.   Feta And Onion Bell Pepper Rolls

Preparation time: 25 minutes Cooking time: 10 minutes Serves: 8

Ingredients

- medium sized bell red and yellow peppers 2 tbps of finely chopped basil 1 green onion, thinly sliced 3½

ounces of feta cheese, grated 8 toothpicks or tapas forks

Cooking Instructions

Heat your Airfryer to 392 ° F.

Place the peppers in the fryer basket and fry for 10 minutes until they are charred.

Mix the feta, basil and green onions in a bowl and set aside.

Take out the peppers and cut them vertically in half, remove the skin and seeds.

Put the feta and onion mixture into each pepper and roll up starting from the thinnest end. Secure the rolls with a toothpick of a tapas fork and serve.

521.   Pumpkin Custard

Preparation time: 10 minutes Cooking Time: 33 minutes Serves: 6

Ingredients :

- egg yolks
- 1/4 tsp cinnamon
- 15 drops liquid stevia 15 oz pumpkin puree 3/4
- cup coconut cream 1/8 tsp cloves
- 1/8 tsp ginger

Cooking Instructions:

Preheat the air fryer to 335 F.

In a large bowl, combine the pumpkin puree, cinnamon, swerve, cloves and ginger together.

Add the egg yolks and beat until blended.

Add the coconut cream and mix well.

Pour the mixture into the six molds and put it in the air fryer.

Cook for 33 minutes.

Allow to cool completely then place in the refrigerator.

Serve cold and enjoy.

Nutritional value (Amount per serving):

- Calories 131
- Fat 11 g
- Carbohydrates 3 g
- Sugar 3 g
- Protein 4 g
- Cholesterol 13 mg

522.   Veggie Spring Rolls

Preparation time: 15 minutes Cooking time: 25 minutes Serves: 8

Ingredients

For Stuffing:

- 2 cups cabbage, shredded thinly 1 big carrot, chopped thinly 2 inch piece ginger, chopped finely 1/2 capsicum, cut thinly 8 garlic cloves, chopped finely Big pinch of sugar 1 tablespoon of pepper powder 1 tsp. soya sauce Spring onion, to garnish 2 big onions, cut thinly Salt - as needed
- 2 tbps of cooking oil For The Sheet:
- 10 Spring roll sheet 2 tbps of corn flour Water, as needed

Cooking Instructions

To make the filling, brown all the chopped vegetables, adding salt and sugar continuously for 2 or 3 minutes. Add the pepper powder and soy sauce, mixing well. Garnish with spring onions.

Make a cream like pasta by adding a little water to the corn flour. Roll the sheets into 4 pieces (for small spring rolls) and arrange them.

Now, place 1 tablespoon of filling in a corner of the pastry, roll it up well so that the spring roll does not become flat. In the other corner, apply the cornmeal paste and stick it on. Do the same with the sheets and arrange.

Preheat the air fryer for 5 minutes at 350 ° F. Brush the spring rolls with a little oil and place the sheets in the basket of the air fryer.

Cook for 10 minutes at 350 ° F. Remove the basket and turn the rolls over, bake another 10 minutes. If the color of the spring rolls remains white, bake for another 2 to 3 minutes.

Remove and serve hot.

523. Breakfast Sandwich

Preparation time: 5 minutes Cooking time: 7 minutes Serves: 1

Ingredients
- 2 Bacon Slices 1 Egg
- 1 English muffin Salt& Pepper to taste

Cooking Instructions

Beat the egg in a soufflé cup and season with salt and pepper.

Heat the air fryer to 390 ° F and place the soufflé cup, English muffin and bacon in the pan.

Cook all the ingredients for 6-10 minutes. Assemble the sandwich and enjoy.

524. Vanilla Orange Custard

Preparation time: 35 minutes + chilling time Serves: 6

Ingredients
- eggs
- ounces cream cheese, at room temperature 3 1/2 cans condensed milk, sweetened
- 1/4 cup swerve
- 1/4 tsp. orange rind, grated 1 1/2 cardamom pods, bruised
- tsp.s vanilla paste 1/4 cup fresh orange juice

Cooking Instructions:

In a saucepan, melt and heat over moderate heat; it takes 10 to 13 minutes. Immediately but carefully pour the melted sugar into six molds, tilting them to coat the bottom; let them cool slightly.

In a baking dish, beat the cheese until smooth; now, add the eggs, one at a time, and continue beating until the mixture is light and creamy.

Add the orange zest, cardamom, vanilla, orange juice and milk; mix again. Pour the mixture over the caramelized sugar. Air fry, covered, at 335 ° F for 38 minutes or until thickened.

Refrigerate overnight; garnish with berries or other fruit and serve.

525. Vanilla Coconut Cheese Cookies

Preparation time: 10 minutes Cooking Time: 13 minutes Serves: 15

Ingredients :
- egg
- 1/4 tsp baking powder 1 tsp vanilla
- 1/4 cup swerve
- 1/4 cup margarine, softened
- tbsp cream cheese, softened 1/4 cup coconut flour
- Pinch of salt

Cooking Instructions:

Preheat the air fryer to 370 F.

Add all the ingredients to a large bowl and mix using a hand mixer.

Pour the batter into the silicone muffin molds and place it in the air fryer and cook for 13 minutes.

Serve and enjoy.

Nutritional value (Amount per serving):
- Calories 65
- Fat 7 g
- Carbohydrates 1 g
- Sugar 0.5 g
- Protein 1 g
- Cholesterol 34 mg

526. Rarebit Air-Fried Egg Preparation

Cooking time: 5 minutes Serves: 2-4

Ingredients
- 4 Slices Sourdough 4 Eggs
- 1/3 cup ale
- 1½ cups cheddar, grated 1 tsp. mustard powder 1/2 tsp. paprika Black Pepper to taste 2 tsp. Worcestershire Sauce

Cooking Instructions

Fry the eggs, sunny side up and set aside. Preheat the air fryer to 350 ° F.

In a bowl, combine the cheddar, beer, paprika, mustard powder and Worcestershire sauce.

Spread only one side of each sourdough slice with the cheddar mixture. Place the slices of bread in the AirFryer tray. Cook for about 3 minutes until lightly browned.

Garnish the rare pieces with fried eggs and season with pepper to taste.

527. Thai Style Omelette

Preparation time: 5 minutes Cooking time: 10 minutes Serves: 2

Ingredients
- 3½ oz minced Pancetta 2 Eggs
- 1 cup onion, chopped 1 tablespoon fish salt

Cooking Instructions

Beat the eggs until they are light and fluffy. Preheat Air-Fryer to 280 ° F.

In a bowl, combine all the ingredients. Pour the mixture into the AirFryer tray.

Remove after 10 minutes or when the omelette is golden brown. Cut and serve.

Made in the USA
Monee, IL
25 January 2021